57 Stories of SAINTS

57 Stories of SAINTS

By
Anne Eileen Heffernan, FSP

Illustrated by
Jerry Rizzo

Pauline
BOOKS & MEDIA
Boston

Library of Congress Cataloging-in-Publication Data

Heffernan, Eileen.
  57 stories of saints / by Anne Eileen Heffernan ; illustrated by Jerry Rizzo.— 3rd ed.
    p. cm.
  Includes index.
  ISBN 0-8198-2681-2 (pbk.)
  1. Christian saints—Biography—Juvenile literature. I. Title: Fifty-seven stories of saints. II. Rizzo, Jerry. III. Title.
  BX4658.H39 2006
  282.092'2—dc22
                                                      2006002707

The Scripture quotations contained herein are from the *New Revised Standard Version Bible: Catholic Edition*, copyright © 1989, 1993, Division of Christian Education of the National Council of the Churches of Christ in the United States of America. Used by permission. All rights reserved.

"P" and PAULINE are registered trademarks of the Daughters of St. Paul.

Published by Pauline Books & Media, 50 Saint Paul's Avenue, Boston, MA 02130-3491. www.pauline.org

Printed in the U.S.A.

Pauline Books & Media is the publishing house of the Daughters of St. Paul, an international congregation of women religious serving the Church with the communications media.

2 3 4 5 6 7 8 9   14 13 12 11 10 09 08

Contents

THE ARCHANGELS
St. Michael, St. Gabriel, and St. Raphael

SEPTEMBER 29

Angels were created by God, just as we were, but they're very different from human beings! Angels have no bodies; they are pure spirits. They never get tired. To talk to one another, they only have to think a thought—they don't have to speak out loud. They never misunderstand one another.

The Bible mentions three angels by name: the archangels Michael, Gabriel, and Raphael. These three angels brought special messages from God to his people.

The Book of Tobit (one of the books in the Old Testament) tells about the Archangel Raphael, who guided Tobit's son Tobiah during a difficult journey and presented Tobit's prayers to God.

We can read about the Archangel Gabriel in the Gospel of St. Luke. Gabriel was the angel who invited Mary to become the Mother of Jesus, God's own Son.

The Bible mentions three angels by name: Michael, Gabriel, and Raphael. Angels are messengers of God, and they also present our prayers to God.

Michael is mentioned several times in the Bible. In a great battle against Satan, Michael led the angels who wished to remain faithful to God. Satan and some other angels had revolted against God. They did not love God and refused to do what God asked them to do. Satan and the other rebellious angels lost the battle. They went to hell. Today we call them devils or fallen angels. After that great battle, Michael became a defender and protector of God's people on earth.

Boys named Michael and Gabriel can think of these archangels as their special patrons (helpers) in heaven. So can boys named Ralph or girls named Gabrielle, Gabriella, or Michelle.

Jesus told us about another group of angels called the guardian angels. Each one of us has an angel to watch and guard us from dangers, especially from evil. We can pray to our guardian angels. They can help us keep calm during times of stress or danger. They can help us think clearly and make good choices when life seems confusing. They can comfort us when we go through difficult times. We celebrate the feast of the guardian angels on October 2.

One way we can be like the angels is to listen carefully to God and try to understand what he wants us to do. We can listen to God by reading the Bible, paying attention to the priest's homily at Mass, and taking time every day to pray. We can pray to the angels when we are afraid of danger or are tempted to do what is not right.

St. Joachim and St. Ann

(First Century)

July 26

Ann and her husband Joachim were prayerful people who tried to obey all the laws of their Jewish religion. At that time, the Jewish people were praying that God would send a leader called the Messiah to save them. They were not a free nation; the rulers of Rome had conquered them and made them pay high taxes. Every young Jewish woman hoped that she might be the Mother of the Messiah. But Joachim and Ann lived together for many years without having any children.

Every day Ann took good care of their home while Joachim brought their flock of sheep out to the pastures. Ann would say many prayers as she carried water from the deep well, or spun the wool from the sheep into fine thread. She prayed that God would bless her and Joachim with a child. At the time when Joachim and Ann lived, people thought that a couple without children must have done something wrong.

An ancient story tells us that one day when Joachim went to the Temple, the priests wouldn't allow him to offer a sacrifice to the Lord. They were afraid that God was not pleased with him. Feeling sad and confused, Joachim left the Temple and went out into the hill country to pray. Suddenly, an angel appeared to him telling him not to be distressed. Soon he and Ann would have a baby!

Joachim had been gone a long time, and Ann started to worry. Just as she was about to go out and look for him, an angel appeared to her also! "Don't be sad any longer," the angel advised. "God has heard your prayers. Soon you'll have a child."

Ann whispered a prayer of thanks and rushed out of the house to find Joachim. She met him by the Temple gate. "Joachim!" she cried, struggling to catch her breath. "Something wonderful has happened! I've seen an angel!"

But Joachim was shouting louder than she was. "Ann, Ann! We're going to have a baby! An angel told me so, too. Surely we are the most blessed couple on earth!"

"We are blessed," Ann agreed, wiping tears of joy from her eyes. "And I think our child must be very special to have an angel come and tell us the good news. We'll consecrate our baby to God."

~~~~~~~~~~~~~~~

Ann eagerly prepared the house and made warm blankets and clothes for the baby. At last the day arrived. How happy the couple was when a little girl was born to them. They decided to call their daughter Mary (Miriam in the Hebrew language). Little did they realize that this beautiful little baby would grow up to become the Mother of the Messiah! Nor did they know that their grandson, Jesus, would be the Savior of the whole world!

Mary grew quickly. She slept, toddled, and soon began to walk and run and dance. Ann carefully taught her daughter the prayers of the Jewish people and told her the stories of how God had protected his people for many long years. But what Mary most loved to hear about was how God had promised to send a Messiah to save his people. She prayed often that the Messiah would come soon.

Seeing how much their daughter loved God and prayer, Joachim and Ann decided to bring her to the Temple school in Jerusalem. They would miss having Mary running about and singing in their home. But they knew that Mary would be happy in the Temple. There she would live with other young Jewish girls and learn more about God and the promised Messiah.

Tradition tells us that Joachim and Ann were already elderly when Mary went off to the Temple. We don't know when they died, but it was probably before Mary became the Mother of Jesus. Certainly, while they were loving and caring for Mary, they didn't know that they would someday be the grandparents of the Savior of the world. But that didn't matter. Ann and Joachim focused all their energy on carrying

Joachim and Ann were happy to do their daily work, loving God and loving their family and friends.

out their daily duties well, loving God, their family, and their friends. They knew that if they did this, God would be pleased, and his will would be done through them.

We can imitate Joachim and Ann by doing our daily duties as well as we can and worshiping God in a special way on his day, Sunday. We can pray that all people will come to know Jesus, the Savior of the world.

St. Joseph

(First Century)

MARCH 19 AND MAY 1

When she was old enough, Mary, the daughter of Joachim and Ann, married a good man named Joseph. According to the custom of the times, the young couple waited a while before beginning their life together.

While they were waiting, the Archangel Gabriel was sent by God to ask Mary to become the Mother of the Messiah, by the power of the Holy Spirit.

"I am God's servant," Mary replied. "Let this happen as you said."

Later, in a dream, another angel told Joseph that Mary was going to have a child by the power of the Holy Spirit. "You must name him Jesus," said the angel. "He will save his people from their sins." ("Jesus" means "God saves.")

Mary and Joseph set up their home in the small town of Nazareth, in Galilee, and eagerly awaited the birth of

Joseph was a carpenter and spent his days making furniture and farm tools for the people of Nazareth.

Mary's son. Joseph was a carpenter and spent his days making furniture and farm tools for the people of Nazareth. Mary took care of their house and got everything ready for the birth of her son. Then, just a few weeks before the baby was to be born, Caesar Augustus, the Roman emperor who ruled Galilee and Judea at that time, announced that he wanted to count all the people in his kingdom. He ordered all the people to go to their hometowns to be registered in a census.

At first Joseph and Mary were worried because they knew that it would soon be time for the baby to be born. But then they remembered that a long time ago, one of the prophets had said that the Messiah would be born in Judea, in the town of Bethlehem. That was Joseph's hometown! They realized that this trip was part of God's plan. They packed some food and extra clothes onto their donkey and set out.

It was almost eighty-five miles to Bethlehem, and the weather was cold. As they got closer to the town, they were joined by many other travelers. Joseph told Mary, "I hope that some of our cousins will have room for us. It looks like all the inns will be full!"

"Don't worry, Joseph," Mary replied. "No matter where we end up tonight, this child belongs to God. God will take care of us."

But the conditions in Bethlehem were even worse than they had imagined. There was no space anywhere. At last they met an innkeeper who felt sorry for them and brought them to his stable. It was a small cave in a hillside, but at least they wouldn't have to sleep outside in the cold wind.

In the cave, Joseph found a pile of fresh, clean straw and spread his cloak over it. Mary rested while Joseph quickly lit a fire to heat their dinner. How safe Mary felt with Joseph there to help her!

A little later, when Joseph thought Mary had gone to sleep, he went out into the cool night. He was wondering how he was going to fit into God's plans.

The sky grew bright with stars, and suddenly Joseph heard a baby's cry! He dashed into the cave.

A little while later, the newborn baby had been wrapped up warmly and had fallen asleep in a manger. Later that night, shepherds from the nearby fields came in to adore the infant. Angels had told them that the Messiah was there in that little cave. How proud Joseph was of Mary and of the child as the shepherds crowded around!

The child was given the name Jesus, the name God himself had chosen.

～～～～～～～～～

Eventually Mary and Joseph returned to their home in Nazareth. Jesus grew quickly, and everyone was happy that Joseph had such a fine son to help him in the carpenter's shop. No one except Mary and Joseph knew that Jesus' real Father was God himself!

Mary taught Jesus his prayers, and Joseph made sure he learned all the skills of a carpenter. In the synagogue, Jesus learned to read the Torah and listened to the explanations of the Jewish Law given by the rabbi.

When Jesus was twelve, the family made a pilgrimage to the holy city of Jerusalem. It was the time of the

Passover feast, and many of their neighbors were also going. Jesus and his parents traveled with people from other small cities of Galilee. In Jerusalem, the little family spent hours in the huge Temple. They also visited with their friends and relatives.

At last it was time to return home. They started out early in the morning. Mary traveled with the women and Joseph with the men, as was the custom in those days. At night, Mary went to find Joseph and say goodnight to Jesus. How surprised and upset she was to discover that Jesus was not with Joseph! And all day Joseph had thought that Jesus was traveling with Mary! They were both very worried and started back to Jerusalem. They had to find their son!

After three days of searching, they went to the Temple. And there was Jesus, in the midst of a circle of rabbis and other teachers. These important men were holding a conversation with Jesus. His wisdom and knowledge amazed them.

Mary hurried over to Jesus. "Son, why have you done this to us? Your father and I have looked all over for you and have been so worried about you!"

Joseph didn't say anything, but his face shone with pride as he took the boy's slim hand into his big rough one. He didn't mind that Jesus had been there in the Temple. He knew that Jesus had been busy with something very important.

They went home to Nazareth, and Jesus obeyed Mary and Joseph. The days and years of hard work and study passed, with Joseph and Jesus working side by side in the carpenter's shop.

And then, one day, God called his good servant Joseph home. Joseph's work was done. It had been done well.

The Catholic Church celebrates two feast days for St. Joseph: on March 19, we honor Joseph as the husband of Mary, and on May 1, we honor him as Joseph the Worker.

What a humble and holy man Joseph was! He did few things that anyone would think extraordinary, but he did everything with great love for God and for his family. Today, we pray to St. Joseph to be with people we love at the moment of their death. We pray that he will watch over and protect the Church, the "family" of Jesus, as he watched over and protected his own holy family. St. Joseph knew what God wanted him to do, and he was happy to do it. He is the special friend of all fathers who work hard to care for their families.

St. Peter

(First Century)

JUNE 29

Simon was strong and tanned, with sparkling eyes that took in everything around him. His gaze most often rested on his treasured fishing boat, his large nets, and the Sea of Galilee—that unpredictable lake where he fished every day. Simon had been born a fisherman, and he planned to die a fisherman.

One day, when Simon had been listening to John the Baptist preach by the Jordan River, his brother Andrew came rushing up to him. "We've found the Messiah!" Andrew excitedly announced. Simon didn't know it yet, but that day his life would change forever.

Andrew brought Simon to Jesus, who gazed long and hard at the sturdy fisherman. At last Jesus said to him, "From now on you'll be called Peter." (In Greek, the word was *Cephas,* which means "rock.")

Simon Peter didn't understand why Jesus had given him that name, but he didn't care. He was convinced that there was something wonderful about this new teacher.

He decided then and there to spend as much time as possible with Jesus and learn all that he could from him.

Jesus had other new followers, too. They were John, Philip, and Nathaniel. One day the little group hiked up the high Galilean hills to the town of Cana. A young couple was getting married. Jesus, his new friends, and Jesus' mother, Mary, had all been invited to the wedding. The party was going well until something unexpected happened—they ran out of wine!

Mary, the mother of Jesus, noticed the problem right away. She didn't want the young couple to be embarrassed, so she went to Jesus and told him what had happened. But Jesus had not planned to do anything extraordinary that day, so he seemed to hesitate. Mary told the waiters, "Do whatever Jesus tells you to do."

The waiters were puzzled when Jesus told them to fill some large stone jars with water, but they obeyed. How amazed everyone was when they saw that the water had become good wine! That day Peter was convinced that Jesus was the Messiah, the long-awaited leader of Israel.

~~~~~~~~~~~~~~

Many months later, Peter was discouraged. He was back home in Capernaum and had spent the whole night fishing, but had caught nothing. Now the hot morning sun beat down on him and Andrew as they bent over their nets, mending the torn parts. Peter's empty boat sat beside them, its prow resting in the sand. Nearby, John, James, and their father Zebedee were mending their nets, too.

Suddenly they heard the noise of a large crowd swarming over the hill. Looking up, they saw Jesus coming toward them. There were so many people with him that Peter was afraid someone would get hurt, or that Jesus would be pushed into the water. Before Peter could say a word, Jesus was stepping into his boat. He asked Peter to pull out a few feet from the shore. Once they had dropped anchor, Jesus continued to teach the people from the boat. This made it easier for everyone to hear Jesus.

When he had finished speaking, Jesus turned to Peter. "Go out into the deep water and lower your nets for a catch," he instructed.

A catch! But night was the best time to catch fish. Surely Jesus knew that. Besides, Peter was tired. "Master," he said, "we've worked hard all night and caught nothing. But if you say so, I'll go out again."

Peter and his crew rowed their boat out into deeper water and lowered their nets. Within minutes the nets were full of fish! They even had to call James and John to come out in their boat and help haul in all the fish. "We almost sank!" gasped Andrew when they finally pulled the boats up onto the beach.

But Peter wasn't thinking of the fish. He was thinking of how holy Jesus must be and how imperfect he, Peter, was. He knelt at Jesus' feet. "Leave me, Lord," he pleaded, "for I'm a sinful man."

"Don't be afraid," Jesus replied. "From now on, you'll be catching people."

That day Peter, Andrew, John, and James left their boats and nets. They had decided to give up everything to follow Jesus.

Religious teachers in Jesus' time and country were called rabbis. Jesus was a traveling rabbi and his followers were called *disciples,* or students.

The group of Jesus' disciples grew. People heard about Jesus' miracles and teachings and came from all over to see and hear him.

One night Jesus went up a hill by himself to pray. His disciples and the crowd camped at the bottom of the hill. The next morning, Jesus came down and chose twelve of the disciples to be his closest followers. "Peter!" Jesus called out. Peter's tanned face broke into a broad grin. He was thrilled to be chosen, along with John, James, and Andrew. Jesus continued to call out names: "Philip. Bartholomew. Matthew. Thomas. James. Simon. Jude. Judas."

The group of twelve was complete. These twelve, called apostles, followed Jesus from village to village. They witnessed many miracles and heard the stories Jesus told. They didn't understand some of the stories right away, but Jesus explained them afterward.

~~~~~~~~~~~~~~~

One evening, after spending several days near the lake with crowds of people, Jesus told the disciples, "Take the boat and cross over to Capernaum. I'm going to stay here for a while, but I'll join you later." So Peter and his companions set sail for Capernaum.

As darkness fell, the wind grew strong and the men had to lower their sail and pull hard on the oars to keep the vessel steady. The boat tossed and pitched, going nowhere.

When they had been fighting the wind for hours, and the waves were growing bigger and bigger, they suddenly saw a tall, pale form gliding across the water toward them. "A ghost!" someone gasped. Frantically, the disciples strained at the oars.

"Be brave," a gentle voice called. "I'm here; don't be afraid."

"Master!?" cried Peter. "Lord, if that's really you," he shouted, "tell me to come to you across the water!"

"Come," invited Jesus.

Immediately Peter was over the side of the boat, hurrying across the waves toward Jesus. Suddenly, he realized what he was doing. How could he be walking on water? Peter stared down in terror. Sure enough, the black water was surging up around his feet and legs. Another second and he would go under. "Master!" he cried. "Save me!"

At once he felt Jesus' strong hand pulling him up.

"You have so little faith," said Jesus. "Why did you doubt?"

Standing there with the Master on top of the wild waves, Peter wondered: *Will I ever doubt again?*

Some time later Jesus asked his disciples, "Who do people say that I am?"

"Certain people say you're John the Baptist. Others think you're Elijah. Some even say you're Jeremiah, or another of the prophets," they answered.

"But you," Jesus insisted. "Who do you say that I am?"

"You are the Messiah, the Son of the living God!" Peter enthusiastically exclaimed.

"Blessed are you, Simon son of John," Jesus replied. "No mere man has revealed this to you, but my Father in heaven. And I say to you, you are Peter, and on this rock I will build my church, and the gates of hell shall not overcome it."

Peter didn't know what Jesus meant by this. But he knew it must be true. Jesus had said it, and that was enough for him.

~~~~~~~~~~~~

The Master had once told a very large crowd that anyone who would eat his flesh and drink his blood would have everlasting life. Many people had stopped listening to Jesus that day. But not Peter. Now, almost three years after Peter had left everything to follow Jesus, he witnessed something amazing. It was the feast of Passover, and Jesus and his apostles were celebrating together in an upstairs room, which they had rented for the occasion.

When it came time for the traditional Jewish blessing of the meal, Jesus took a loaf of bread. He passed it around for them to share, saying, "This is my Body, which is being given for you; do this in remembrance of me." Next, Jesus took a cup of wine and passed it around. He said, "This cup is the new covenant in my Blood, which will be shed for you."

Peter was thinking about these strange words when the Master began to speak again. Jesus told his apostles to serve each other. He said that the most important person among them should behave like the least important. Just before supper, Jesus had washed their feet as an example of the service they should give one another. Now he turned to Peter and added, "Simon, Simon, Satan wanted to have you, to sift you like wheat. But I've prayed for you, that your faith may not fail. Someday, you must strengthen your brothers."

"Lord," said Peter, not understanding what Jesus was saying, "I'm ready to go to prison with you. I would die for you!"

But Jesus answered, "I tell you, Peter, before a rooster crows, you will deny three times that you even know me."

~~~~~~~~~~~~~~~~

Later that night, Jesus and the disciples went to the Garden of Olives, a place near Jerusalem, where Jesus liked to pray. Jesus took Peter, John, and James farther into the garden, and then he went a short distance away from them to pray by himself. The three men grew drowsy as they waited for Jesus. Soon they were sound asleep.

Suddenly, Peter felt a hand on his shoulder, shaking him awake. "It's time," Jesus was saying. "The Son of Man has been betrayed into the hands of sinners. Come, my betrayer is here."

The disciples staggered to their feet. Flickering lights drew near, casting strange shadows in the night. A large group of men came crashing through the trees, carrying clubs and swords. Leading them was Judas, one of the apostles.

"Hail, Master," said Judas, kissing Jesus in greeting. Jesus looked sadly into his eyes and asked, "Are you betraying the Son of Man with a kiss?"

The other men rushed forward and seized Jesus. The Master did not resist. Peter was frightened and angry. He grabbed one of the two swords they had brought and lunged at the high priest's servant, cutting off his ear.

"Put your sword away," Jesus told him. "Those who use the sword will die by it. Don't you know that my Father would send thousands of angels if I asked him?" Reaching out, Jesus touched the servant and immediately healed his ear.

The mob was hemming Jesus in now. Jesus calmly asked why they had come at night, with weapons, as if he were a criminal. Peter slipped into the shadows. From his hiding place, he watched them lead his Master away. Then he followed.

Jesus was led to the palace of the high priest. The building was heavily guarded. Peter saw John go in through the gate. John had been allowed in because he knew the high priest. Soon enough, John approached the gatekeeper and asked her to admit Peter. The woman peered at Peter in the dim light. "Are you also one of this man's disciples?" she asked.

"I don't know what you're talking about!" Peter nervously replied, pushing his way past her. In the courtyard of the palace he joined some servants who were warming themselves around a fire. He strained to hear any news of what was happening to Jesus. The crowd in the courtyard was growing restless. Some of the men were calling for Jesus' death. Peter shuddered. In the dancing light of the fire, fear clouded his face.

"This is one of that man's followers!" someone shouted, pointing at Peter.

"No," he replied. "I'm not!"

But a relative of the man whose ear had been cut off was staring at him. "Weren't you there in the garden with him?" he demanded.

This time Peter made his point loudly. He swore with an oath, "I don't know this man you're talking about!"

The shrill crowing of a rooster suddenly pierced the air. Just then a group of guards led Jesus into the courtyard. For an agonizing moment, the Master turned and looked straight at Peter. And Peter realized what he had done.

He turned and fled out through the gates and into the night, hoping that the darkness would swallow him up. He stumbled as he ran, hot tears searing his face.

No one knows where Peter went or what he did during the next two days. Perhaps he stayed at the edge of the crowd that gathered to watch Jesus' trial before Pilate. He may have heard the people in the crowd who screamed, "Crucify him! Crucify him!" Maybe he even followed the painful procession to Calvary and watched from a distance as Jesus suffered and died on the cross. Peter didn't dare approach the cross, where Mary stood. How could he ever face Jesus or his mother after what he had done?

On Sunday, Mary Magdalene, a good friend of the Master, came rushing into the room where the apostles were staying. "The body of Jesus isn't in the tomb!" she sobbed. Peter and another disciple ran to the tomb and found it empty, but they were not sure what all of this meant.

Later that same day, the risen Jesus appeared to Peter alone. No one knows what happened at that meeting. But we can imagine how happy Peter was to see his Master again and how grateful he was to know that Jesus had forgiven him.

In Galilee a few weeks later, Peter and some of his companions were out fishing on the lake when Jesus called to them from the beach. As soon as Peter realized it was Jesus, he plunged into the water and swam ashore. The others brought the boat in, and they ate breakfast with Jesus on the beach.

After the meal, Jesus turned to Peter and asked, "Simon, son of John, do you love me more than these men do?"

"Yes, Lord, you know that I love you!" Peter exclaimed.

"Feed my lambs," said Jesus. Then he repeated his question, "Simon, son of John, do you love me?"

"Yes, Lord, you know that I love you!" Peter again responded.

"Tend my sheep."

A third time Jesus asked Peter, "Simon, son of John, do you love me?"

"Lord," said the big fisherman, "you know all things; you know that I love you!"

"Feed my sheep," Jesus said.

Just as Peter had denied knowing Jesus three times, he had now declared his love for the Master three

Just as Peter had denied knowing Jesus three times, he now declared his love for him three times. At the same time, Peter received the command from Jesus to take care of the entire Church.

times. And he had received from Jesus the mission to take care of the entire Church.

Forty days after his resurrection, Jesus ascended into heaven. His mother, Peter, and the other disciples and apostles stood on the top of Mount Olivet watching their Master rise steadily into the sky. Finally a small cloud hid him from view. They were alone, but Jesus had said, "I won't leave you orphans; I'll send you another Advocate." The little group made their way back to Jerusalem to wait for what would happen next.

For nine days they prayed together in a large room. On the morning of the tenth day, they heard a loud roar, like a strong wind blowing. Tongues of fire appeared above their heads. And all at once, what they had found difficult to understand about Jesus and his teachings became clear in their minds! They began to really understand Jesus' mission—and their own.

Peter and his companions hurried out into the street, where they found a growing crowd of people who had traveled from many lands to celebrate the harvest feast of Pentecost. These people had also heard the rushing wind and had come to see what was happening. Peter and the other apostles began to tell them about Jesus—how he had fulfilled the prophecies of the Messiah, how he had been crucified, how he had risen from the dead and ascended into heaven. They explained that Jesus is God and the Savior of the world!

Although the people listening spoke many different languages, they all understood what Peter was saying. The Holy Spirit had made this possible. "What shall we do, brothers?" they eagerly asked the disciples.

"Be sorry for your sins and be baptized in the name of Jesus Christ," Peter answered.

By that night about three thousand people had been baptized!

~~~~~~~~~~~~~~~~~~

The lives of the followers of Jesus centered around the Eucharist, which renewed Jesus' presence among them. They found themselves being transformed by the Eucharist and by the Holy Spirit, until they were living more and more as Jesus had lived—with great love for all people, with humility and patience, spending time in prayer to their heavenly Father. The Acts of the Apostles, which tells us how the first followers of Jesus lived, says, "The whole group of those who believed were of one heart and soul" (4:32). This was the beginning of the Church.

The Church grew in spite of being persecuted and misunderstood. People who were not Jewish also began to believe in Jesus and received baptism.

Soon Peter went to live in Antioch, a city much larger than Jerusalem. It was there that members of this new Church were first called "Christians." Later, Peter went to Rome, the center of the Roman Empire.

In Rome, Peter encouraged, comforted, and taught Christians, especially those who were being mistreated because of their faith. He urged all Christians to be humble and kind and to give good example to everybody.

During Nero's rule as emperor, a fierce persecution of Christians broke out in Rome. Nero didn't understand why Christians wouldn't worship him, as Roman law required, and why they wouldn't pray to the Roman gods.

Peter was taken prisoner and put on trial. He was sentenced to death together with Paul, another great disciple of Jesus. Since Paul was a Roman citizen, he would be beheaded. Not being a Roman citizen, Peter would suffer the crueler punishment of crucifixion.

While the soldiers were leading him out to a hill called the Vatican, Peter remembered the day that Jesus had been led up another hill—called Golgotha— and to another cross. *I'm not worthy to die in the same way as Jesus,* he thought.

"Please," Peter asked the soldiers, "crucify me upside down."

They fastened him upside down on the cross, and the agony began. Pain tore at every part of Peter's body until his half-closed eyes could see no more and numbness overcame him. But suddenly Paradise opened wide before him, and Peter saw with joy once more the gentle Master whom he had loved so much.

One of Peter's most beautiful attitudes was his humility. He often spoke at the wrong time or said things before thinking. But when he had made a mistake, he always admitted it, and he let Jesus correct him and teach him. We can be like Peter by admitting our mistakes and apologizing when we have hurt anyone.

St. Paul

(First Century)

JANUARY 25 AND JUNE 29

While Jesus walked the dusty roads of Palestine, a young Jewish boy named Saul was growing up in a seaport city in Asia Minor called Tarsus. Many wealthy Jewish families lived in Tarsus.

Saul's father was a Pharisee. This meant that he followed many strict religious rules. Saul had to live by those rules too.

The boy was intelligent and lively. At the age of five, he began his schooling with the study of the Bible. As soon as he was old enough, Saul also began to learn a trade, as was the custom at that time. His father taught him how to make tents.

"Come, O Lord, and don't delay," the boy often prayed as he worked. Like all Jewish children, he was waiting for the coming of the Messiah whom God had promised to send to his people. Saul didn't know that the Messiah had already come. He was Jesus, God's own Son. He was living in a town called Nazareth, where he learned the carpenter's trade from his foster father. People were expecting the Messiah to be a mighty prince who would free Israel from the Roman armies and conquer the whole world. What a surprise Jesus would be to everyone!

While Jesus was still living a quiet, hidden life in Nazareth, twelve-year-old Saul set out with a camel caravan for the great city of Jerusalem. There, at the magnificent Temple, he studied to become a rabbi—a teacher of the Hebrew Law.

Years passed. Saul became a rabbi and returned home to Tarsus. Saul was in Tarsus when Jesus began his public ministry and revealed that he was the Messiah. He was in Tarsus when some of the Pharisees refused to recognize that this poor Man who spoke of a spiritual kingdom was really the leader sent by God to his people. Saul was in Tarsus when word came that the leaders in Jerusalem had killed Jesus by nailing him to a cross.

At some point, Saul returned to Jerusalem. There, one day, he joined a crowd of people who were determined to punish a man named Stephen. Stephen was a disciple of Jesus and had been teaching others about him. This angered Saul and some of his friends. They felt that Stephen had betrayed their religion and must be killed.

The crowd dragged Stephen outside the city. As the men hurled stone after stone at him, they piled their cloaks at Saul's feet. Just before he died, Stephen fell to his knees and cried out, "Lord, don't hold this sin against them." Saul didn't understand how Stephen could forgive the men who were killing him. But he was still determined to stop these "Nazarenes." From that day on, Saul became one of the fiercest and most violent persecutors of the followers of Jesus. He rushed from city to city capturing the Nazarenes and having them thrown into prison.

Saul was soon on his way across the desert to Damascus—a city that had become a new center for Jesus' followers. After long days of travel, Saul and his companions saw Damascus before them. Saul felt a new burst of energy. *Nobody will escape this time,* he silently vowed. Suddenly, the very air about him seemed to explode with light, and an unknown power knocked him to the ground. Dazed and confused, Saul struggled to open his eyes. A voice rang out, "Saul, Saul, why are you persecuting me?"

"Sir," he cried, "who are you?"

Terrified, Saul heard the reply: "I am Jesus, whom you are persecuting."

Jesus! The one who had been crucified really *was* the Messiah, and was alive...just as his followers claimed! Not only that, but Jesus was identifying himself with the people Saul was persecuting. Saul felt sick. What a terrible mistake he had made!

"It's hard for you to accept this," came the voice again.

Yes, Saul thought, *it's very hard indeed.* But now that he knew the truth, he had to swallow his pride and forget his plans. "Lord," he asked, "what do you want me to do?"

Jesus told Saul to go into the city to the house of a man named Jude. Saul stumbled to his feet. His eyes were open, but he could see nothing. His startled companions, who had seen the brilliant light but not heard Jesus' voice, had to lead him by the hand into Damascus.

~~~~~~~~~~~~~~~~

A few days later, Jesus appeared in a dream to Ananias, one of the disciples who lived in Damascus. The Lord instructed him to go to the house of Jude, where he would find Saul praying. Ananias knew that Saul had been persecuting the disciples, and he was afraid. "Go," Jesus insisted. "This man is the one I have chosen to make me known throughout the world. I'll show him how much he will have to suffer for my name."

When Ananias arrived at Jude's house, he found Saul praying, just as Jesus had said. "Saul, my brother," said Ananias, laying his hands on him, "the Lord Jesus has sent me to you so that you may see and be filled with the Holy Spirit." When Saul heard Ananias's voice and felt his touch, peace filled his heart and he was able to see again!

Then Ananias baptized Saul, making Saul a member of the same group he had been so violently persecuting. Now Saul promised to do everything he could to spread the Good News about Jesus.

Saul immediately began preaching in the synagogues of Damascus, proclaiming that Jesus is the Son of God. He kept this up for a long time until some people decided to kill him. But the followers of Jesus learned about the plot and warned Saul. Disguised as an Arab, Saul left Damascus and went out alone into the desert.

Saul stayed in the desert for many months. While he was there, Jesus instructed him through inspirations and revelations. Saul prayed and fasted. Finally he returned to Damascus and began to preach again. Again there were rumors that some men wanted to kill him. The gates were being watched, so this time his friends had to lower him over the city wall in a huge wicker basket!

Saul traveled to Jerusalem, but he had trouble there, too. Many of Jesus' followers, who knew what a fierce enemy he had been, didn't believe that Saul had *really* been converted. Even the apostles, who led the young Church under the guidance of Peter, wondered whether Saul could be trusted. A disciple named Barnabas finally came to the rescue. Barnabas believed that Saul was sincere, and he told the apostles so. Barnabas was able to convince them to accept Saul as a new apostle.

Saul spent fifteen days in Jerusalem. With Peter he walked the road that Jesus had followed to Calvary, prayed at Jesus' tomb, and remembered the suffering he himself had caused Jesus.

"I persecuted him," cried Saul.

"I denied him," recalled Peter. Together they thanked God for the mercy and love he had shown both of them. Together they continued to preach about Jesus to the people living in Jerusalem. But many of the people still would not listen to Saul. One day, when Saul was praying in the Temple, Jesus appeared to him. "Don't be discouraged," the Lord told him. Hurry and leave this city. I'll send you to the people of distant nations."

Saul obeyed. He went home to Tarsus and began to tell friends and relatives about Jesus, while he waited to learn what to do next.

~~~~~~~~~~~~

After a few years had gone by, Barnabas arrived in Tarsus, looking for Saul. "Come with me to Antioch, Saul," he invited. "We need you there."

So Saul eagerly set out with Barnabas. Antioch, in Syria, was the third largest city in the Roman Empire, and many of Jesus' followers were already living there. In fact, Antioch was where members of the Church were called "Christians" for the first time.

Saul found that his days were busy and full as he preached the Gospel in Antioch. More and more people came to believe in Jesus.

Time passed. Once, while the disciples were praying, the Holy Spirit let them know that Barnabas and Saul were to be missionaries, bringing the Good News of Jesus to many different people and nations.

Saul and Barnabas took Mark, Barnabas's young cousin, with them on their first journey. Their hearts pounded with excitement as they set sail for the Mediterranean island of Cyprus.

The trio had been preaching on the island for several days, and had baptized many of the people, when they received a summons to appear before Sergius Paulus, the Roman governor of Cyprus. The disciples felt honored to be called before the governor. They thought that he, too, wanted to learn about Jesus. But trouble was waiting for them at the governor's home. Sergius Paulus had a crafty magician named Elymas living in his household. "Don't listen to them, Paulus!" Elymas urged. "They're speaking a lot of nonsense."

"Son of the devil!" retorted Saul, feeling himself full of the power of the Holy Spirit. "As a punishment you will be blind for a while!" At that moment Elymas gasped and began groping about. He was blind!

Governor Paulus was amazed. *Men with such power,* he thought, *must be representatives of the true God.* "Saul, will you baptize me into your faith?" he asked. And so Sergius Paulus became a Christian.

It was after this that Saul (who was now called Paul) and his companions set off for Asia Minor. When they reached the coast, Mark returned home to Jerusalem. Paul and Barnabas traveled on foot from city to city, establishing Christian communities. Because the Christian religion was not understood, Paul and Barnabas were persecuted almost everywhere and had to keep moving on.

In a city called Lystra, Paul and Barnabas met a crippled man, who listened to them intently. Paul looked at the man and knew that he had faith. "Get up," said Paul, "and walk." The man stood up, healed!

"It's Hermes himself," whispered a man in the crowd to a companion. "It's Zeus and Hermes!" cried another. The crowd was in an uproar, convinced that Barnabas and Paul were two of their pagan gods.

"Bring them to the temple!" they cried. "Cover them with flowers! Call the priests!"

When Paul and Barnabas realized what was happening, they began to protest, "We're not gods, but human beings—just like you!" But then a new rumor started. The people began to shout, "They've tricked us! Stone them! Stone them!" Instead of being draped with flowers, Paul and Barnabas had to run for their lives. Stones whizzed through the air, pounding them on every side. Finally, Paul and Barnabas sank to the ground. Members of the angry mob dragged them outside the city, leaving them for dead.

Fortunately, Paul and Barnabas had made some friends in the city. When some of them heard what had happened, they rushed out to find the two missionaries. As Paul and Barnabas opened their eyes, they saw a circle of anxious and compassionate faces looking down on them.

The new Christians tenderly cared for the apostles, and Paul and Barnabas recovered enough to move on. The next day saw them limping away to the next city. They had to tell others the Good News of Jesus.

Four years later, after having preached in many cities and towns, the two friends returned to Antioch. They also went to Jerusalem, where they spent time with Peter, telling him of the many new Christian communities in Asia Minor. Peter happily sent Paul back to evangelize other parts of Asia Minor.

This time, Paul's companion was Silas instead of Barnabas. The two men passed through many of the towns Paul had visited on his previous trip. At each stop, Paul encouraged the Christians. In Lystra, a young man named Timothy joined Paul and Silas.

One night, while the three men were in Troas, a city on the coast of Asia Minor, Paul had a vision. A man from Macedonia stood before him and begged, "Come over to Macedonia and help us!" Though close to Asia Minor, Macedonia was part of a different continent—Europe. The next morning, Paul excitedly told Silas and Timothy what had happened. "God must want us in Macedonia," Silas agreed. Timothy nodded. So the missionaries immediately made plans to sail for Europe.

In Philippi, the first European city they visited, a woman named Lydia was baptized. She opened her home to the three apostles, and many of the new Christians also gathered there to pray. In Philippi, a doctor named Luke also joined Paul, Silas, and Timothy. Luke would one day write down all he knew about Jesus and the early Christian communities. The books he wrote are what we know as the Gospel of St. Luke and the Acts of the Apostles.

But Paul and Silas soon found themselves in trouble again. When Paul freed a slave girl from an evil spirit, her owners became very upset. Now she could no longer tell people's fortunes—which meant she could no longer earn money for them. The girl's masters stirred up anger against Paul and Silas and had the city officials of Philippi arrest them. "Beat them with rods and throw them into jail!" came the order. That night, bruised and bleeding, and with their feet tied to a stake, Paul and Silas thanked Jesus for having made them worthy to suffer for his name. To the amazement of the other prisoners, they even began to sing!

God had given Paul such great powers to heal that sick people only touched his clothes or objects that belonged to him and they were cured!

Around midnight, while Paul and Silas were praying and singing, a violent earthquake shook the prison. The cell doors flew open, and all the prisoners' chains were pulled loose. When the jailer woke up and learned what had happened, he panicked. *If the prisoners have escaped, I'm doomed! Better for me to take my life than to be killed,* he reasoned. The jailer was ready to commit suicide with his own sword, when Paul's voice echoed in the dark jail, "Don't harm yourself! We're all here!"

Calling for a torch, the jailer ran in and fell to his knees before Paul and Silas. "What must I do to be saved?" he asked.

"Believe in the Lord Jesus, and you and your family will be saved," Paul and Silas promised him. That night the jailer and his whole family were baptized.

Paul and his companions moved on to Thessalonica. But they had to leave when some men there stirred up the people against them. Paul went on to Athens and then to Corinth, where he waited for Timothy and Silas to join him.

After spending a year and a half in the busy port city of Corinth, Paul and his companions returned to Jerusalem.

But soon Paul was back in Asia, where he stopped in the city of Ephesus. He stayed there for almost three years, preaching and working miracles. God had given Paul such great powers to heal, that sick people only touched his clothes or objects that belonged to him and they were cured!

Once, the Christians of Ephesus brought Paul all the books they could find that taught magic or superstitious practices. He made a huge pile and burned them in the city square. The bright bonfire reminded the people of the light of the new faith in Jesus that Paul had brought them.

Soon Paul's restless spirit urged him to search for other people to bring to Christ. He traveled again to Macedonia and Greece. Then he returned to Troas in Asia. There an amazing thing happened.

One evening, Paul was celebrating Holy Mass in an upper room. The room was crowded with Christians eager to take part in the Eucharistic Celebration and to hear Paul speak. During the sermon, some of the boys sat on the windowsills. As Paul spoke on and on about the love of Jesus, one of the boys became sleepy. His head began to sag. He nodded, caught himself, then drooped again...and all of a sudden it was too late! He was falling!

"Eutychus!" screamed one of his companions. The people rushed wildly down the stairs and out into the street. "Paul," a terrified voice cried, "Eutychus is dead!"

Paul had raced down the stairs behind them. He shouldered his way through the crowd and knelt beside the lifeless form. The boy had fallen three stories onto the hard stones of the street. What could save him? The power of God!

Paul quickly threw his own body onto the boy's, praying silently. Then, wrapping his arms around the boy, he said, "Don't be afraid. He's alive!"

Sure enough, Eutychus was moving! His eyes opened. He blinked and smiled up at Paul. "Praised be

Jesus Christ," murmured one of the onlookers. Exclamations of joy ran through the crowd. With their hearts full of love and thanks, the Christians returned to Mass.

Paul wanted to go to Jerusalem again. On the way, he stopped in Miletus. Many of his friends from Ephesus met him there. *Perhaps I'll never see them again,* Paul thought. "Be real followers of Jesus," he urged them. They cried for sorrow as he prepared to board a ship for Jerusalem. Paul himself had to wipe tears from his eyes.

The last part of Paul's journey was over land. On the way, he and his companions met an old prophet named Agabus, who was enlightened by the Holy Spirit. Agabus came up, took Paul's belt, and tied his own hands and feet together with it. "The man who owns this belt will be bound just like this in Jerusalem," he said. There was no doubt that he was talking about Paul!

"Turn back, Paul, before it's too late," his friends urged him. "You're risking your life to go to Jerusalem now!"

"Why are you crying and breaking my heart?" Paul asked with pain in his voice. "I'm ready to be chained and even killed in Jerusalem. It will be for the honor and glory of Jesus, my Lord."

Tense and expectant, Paul and his companions finally reached Jerusalem. They found the place where the Christians met for prayer, and were greeted by James, the cousin of Jesus. James was in charge of the Jerusalem church. Peter had moved on sometime before.

Soon a false story began circulating among the people in Jerusalem. Rumor had it that Paul had brought non-Jews into the Temple. This was forbidden, and an angry mob pounced on Paul. They would have killed him if Roman soldiers hadn't stepped in. Thinking that Paul must be a criminal to have started such a riot, an officer barked to his soldiers, "Arrest this man! Bind him in chains, and take him to the prison."

Some men were still determined to kill Paul. Paul's young nephew overheard them plotting and told the Roman commander. "Don't tell anyone that you gave me this information," the officer instructed the boy. "I'll keep Paul safe."

The commander immediately arranged for a group of armed soldiers to bring Paul to the palace of Felix, the governor, in the city of Caesarea. Paul would be safe there until his trial. Paul and his guards left Jerusalem that very night.

For two years, Paul remained in the dungeon of Felix's palace. It was not until a new governor, Festus, took office that the apostle was brought forward and questioned. Festus didn't find Paul guilty of anything, but decided to keep him in prison to please some of the people.

"I appeal to Caesar," Paul declared at last. Such an appeal was the right of every Roman citizen, and Paul had inherited Roman citizenship from his father. When a man appealed to Caesar, he had to go to Rome for his trial.

Two of Paul's friends, Luke and Aristarchus, started out for Rome with him. Of course, Paul was still a prisoner, so a Roman soldier was sent along as a guard. The soldier, Julius, was a kind and considerate man who grew to admire and respect Paul during the long and dangerous sea voyage.

After many adventures, including a shipwreck on the island of Malta, Paul, Luke, Aristarchus, and Julius walked the last few miles to Rome. Christians living near Rome came out to greet Paul and encourage him along the way.

In Rome, while Paul was waiting for his trial, he met often with the Christians. Even though he was under arrest, he was allowed to live in a rented room and have visitors. From that room, Paul wrote many letters to his friends in the communities of Greece, Macedonia, and Asia Minor. At last his trial came to court. He was found innocent of any major crime and set free!

Paul continued his travels and preaching. At one point, he met Peter in Corinth. The two apostles decided to return to Rome to help and comfort their fellow Christians, who were undergoing a terrible persecution. The cruel and insane Emperor Nero had set Rome on fire—and blamed it on the Christians!

Peter and Paul were not in Rome long when they, too, were arrested and flung into prison. Both apostles were sentenced to death.

Paul was led outside the city walls, whipped, and blindfolded. He was told to rest his head on a low pillar. The executioner raised his gleaming sword and brought it down with all his strength. The apostle's head fell to the ground. But his soul flew to God.

From heaven, St. Peter and St. Paul have watched over the Church down through the centuries. Their spirit lives on in the Church even today. Their letters to various

Christian communities are part of the New Testament and are often included in our readings at Mass.

The Church celebrates the Conversion of St. Paul on January 25, and the Solemnity of Peter and Paul on June 29.

> *St. Paul's letters speak to us today, just as they spoke to the people to whom they were first written. In reading and studying them, we can become filled with faith and love for the Lord Jesus just as Paul was. We can pray to St. Paul for the strength to live and spread our faith in Jesus as he did.*

St. Thecla

(First Century)

SEPTEMBER 23

Tradition tells us that St. Thecla was the first martyr among Christian women, as St. Stephen was the first of the men.

Thecla was born around A.D. 30 in the city of Iconium, in Asia Minor. It is said that she was the daughter of an important citizen, whose house was noted for the expensive banquets that were given there.

Thecla's family believed very strongly in the pagan gods and magical superstitions, which were popular at the time.

Thecla liked to spend her time studying great works of art and literature. But the more she learned, especially about philosophy, the more unhappy she felt. It seemed that none of the many books she read, or the many teachers she had, could answer her deepest questions about life.

Often, after long hours of study, she would go out on the balcony and gaze at the sunset, wondering silently, *If my soul is to die out like that setting sun, why was it created? If it is to go on living after death, what will happen to it? Will some God take it to live with him? If so, who will he be?* In her heart, Thecla would say to that unknown God, *O mysterious Being, if you exist, if you love me as I believe, let me know about you!*

Thecla was eighteen when her parents began to think of finding a husband for her. She seemed to have no interest in marriage, but her father chose a rich and powerful young man named Tamiridus to be her fiancé.

Tamiridus was extremely happy to be Thecla's fiancé, and everyone envied him. Thecla was not only rich—she also had a reputation for being mature, intelligent, and gracious. Her sense of modesty showed off her natural beauty the way a white background shows off a bright bouquet of flowers.

But while her parents and fiancé were busily preparing for the wedding, something happened that would change the whole course of Thecla's life. The apostles Paul and Barnabas arrived in Iconium.

Coming home one night, Thecla passed by the temple of Castor and Pollux. She heard the voices of two speakers who were teaching the people.

"Who are those philosophers?" Thecla asked, ordering her servants to stop.

"Two preachers who come from Antioch," she was told.

"What are they talking about?"

"They are teaching about a God, who created heaven and earth and is our Father."

Thecla was excited. Could this be the God she had been looking for? Could this be the God whom she loved?

Thecla couldn't sleep that night. What she had heard fired her imagination, and she felt sorry that she had not spoken to the two preachers.

At sunrise, she knew what she must do. Calling one of the servants to go with her, Thecla hurried to the temple of Castor and Pollux, where she found Paul and Barnabas.

"Speak to me," she begged them. "Tell me about your God. I need to know all about him!"

Paul greeted Thecla kindly. In his heart he thanked God for the young woman's sincere desire. He began to teach her about Jesus. When he told her about the mystery of the Eucharist, Thecla was astonished at God's infinite love. This God was so unlike any god she had learned about before. Warm and tender tears flowed down her cheeks. She asked to be baptized immediately, and to complete her religious instruction as soon as possible.

Together with her servant, who also became a Christian, Thecla often took part in the Eucharistic Celebration. When she received the Body and Blood of Jesus, she was filled with a love that made her completely forget everything else.

Thecla's family and Tamiridus were very angry when she told them that she was now a Christian. She also told them that she would not marry Tamiridus because she was consecrated to God. First with kindness and then with threats, they tried to change her mind, but it was no use. Thecla refused to give up her Christian faith.

Finally Thecla was taken before the governor, who tried to make her give up her belief. "For your own good, leave this new religion to the miserable and to the poor for whom it seems to have been made. Sacrifice to the gods of Greece with me!" the governor urged.

"No, I cannot obey you," Thecla bravely replied. "It is not right to disobey God in order to obey a human person."

"You will not even obey your governor?"

"No, for God is much greater than you are."

"You are a proud and superstitious girl," the governor retorted. "You no longer listen to reason. Guards, take her to the prison!"

Thecla was put in chains and shut up in a dark, filthy cell. Anyone else might have been overwhelmed by hunger, fear, loneliness, and the terrible odor of the prison. But not Thecla, who placed all her hope in the Lord. It is said that angels came from heaven to comfort her in the silence of that dark cell.

Eight days later, Thecla was taken before the governor in the arena. She appeared more beautiful, more joyful, and more radiant than ever before. She still refused to give up her faith, so the governor ordered a tall stake to be erected. The trumpets sounded, announcing a death sentence.

The soldiers tied Thecla to the stake, piled wood around her, and lit a fire. Soon thick smoke filled the air. Tall flames leapt and crackled.

A shiver of horror ran through the crowd. Some people screamed. Others called for silence. Some hoped that she would change her mind. Others wished that they could save this noble and beautiful girl.

But what was happening? Thecla made the Sign of the Cross and stood calmly amid the flames. Her face shone with heavenly beauty. Her gaze was fixed on the sky, for she was deep in prayer.

A miracle! God had saved his faithful servant! The fire did not touch Thecla.

But the governor was not to be outdone. He ordered that Thecla be heavily guarded and sent to the city of Antioch. There she was to be taken to the arena and fed to the lions.

A large crowd turned out to see the spectacle. The people murmured excitedly as Thecla's slender form appeared at the edge of the arena. They grew silent as she walked out into the center, knelt down, and prayed. Even some of the most heartless and cruel people felt pity for her. Mothers embraced their daughters, as they thought with horror of what would soon happen to the young Christian. Even the governor's heart was touched—and that had never happened to him before! Someone suggested that Thecla be freed, but then superstition won out again, and the crowd began to yell, "The Christian to the lions! The Christian to the lions!"

The attendants opened the cage door. A huge, fiery-eyed lion leaped out. He stretched himself and roared, showing two rows of fierce teeth in a mouth that made even the governor shiver.

The lion pawed the ground and shook his long mane. After circling the arena, he stopped and looked at Thecla. He switched his sides with his tail, then let out a great roar and crept toward her. The people held their breath.

Only Thecla seemed unworried. Although the lion's breath was now hot on her face, she stood peacefully, looking toward the sky. The lion lowered his large head and lay down beside her. He began to lick her feet!

A murmur of astonishment arose from all sides.

"Another lion!" the governor shouted angrily.

A short-furred lioness leaped out of the cage. She also ran around the arena, roared fiercely, and pawed the ground. Then, attracted by the peaceful girl, she rubbed up against Thecla's hands as a little kitten might have done!

At this sight, the wonder and anger of the spectators grew. The governor was furious.

Two more unsuccessful attempts to take Thecla's life convinced a few important citizens that she should be freed, and she was.

Thecla went to live by herself in a small cave in the country, where people from nearby towns and cities came to hear her talk about Jesus and his love for all of us—love so great that he died on the cross for everyone. Many people became Christians. Thecla had been so generous and trusting in God that he now used her to bring others to believe in him.

Thecla died a holy death at the age of ninety. Even though she had survived the attempts on her life, she

Although the lion's breath was hot on her face, Thecla stood peacefully, looking toward the sky. The lion lowered his large head and lay down beside her.

is honored as the first woman martyr because she was ready to die for her belief in Jesus Christ.

When early Christians wished to praise a woman for her courage, they would say, "She's like Thecla!"

Thecla was brave in the face of death because she knew that her faith in Jesus was a great treasure. She knew that if she died, she would be with her Lord in heaven. She knew that if she lived, she would tell others about the love of the true God, Creator and Father of all people. Like Thecla, we should always thank God for our faith.

St. Cecilia

(Third Century)

November 22

Cecilia was born in the city of Rome during the third century. Her father was a Roman senator, and her family was very wealthy. Although her father was not a Christian, he allowed his Christian wife to baptize Cecilia when she was still a young child.

Dressed in her tiny tunic and sandals, little Cecilia would go around the large family estate singing, dancing, and amusing everyone. Her mother taught her Christian prayers and told her many stories about Jesus. Together they would often pray for an end to the persecution of their Christian brothers and sisters.

Although she was young, Cecilia understood what the persecutions meant. "Mother, won't they ever stop killing Christians?" she asked. "Every day so many die in the arena while people laugh at them. I feel so sorry for them."

Cecilia's mother told her, "It's good to feel sorry for people who die because of their faith in Jesus. But we should be happy for them, too. The martyrs are killed because they love Jesus and believe he is God. They go straight to heaven to live with Jesus forever."

Cecilia asked, "Can only poor people become martyrs?"

"Oh, no, Cecilia! All of us must be ready to die for our faith."

With eyes shining, Cecilia exclaimed, "I want to be a martyr, too!"

Cecilia could not hide her great desire for martyrdom, and often talked about it with her mother. If her mother was busy, Cecilia would talk with Lyda, one of the family's servants, whom she loved like a sister.

The years passed, and finally it was Cecilia's fourteenth birthday. In the family's large courtyard, many of the young woman's friends had gathered for her party. It was already time for the celebration to begin, but Cecilia had still not come down from her room. Her mother went up and found her crying.

"Why are you crying?" she asked in surprise. "You should be happy. Today you are a young lady! All your friends are waiting downstairs for you."

Smiling through her tears, Cecilia stood up and straightened her dress. "I'll go down now, Mother," she answered. "Thanks for coming to get me."

Cecilia hurried downstairs to the party. For the rest of the afternoon, she and her friends had a good time. They played games and ate all the good food that had been prepared for them. In the late evening, the young people began to leave. Cecilia disappeared, too. Her mother searched all over for her and finally found her in the kitchen, washing the dishes.

"Cecilia, what are you doing?" Cecilia's mother was shocked to see her daughter working like a servant. "You know Lyda and the other servants will take care of all this!"

"I'm no better than Lyda, Mother," Cecilia calmly answered. "I must work, too."

"Never mind that now," her mother replied. "Let's go up to your room. I want to talk with you."

Silently the mother and daughter climbed the marble staircase. "Now tell me, why were you crying this afternoon?" Cecilia's mother finally asked. "Did someone hurt you?"

"No, Mother," Cecilia quietly answered.

"Are you unhappy? You know you can have anything you ask for," her mother continued.

Cecilia smiled. "I'm very content with what I have, really, Mother. I was crying today because I am so happy to be a Christian. But I want to be more. I want to love and please Jesus by doing something special for him. I've talked with our priest, and I've decided to consecrate myself—body and soul—to Jesus forever. I've made a vow to do this."

Cecilia's mother was silent for a few moments. Finally, she said, "You're still very young. Why not wait a few more years? Besides, I'm afraid that your father will not understand this!"

Cecilia's mother began to cry then, for she knew that her husband, the senator, would be very upset with this news. Leaving her daughter's room, she met her husband in the hall.

"What's wrong?" he asked, seeing her tears.

"I must talk to you about Cecilia. She told me that she never wants to marry. She is in love only with God."

Cecilia's father grew angry. "In love with God? What foolishness is this! Of course she'll marry. And she'll marry a wealthy Roman senator. I'll see to that."

Cecilia's father calmed himself and went to confront his daughter. "Tell me that what your mother says isn't true," he demanded. "You don't want to hurt me by remaining unmarried all your life, do you?"

"I don't intend to hurt you, Father," Cecilia replied. "You've always told me that you wanted me to be happy. To give my life to Jesus will make me happy."

"Never speak of this nonsense again," her father ordered as he turned away. "I won't hear of it."

Cecilia didn't sleep that night. She kept thinking about what her father had said. She never spoke again about consecrating her life to Jesus, but she prayed that God would guide her in the years ahead.

~~~~~~~~~~~~

Three years passed with nothing more said about marriage for Cecilia. Then one day, her father brought a handsome young man named Valerian home to meet her. Valerian wanted to marry her, and her father soon began arranging for the wedding. Cecilia had no choice in the matter. In those days, marriages were always arranged by the parents.

On the day of the wedding there was great excitement in Cecilia's home. The servants decorated a large room and spread tables with all kinds of food and drink. Cecilia looked especially beautiful in her lovely white tunic. White roses adorned her hair.

All through the wedding ceremony, Cecilia thought about the vow she had made to Jesus. But she did her best to be a good hostess and make sure that her guests enjoyed themselves. The party lasted all day and part of the night. Finally, she took Valerian aside and told him about her vow. She told him that she was the bride of Jesus Christ. Valerian was not a Christian, but he wanted to know more about her "Bridegroom." As Cecilia explained, he understood more and more. He accepted Cecilia's situation and asked to become a Christian.

After some months of instruction about Jesus Christ and the Church, Valerian was baptized. His brother Tiburtius was also baptized. Together, the three young Christians helped the poor people of the city and buried the martyrs. But one day the emperor found out that Valerian and Tiburtius were Christians. Since this was against the Roman law at that time, he had both men arrested and ordered them to be killed in the arena. They were happy to die for Jesus, because they wanted to go to heaven. But poor Cecilia! Now she was left alone.

After the two young men died, Cecilia waited until everyone left the arena. Then with the help of friends, she took the bodies to the catacombs. The catacombs were underground tunnels where the Christians buried their dead.

Each day Cecilia prayed that God would grant her the joy of dying as a martyr for him. She did not have long to wait. Soon two Roman soldiers came to take her to the emperor, who condemned her to death. She was to be martyred in a large room that would be heated until she suffocated.

Finally, Cecilia took Valerian aside and told him of her vow. She told him that she was the bride of Jesus Christ. Valerian was not a Christian, but he wanted to know more about her "Bridegroom."

Cecilia entered the death room, knelt down and said, "Oh, Jesus, I thank you for having given me the grace to die a martyr. I believe and hope in you, O Lord. I love you with all my heart! Now I'm going to my death, a day for which I've waited so long. I will die for you, dear Jesus. Take me to heaven quickly. Have mercy on all the people who don't know you yet. Bless and protect all Christians, that they may worship you in peace. Amen."

The soldiers closed and locked the door. For about three hours they left her alone, expecting to find her dead when they returned. Instead, they heard music coming from the room. The soldiers rushed in and found Cecilia, standing up with her arms outstretched, singing and praising God.

The captain was startled. After a few moments he ordered a soldier, "Go tell the emperor about this!"

Minutes later the royal carriage arrived. The emperor, in all his glory and majesty, walked into the building. He had never been so angry. "So, she did not die?" he roared. "Then we will kill her in another way! You fools didn't heat the room enough, that's why she's still alive. But now she'll suffer more. Take your sword and cut off her head!"

Two soldiers stepped forward. Before they reached her, she had already put her head down, pushing her long hair to one side. The captain let his sword fall once swiftly, then again. But the blows weren't enough to sever Cecilia's head. Although mortally wounded, she was still breathing.

The cruel emperor smirked. "Let her suffer," he commanded. "Let her die in misery." Then he turned and left the room.

Cecilia's friends gathered around her, crying. Her eyes opened and she gazed upon them all. She was silently praying for them. Then her eyes closed and remained that way. At the end of the second day, Cecilia again opened her eyes. She looked at her friends, and then toward heaven. Her friends gathered closer, hoping that she would say something. But, no, she was looking at Someone whom they could not see. In her heart, she was talking with God.

The hours passed slowly, while Cecilia remained in the same position. At the beginning of the third day, she moved a little. Her eyes opened once again, and she looked up. One friend drew close to her and watched her for a few moments. Then she turned to the others and whispered, "Jesus Christ came to take Cecilia just now. Let's pray for our dear sister, who is now a saint in heaven."

All her friends knelt down to pray for Cecilia. They also prayed to her, asking her to intercede for all the Christians, for they knew that she was now with Jesus and Mary.

St. Cecilia loved and respected everyone sincerely, whether they were rich or poor, servant or noble. She tried to help anyone in need and knew that all people were children of the same God. We can imitate Cecilia by showing respect for each person we meet.

St. Tarcisius

(Third Century)

AUGUST 15

Under the rule of the Roman Emperor Valerian, the Christians lived in peace for several years. But in A.D. 258, an official convinced the emperor to begin a new persecution of the followers of Jesus. "All Christians will be put to death," Valerian declared. "Only those who deny Jesus Christ and honor the gods of Rome will be set free."

That very night, the elderly Pope Sixtus II called the Christians together in the catacombs. "My brothers and sisters and beloved children in our Lord Jesus Christ," he began, "as you already know, we are under persecution once again! Some of the faithful have already been taken to prison. Let us pray for them!"

The search for Christians grew more intense with each passing day. The emperor's soldiers went house by house, arresting Jesus' followers. Soon the city's prisons were full. Every evening when the sun was setting, the condemned Christians sang hymns to God.

The beautiful sound of their singing floated up from the damp underground cells.

One evening, a young boy was walking near the prisons. His name was Tarcisius, and he was the son of Senator Tarsente, a wealthy Christian. Tarcisius heard the condemned Christians singing, and his heart filled with pity. The boy knelt, listening, for a long time by the barred windows.

Tarcisius returned home late. His governess was waiting for him in the doorway. "Why are you so late, Tarcisius? I was worried about you, especially since your father isn't home. He had to go into hiding. They're trying to find him to question him."

"He's hiding?" Tarcisius repeated in alarm.

"Yes. For your sake," the governess answered.

"But if they find him, he won't deny Christ, will he?" the boy asked.

"Of course not," the elderly woman responded. "Your father is a brave man, and he loves Jesus more than life itself. He won't betray his faith. Now come and eat. Supper is ready."

Tarcisius ate slowly. It was a sad supper without his father. Suddenly he asked, "I've heard people say that my mother was a martyr. Is that true?"

"Yes," replied his governess. "She was killed when Decian was emperor. Your father was going to tell you when you were older."

"But I'm already old!" exclaimed Tarcisius. "Please tell me more about my mother," he pleaded.

"Yes, yes, I'll tell you tonight, Tarcisius. Your mother told me that she would be waiting for you in heaven. She loved you very much."

Tarcisius's eyes glowed at the words of his governess. "Tell me more," he begged.

"Your mother was young and a very kind woman, Tarcisius. Although she loved you very much and would have wanted to stay with you, she was faithful to Christ." Later that evening, after the governess and Tarcisius had talked for a long time about his mother, they went down into the catacombs to meet with the other Christians.

The Pope was facing them, seated on a stone chair, the chair of Peter. His face was pale and marked with suffering, but his bright eyes shone.

"My brothers and sisters, many Christians will be judged tomorrow," he said. "Their fate is certain—they will all be killed!" Sighs and moans rippled through the crowd. Quadratus, a strong young man, stepped forward. He was a soldier who had become a follower of Christ. "Holy Father," he said, "today I was on guard at the prison. I've seen our brothers and sisters. They told me to ask you to send them the Bread of Heaven."

"How can we get the Holy Eucharist to them?" sighed Pope Sixtus. "Who will dare to go into the prison? Can you, Quadratus?"

"That would be impossible, Holy Father," he answered. "Tomorrow I'm assigned to guard the Appian Way."

"Who dares to undertake this dangerous mission?" asked the Pope, glancing around the underground room. "Who will take the risk?"

There was a chorus of "I!" "I!" "No, I!"

Tarcisius made his way forward through the crowd until he was standing directly in front of Pope Sixtus.

"Holy Father, send me!" he cried.

"You, Tarcisius—so young?" exclaimed the Pope in surprise. "Why, you're just a boy!"

"Because I'm just a boy, no one will pay any attention to me," Tarcisius answered hopefully.

Pope Sixtus looked at him intently. In Tarcisius's eyes he saw a strong desire to carry the Eucharist to the prisoners.

"All right," he decided, "you shall be the one. I'll entrust the Eucharistic Jesus to you, in this little case."

"I'll carry Jesus on my heart," Tarcisius promised. "I'm ready to die to protect the Holy Eucharist."

The next day, some schoolmates of Tarcisius were sitting on a pile of stones along the Appian Way. One of them was Fabian, a good friend of Tarcisius.

"Fabian, where's Tarcisius?" asked one of the boys.

"Oh, he'll be coming. He always comes to play."

"When he gets here we'll have a stone-throwing contest," said Mark. "I've been practicing, and I'm sure I'll beat him this time!" he boasted.

The other boys laughed in support. Mark was a bully, and the others were afraid of him.

Mark grew impatient as the minutes slipped by with no sign of Tarcisius. He was anxious to begin the contest and prove himself the best of the group for once.

Tarcisius made his way forward through the crowd until he was standing in front of Pope Sixtus. "Holy Father, send me!" he exclaimed.

"Tarcisius is taking his time," said Fabritius. "Let's start without him."

"He'll come, and he'll win the contest," promised Fabian. "He's the best stone-thrower, just as he's the best at school."

"He *was* the best at school," broke in Mark. "Lately, he's always sleepy. His head rolls from side to side...like this!" The boys laughed as he imitated Tarcisius.

"Even the teacher has been noticing it," Fabritius admitted.

"Maybe Tarcisius doesn't feel well," Fabian defended. "Anyway, he'd beat you just the same—he's a born winner!"

"And what were you born for? To defend him?" retorted Mark.

"I like him a lot, that's all," replied Fabian. "He treats me like a brother."

Fabritius caught sight of Tarcisius coming along the road. "Here he comes!"

Tarcisius was walking toward them silently and cautiously, his arms pressed firmly to his chest.

"Come and play!" called Mark. The other boys took up the cry. "Come on, Tarcisius! Mark has challenged you!"

But Tarcisius answered, "I can't. I've got an errand to do."

"Oh, so you're important now!" sneered Mark. "Cut it out! Come on, let's play."

"I really can't," Tarcisius said firmly. "I'll play tomorrow."

"No," said Fabritius, "we'll play today. Right now. Choose your stones."

"I can't," Tarcisius said again. "I really can't."

"Oh," sighed Mark in disgust, "you're whining like a baby! Why do you have your arms like that? What are you hiding?"

"I can't tell you," protested Tarcisius.

"You *will* tell us," threatened Mark. "What can you have that's so important?"

In his heart, Tarcisius prayed: *Please, Jesus, make my arms as strong as steel! I'll press you close to me! I'll defend you!*

The circle of boys closed in around him. Tarcisius's heart was pounding.

"We've had enough," warned Mark. "I'll give you time to tell us what you have there. I'll count to three. One..."

Tarcisius prayed silently, *Please, Lord, help me!*

"Two!" yelled Mark.

"Mark, stop it!" cried Tarcisius. "Let me go. I'll give you my bow and arrows, all of them. I'll give you anything you want, but please let me finish my errand!"

"It's no use!" Mark shouted. "You're hiding something, and we're going to find out what it is! I'm going to count one more time." Glaring at Tarcisius, he began, "One, two..."

"No!" cried Tarcisius.

"I'll repeat it!" Mark's eyes were flashing angrily. "Two..."

"Listen, Mark," interrupted Fabritius, "I think I know what he's carrying."

"Yeah!" shouted Mark. "I had the same idea myself. Tarcisius must be a Christian. And maybe he's carrying the mysteries!" By that word Mark meant the Holy Eucharist.

"Yeah, the mysteries! The mysteries!" shouted the other boys, none of whom were Christian.

Mark stared hard at Tarcisius. "Have you made up your mind?" he demanded. "I said two and—and—"

"I said no, and I meant it!" cried Tarcisius.

"Leave him alone!" pleaded Fabian.

"No, no, Mark, go ahead!" yelled Fabritius.

Tarcisius prayed earnestly, *King of Martyrs, I beg you, don't let me be separated from you. I'd rather die.*

"Three!" shouted Mark.

There was a scramble, and several voices screamed, "Hit him! Hit him!"

Tarcisius fell to the ground, and the boys jumped on top of him. Still his arms remained crossed over the Eucharist like two iron bands.

With terrific effort, Tarcisius struggled to his feet and managed to run a few steps.

"Grab some stones!" yelled Fabritius. "Let him have it!"

One after another, stones struck him from all sides, until there was no part of his body that wasn't bleeding.

Tarcisius managed to stumble on, but fell when a stone struck his forehead.

"Tarcisius! Tarcisius!" sobbed Fabian in terror. "Leave him alone!" he cried to the others. "Look what you've done!"

But Mark urged them on. "Come on, let's have a look at those 'mysteries.'"

Just then Fabritius yelled, "Look out! A soldier's coming!"

"Let's get out of here!" cried someone else. In an instant the boys were gone.

Only Fabian didn't run. He stayed beside his friend, who was in terrible pain.

"Jesus," murmured Tarcisius. "I'm dying, but I defended you. Forgive my friends, forgive them!"

Meanwhile, the soldier had reached them. It was Quadratus, the Christian. When he saw Tarcisius lying on the ground, he exclaimed, "Poor boy! What have they done to you?" Turning to Fabian, he sternly demanded, "What are you doing here?"

"I'm Tarcisius's friend," wept Fabian. "I didn't throw any stones. Let me stay with him."

"Tarcisius, open your arms," Quadratus urged tenderly, bending over the boy.

"No," whispered Tarcisius. "I won't open my arms. Bring me to Pope Sixtus. I'll give my treasure—Jesus—only to him."

"Are you in great pain?" asked Quadratus, gently raising the boy's head.

"Yes," panted Tarcisius. "But that doesn't matter. Nobody touched Jesus. He's here, right here with me." He was breathing hard, struggling to talk. Suddenly he said, "I already see the angels. Take me to the Pope!"

"Don't die, Tarcisius! Please don't die!" Fabian wailed.

"I see the angels," Tarcisius repeated. "My faith is true. And you,"—he gasped for breath—"you, Fabian, do you believe?"

"Yes," declared Fabian. "I believe, Tarcisius. I want to become a Christian, too. Then we'll be together again some day."

Quadratus picked up the dying boy in his arms and carried him to the catacombs.

"Tarcisius," Pope Sixtus whispered gently, shocked at seeing the boy in such condition. "Tarcisius, Jesus is safe because of your loving sacrifice."

Tarcisius tried to smile. Then, pressing Jesus in the Eucharist close to his heart, he died. Only then did his arms fall away from his chest.

A strong, sweet odor of lilies filled the air at that moment. And Tarcisius's soul ascended joyfully to the throne of God, to the throne of the King who is waiting for all of us in eternal glory.

Although we may never have to defend the Eucharist with our lives, we can show our love for Jesus in the Blessed Sacrament by receiving Holy Communion reverently and with love. We can make a visit to the Blessed Sacrament when we pass by a church. And we can show love for the Eucharistic presence of Jesus in the tabernacle by always dressing modestly in church and behaving respectfully there.

St. Sebastian

(Third Century)

JANUARY 20

Sebastian, a young officer in the Roman army, had just found out that two young men had been put in prison and sentenced to death because they believed in Jesus Christ. Sebastian was a Christian, too, although the other soldiers didn't know it. In fact, he had become a soldier of Rome with the hope that he would be able to secretly comfort and assist Christian prisoners. With deep concern he thought of the twin brothers, Mark and Marcellinus, who were newly baptized and the only Christians in their family.

Lord Jesus, prayed Sebastian silently as he hurried toward the prison, *let me die, if need be, but please give Mark and Marcellinus the courage to remain faithful to their baptism!*

As he entered the cell, Sebastian found the brothers surrounded by a group of friends. Their father was there, too. Everyone was urging the twins to give up their Christian faith and save their lives. Mark and

Marcellinus were torn between love for their Heavenly Father and love for their earthly father.

Sebastian's clear voice rang out. "My brothers in Christ!" All heads turned in his direction as he continued, "You have always shown yourselves brave and courageous. Will you now turn your backs on the Lord Jesus, the heavenly King who has prepared a place of eternal glory for you?"

All were silent. Sebastian's face glowed with supernatural light as he continued, "What has this poor world to offer in the end but death? Will you exchange an eternity of joy for a few years of passing pleasure?"

The brothers looked at one another silently and bowed their heads. They had chosen God! Even their father and friends were impressed. They crowded around Sebastian, asking him questions about Jesus. And Sebastian spoke on and on, with the enthusiasm of an apostle.

"I want to be baptized," said one of the men.

"And I!" cried another.

"And I!"

Only one man remained unconvinced. "I need more proof than your words," he told Sebastian. This man was Chancellor Nicostratus, and he was known for his stubbornness. But Sebastian saw Nicostratus's wife beside him, her eyes full of belief. "You believe, don't you?" he asked. "Why don't you speak to your husband? A word from you might convince him, too."

To Sebastian's surprise, tears began to stream down the woman's cheeks. What had he said? Why should she start to cry like this?

Sebastian's face glowed with supernatural light as he continued, "What has this poor world to offer in the end but death? Will you exchange an eternity of joy for a few years of passing pleasure?"

Nicostratus stepped forward. "My wife Zoe is mute," he explained.

No wonder she hasn't spoken, Sebastian thought. Lifting his eyes, the young soldier prayed silently for a moment. Then he turned to the woman.

"Zoe, look at me."

She turned her sweet, sad eyes toward him. Sebastian made the Sign of the Cross on her lips and asked, in a voice that trembled with emotion, "Zoe, do you believe in our Lord Jesus Christ?"

The woman opened her lips and said clearly, "I do believe in Jesus, our Lord!"

Hardly had she finished speaking when her husband threw himself at Sebastian's feet. He, too, had been won to Christ!

~~~~~~~~~

Shortly afterward, the privilege of martyrdom came to Mark and Marcellinus. Surely they were received in heaven with great joy!

Sebastian continued his work of preaching and of comforting the Christians who had been captured and sentenced to death. The persecution grew worse than ever, and the prisons were filled. One night, in a vision, Sebastian was warned that his own death was near.

~~~~~~~~~

"That's the man! Seize him!"

Soldiers closed in on Sebastian and quickly bound him in chains. *How was my faith discovered?* Sebastian wondered. Then he saw the face of one of the newly baptized Christians smirking at him from the shadows. This was his betrayer.

Sebastian was brought to Emperor Diocletian, who had always considered him to be one of his best soldiers. Now that Diocletian knew the truth about him, he was very angry. "Death!" he shouted. "Death by arrows!"

Sebastian was securely tied to a tree. Then the guards stepped back to let the archers do their work.

Arrow followed arrow, sinking deep into Sebastian's body. He writhed in pain, but didn't cry out. Sebastian was willing to suffer this, and even more, for the Lord Jesus.

The archers left the field satisfied that Sebastian would die after several hours' torment. They had purposely avoided shooting him in the heart, for that would have caused a quick death.

Alone and bleeding, Sebastian could almost *feel* the life leaving his body. Abandoned by everyone, he prayed to God.

But had he been abandoned? There was a sudden rustle in the bushes as someone came toward him. Sebastian blinked the blood out of his eyes, and gazed weakly on the face of a woman whom he had seen among the Christians in the catacombs.

"I had come to give you a decent burial, my son," she murmured, "but I see there's still hope for you. Let's get you to shelter."

~~~~~~~~~~~~

In the security of the good woman's home, Sebastian slowly regained his strength. *Perhaps God has spared me for a reason,* he thought. *Perhaps I may be able to convert Diocletian from his cruel ways.* Sebastian pondered and prayed over the question.

At last, a little unsteady on his feet, but with the old fire in his eyes, Sebastian put on his soldier's uniform and went to stand guard where he knew the emperor would pass by. "The hour of justice has come!" he called out as Diocletian came near. "Repent. Ask God's forgiveness for the sins you have committed!"

For a moment Diocletian stood in shock at seeing Sebastian alive. But then he screamed in rage, "Take that man! Beat him until he dies!" At once the soldiers fell upon Sebastian. He felt blow after blow, then...nothing.

The soldiers took Sebastian's body and threw it into the sewer. The Christians later rescued and buried it. In time, a beautiful church was built above the grave. But Sebastian's soul was already happy with God, where it will be happy for all eternity.

St. Sebastian always had one thought before him: heaven. That goal was so precious that he would never do anything that might make him lose it. We all can work for heaven by doing what is right and avoiding what we know is wrong.

St. Lucy

(d. 304)

December 13

During the time when Diocletian was emperor of Rome, a daughter was born to a wealthy family on the island of Sicily in the Mediterranean Sea.

The little girl's eyes sparkled so brightly that she was named "Lucy," which means "light." Lucy's father died when she was about six years old, but the family had enough money to live comfortably in their home in the city of Syracuse.

Lucy and her mother were both Christians. They often met secretly with other Christians in tunnels and caves beneath the city to pray and to celebrate Mass. At that time, Christians were being persecuted and put to death for their faith in Jesus Christ.

As Lucy grew older, her love for Jesus grew stronger. She saw the great difference between the way of life that Jesus had taught his followers and the way in which the non-Christian Romans lived. The world was full of violence, injustice, and immorality, but Lucy refused to be drawn into the sinful lifestyles of many of her friends. For Lucy, God's love was infinitely more precious than anything else in the whole world.

In those days, every young girl was expected to marry and have children. Not to marry was considered a social disgrace. Lucy had often dreamed of the day she would have her own family. But after praying about it, she believed that Jesus was asking her to remain his, and only his, forever. By giving up marriage and her own family, she could dedicate all her time and energy to praying and to serving people in need.

Lucy accepted Jesus' "proposal." She didn't mind when a small voice inside her said that she would suffer because of this choice. She loved Jesus, and she already knew that suffering often goes with love.

Having made her decision to consecrate her life to Jesus, Lucy felt great peace for several days. Then her mother announced that she had arranged for Lucy to marry a young man. The engagement would soon be announced! Lucy felt surprised and anxious, but she said nothing to her mother—not at first, anyway.

Lucy's mother had been ill for years, and the girl decided to ask St. Agatha to cure her.

So the mother and daughter set out for the neighboring city of Catania, where they visited the tomb of the virgin martyr, Agatha. After participating at Mass, they remained praying before the tomb. Suddenly, in a vision, Lucy saw St. Agatha coming toward her. Agatha was dressed in radiant garments and sparkling jewels and was surrounded by angels.

"Dear sister," said the saint, "why do you ask *me* to obtain your mother's cure? Your mother is now well, because of your own great faith. And the Lord is pleased with your promise to be his alone."

St. Agatha continued, "Soon you will become the splendor of Syracuse, just as Jesus has made me the glory of Catania."

The saint then disappeared. Lucy stood up and went over to her mother. It was true. She had been cured!

This seemed to be Lucy's chance to ask her mother two favors. One was not to go through with the marriage engagement. The other was to give the family's wealth to the poor. Her mother agreed to both, but she hesitated to tell the young man, who was not a Christian.

The young man was shocked to learn that the poor were swarming to Lucy's home to divide among themselves the wealth he had expected to be his. Early one morning, he arrived on Lucy's doorstep. Ushered inside, he waited nervously in the entrance hall. As soon as Lucy appeared, he said, "Your mother has promised you to me!"

The dreaded moment had come. Steadily, Lucy replied, "I have already been pledged to Another. Please leave, and permit me to remain true to him."

Like a flash of light, the young man saw the truth. Lucy was a Christian! He was furious. Storming out of the house, he rushed to the governor's palace.

Very soon, soldiers were at Lucy's door. "You are summoned to appear before Governor Paschasius," they declared. Grimly the soldiers marched Lucy through the streets. When they arrived at the palace, she was calm.

Paschasius was stern. "You must offer a sacrifice to the gods of Rome!" he told her.

"I've sacrificed my riches to help the poor, as my heavenly Bridegroom wished," replied the girl. "The only other possession I have is my body, which I've also given to God."

"Don't speak such nonsense!" retorted the governor. "It's my duty to carry out the commands of the Roman emperor, and his command is that you worship the gods of Rome."

"Just as you respect the emperors and their laws, so I respect God and his laws," Lucy explained. "In fact, nothing will stop me from obeying his laws and worshiping him alone."

Paschasius stiffened. "You're bold enough now, but the torturers will change you."

"The words of God are changeless," replied Lucy. "Jesus said that whenever his disciples would be brought before a judge, the Holy Spirit would speak through them."

"So you think this Holy Spirit is speaking through you now?"

"He is in everyone who lives in chastity and purity, because such a person is a temple of God."

With fire in his eyes, the governor shouted, "Unless you worship our gods, I'll have you taken to a place where you will be forced to sin. Then the Holy Spirit will leave you!"

"*Just as you respect the emperors and their laws, so I respect God and his laws,*" *Lucy explained.* "*In fact, nothing will stop me from obeying his laws and worshiping him alone.*"

The threat frightened Lucy. She had heard of other young Christian girls being forced to go to places where sinful things were done. But Lucy hid her feelings and said firmly, "The body doesn't sin if the will doesn't consent. Even if you took my hands by force and made me offer incense to idols with them, God would know that I didn't want to do it. It would be the same if you tried to make me commit any type of sin by force. Because it would be against my will, I would have done no wrong in God's sight."

Nevertheless, Paschasius commanded that Lucy be taken to a sinful place. Four soldiers stepped forward to drag her away, but the calm young woman prayed fervently. The combined strength of all four men couldn't move her!

Other soldiers sprang forward, but their help was of no use. At last Paschasius ordered that Lucy be dragged away by a team of oxen, but even those strong animals couldn't budge the girl.

The pagan magicians whom Paschasius called in couldn't move her either. "What's the secret of your magic?" the governor asked Lucy in a rage.

"It's not magic," replied the girl. "It's God's goodness toward those who are true to him."

Curious spectators were crowding around on every side. Governor Paschasius's anger mounted, because he was looking foolish in front of everyone. "Bring wood and oil!" the governor roared. "Light a fire and burn the Christian girl!"

The soldiers obeyed, and a fire was lit. As the flames blazed up, licking hungrily at the wood, Lucy remained unharmed. She knelt in prayer, now and then speaking to the crowd. "I have asked God to spare me from the fire," she explained, "so that the faithful may gain courage from my tortures, and so that unbelievers may see the beauty and glory of the Christian religion."

But now Lucy's mission had been accomplished. It was time for God to take her to heaven. An execution-er came forward with a sharp-bladed dagger and plunged it into Lucy's throat. The young martyr left this earth to be safe and happy with God forever.

St. Lucy had a deep love for God. Love like this comes from prayer. The more we pray and speak to the Lord, the more we will love him and remain close to him.

St. Agnes

(d. 304)

JANUARY 21

Almost three hundred years after Jesus died for us on the cross, a family named Clodius lived in the city of Rome. They were a noble family who lived in a magnificent palace and had many servants. But the most precious treasure of the Clodius family was their daughter, Agnes.

The name "Agnes" means "lamb." It fitted the young girl well, because she was very gentle. Agnes had eyes that shone with a beautiful light. She was warmhearted and kind to everyone, always doing good things for others.

By the time Agnes was thirteen, she was already tall and graceful. She often wore a snow-white dress with no ornaments or jewels, which made her look very much like a bride. And she always looked as happy as a bride, as if she was thinking of someone very special to her.

The name "Agnes" means "lamb," and it suited the young girl well, because she was very gentle.

People couldn't help noticing her beauty, graceful-
ness, and goodness.

One day a boy named Procop, the son of the prefect of Rome, met her as she was out walking. "Agnes,"
he said, "I'd like to talk with you."

"About what?" she asked.

"I'm in love with you," Procop admitted. "Will you
promise me that you'll marry me someday?"

"But I'm already engaged!" Agnes replied.

"You're engaged?" Procop repeated in surprise. "To
whom?" he demanded. "Who is richer or more honor-
able than I? Who has more gold or more servants?"

"He who has angels for servants and owns heaven
and earth," Agnes answered. "He who has put a neck-
lace of precious gems about my neck and has dressed
me in white linen woven with pearls. He who loves
the pure and sweet scent of lilies. He will be my
Husband, and he alone!"

Procop went away sad. Because he didn't understand what Agnes had said, he thought that she had
been teasing him, or that she was daydreaming.

Procop began to feel sorry for himself. He was no
longer interested in sports or games. He didn't even
read or study any more, even though he was supposed
to be preparing to become an important leader.

One night, an old servant told Procop's father, the
prefect, "I know why Agnes refused your son! She
must be a Christian. There are many young women
who are...and some refuse to marry because they say
they love someone named Jesus Christ!"

The prefect was startled. He wasn't a Christian,
and, like most of the Romans, he hated the Christians

because they refused to worship the Roman gods. Procop's father decided to force Agnes to marry his son by threatening to kill her.

The prefect went to talk to Agnes's parents. "Either Agnes will marry my son, or I'll summon her to court," he declared. "If she confesses to being a Christian, I'll have her killed. You know the law of Rome. It's severe, and it commands enemies of the gods to be condemned without pity."

Agnes's parents—who were also Christians, like their parents before them—were terrified. They tried to remain calm in front of the prefect. But as soon as he left, they called Agnes and told her what Procop's father had threatened to do.

"Mother! Father! Have courage," she replied. "I won't betray the faith you've given me. I won't be a traitor to my faith even if it means suffering and death! Don't cry for me."

A few days later, the palace of Agnes and her parents was surrounded by armed guards. Agnes was taken to the court, where the prefect came forward to accuse her.

"Do you know why you're here?" he asked.

"Yes. It's because I'm a Christian," Agnes calmly responded.

"Foolish girl!" the prefect exclaimed. "You admit to something so serious and dangerous and you do it with a smile? You should be trembling. Do you know what's going to happen to you?"

"I know," Agnes answered. "But Jesus said, 'You will be persecuted and tortured because I was. Remember that you were made for my kingdom and not for this world.' I would give up my life a thousand times rather than give up my faith in Jesus Christ."

"Enough!" the prefect cried. "My son is suffering on account of you. I'll set you free if you promise to marry him."

"I'm the bride of Jesus, and his alone. I'm not afraid of you or your soldiers! For Jesus' sake, I'm not afraid. There's an angel always guarding me, and he won't let Christ's handmaid suffer any harm!"

"Guards!" shouted the prefect, "take this stubborn girl to the Arena of Alexander! Take her clothing and make her walk through the streets. That should humiliate her."

The guards carried out the cruel command. But a miracle happened. Agnes's hair began to grow...and grow. It quickly grew so long that it completely covered her from head to foot! The guards were amazed. *Thank you, Jesus, for saving me from this humiliation,* Agnes prayed in her heart. *If only everyone knew your goodness and love, the world would be such a different place.*

The prefect, his son Procop, the nobles, and crowds of people were waiting at the arena when Agnes arrived. Guards led her to the center of that huge open area. Agnes calmly refused to sacrifice to the pagan idols. She made the Sign of the Cross instead.

Angrier than ever, the prefect left the arena, commanding an official named Aspasian to take his place. "Light the fire!" Aspasian ordered the soldiers. "The Christian will be burned to death."

Agnes bravely climbed the pile of burning wood. To the astonishment of everyone, the flames divided in half, leaving her completely untouched. There the girl stood, a witness to the great King of heaven. In a loud voice, Agnes cried, "O Jesus, thank you for this new proof of your love. But if you wish, give me martyrdom. I want it. I want to come to you and never leave you."

The sight of young Agnes standing there, so strong and so calm, made others in the crowd want to learn about Jesus, for whom she was willing to suffer so much. They, too, wanted to embrace her religion.

Aspasian scanned the arena. Many of the onlookers were falling to their knees, shouting, "I want to be a Christian!" "I'm a Christian, too!"

Aspasian was furious at what was happening. "Behead her!" he screamed. As Agnes knelt down, an executioner carrying a gleaming sword drew near. Many in the crowd began to cry.

Calmly, Agnes bowed her head and awaited the death blow. The crowd grew still when the soldier lifted his blade. "Take me, O Lord," Agnes prayed. "Death is really life, the sweet life of eternity. Take me, O Lord."

The executioner was trembling. For a moment, he seemed almost paralyzed. "Discharge your duty!" Aspasian angrily shouted. The soldier obeyed, and the blow fell. Agnes's head was cut off.

The body of Agnes was taken to a spot near the Nomentana Road, not far from Rome. Later on, during the reign of Emperor Constantine, a church would be built over the place where the young martyr was buried.

Tradition tells us that on January 28, a week after she was killed, Agnes appeared to her parents as they were praying at her grave. She was surrounded by a group of holy virgins, and in her arms she held a little white lamb.

"Don't cry for me, my dear ones," she said. "I'm very happy with all those who have consecrated their lives to Jesus. Jesus will have as many spouses as there are stars in the sky—young women who will consecrate themselves to him in the centuries to come. And I'll be waiting for them near the God of the pure and the strong!"

Every year on January 21, the feast of St. Agnes, the Pope blesses two lambs in memory of the young martyr. Their wool is then shorn off and given to the Benedictine Sisters of St. Cecilia Convent in Rome. The sisters use the wool to knit *palliums,* strips of white wool worn by the Pope and archbishops as part of their sacred vestments.

St. Agnes knew that keeping our souls and bodies pure is very precious to God. One way we can follow her example is always to dress modestly, and to refuse to listen to crude jokes or to watch programs or movies that are disrespectful of the human person.

St. Helen

(d. 330)

AUGUST 18

In the late third century, in a small province of the western part of the Roman Empire known as Bithynia, a daughter was born to an innkeeper and his wife. The little girl was named Helen, and as she grew up she learned to help her parents care for the travelers who stopped at the inn. Like most of their neighbors, the family was not Christian. They were pagans who worshiped the gods of the Roman Empire.

One day there was great excitement in the town. "General Constantius is coming!" some men shouted. "Constantius Chlorus is coming with his troops!" Constantius and his men stopped at the inn. Helen helped her parents serve the soldiers their meals. She must have been a very gracious hostess, for General Constantius fell in love with her and asked for her hand in marriage. Her parents were sorry to lose their daughter, but they were happy for Helen. "As the general's wife, you will be well cared for," Helen's father told her. "You'll never have to worry about finances, and you'll get to travel all over the empire."

Helen was in her late twenties when she married Constantius. Soon enough, the couple had a son, whom they named Constantine.

Constantius was a brilliant soldier and won many victories. He became more and more important in the army. Then he was appointed Caesar (ruler) of the western empire. That was when the blow fell. Constantius was persuaded to divorce Helen and marry the stepdaughter of Emperor Maximian—for political reasons! This type of political marriage was common at the time, and Helen had no choice but to agree with the divorce.

Poor Helen! She loved her husband and her son, and it was hard to leave them. But she accepted the situation as best she could and began to live her lonely life of exile. We're not sure, but perhaps it was during this period that Helen became interested in Christianity and began to learn all she could about it.

We don't know much about Helen's life over the next twenty years. But at last her ex-husband, Constantius, died and their son Constantine became emperor. Helen was now almost sixty-five years old.

One of the first things that Constantine did was to call his mother back from exile. He gave her the title of empress, and even had coins made in her honor.

At the same time, Helen finished her instruction in the Christian faith and received Baptism. With

Constantine's permission, she spent great sums of money to provide food and clothing for the poor and to free many people from prison. She invited the men and women who were specially consecrated to God to dine at the palace, and she herself served them. She also had many churches built and decorated with beautiful artwork and gold.

The Romans, who had long governed Jerusalem, had built a temple to Venus, a pagan goddess, on Mount Calvary. Helen went to Jerusalem and ordered the temple torn down. Then she had a church built over the tomb where Jesus had been buried. Helen had another church built on the Mount of Olives.

At Calvary, Helen searched for the cross on which Jesus had been crucified. Although it had been preserved by the first Christians, it had been lost later when the Romans scattered the Christians and Jews. Workmen began to dig, and soon three wooden crosses were discovered! In the earth nearby they found long, sharp nails.

Helen was overjoyed—but which cross was the cross of Jesus? She turned for help to the holy Bishop Macarius. "Your Excellency, how are we to distinguish the true cross?"

"Your Highness," he replied, "let us ask God's help in this matter."

So the bishop and the empress, together with several other people, took the three crosses to the home of a lady who was ill. They said a prayer, and then

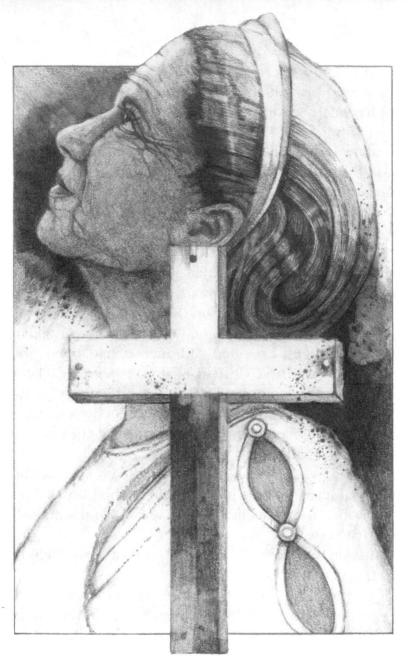

With Constantine's permission, Helen spent great sums of money to provide food and clothing for the poor and to free many people from prison.

touched the sick woman with the crosses. At the touch of the true cross, the lady was miraculously cured!

Helen had a beautiful church built, where the relic of the true cross could be kept. News of what she had done spread throughout the empire. Everywhere people learned or were reminded that Jesus died on his cross to redeem us. Thousands and thousands of people were baptized in the following years. Many of these made a pilgrimage to Jerusalem to see the holy cross for themselves.

Having been God's instrument in reawakening the Christian world, Helen died peacefully at the age of eighty. She had been a strong and faithful woman, able to accept difficult circumstances and grow from them.

Sometimes things happen to us or to our families that are beyond our control. St. Helen's life shows us that God can help us find peace and strength no matter what situation we find ourselves in.

St. Martin of Tours

(317–397)

November 11

"Take me with you, Father! I'm not afraid of the long journey." Young Martin's eyes were wide with excitement as he pleaded with his father, a strong Roman officer.

"Yes," agreed Martin's father. "Now you can come to live in Italy with your mother and me. You will be living in a land very dear to the gods."

"Do you still believe in the gods, Father?" Martin asked. "Don't you realize that there is only one God?"

Martin's father didn't reply. He wondered—as he had wondered before—who had told his son such strange things.

The truth was that Martin, born in the Roman province of Hungary, had learned about the Christian faith from the woman who had cared for him during his early childhood. She had taught him about Jesus and the Christian martyrs.

Now Martin's father was going to take him to Italy. The boy was very excited. Soon he would see Rome, the "capital of the world"!

It was a long journey. Mounted on a single horse, father and son rode through green valleys and up rocky mountain passes. At night they would roll up in their blankets beneath the stars. Sometimes Martin would dream of Jesus. The boy was only ten, but he already felt a strong desire to become a Christian.

Life in Rome was exciting for Martin. Before he knew it, he was celebrating his fourteenth birthday. Martin's father told him, "I've always wanted you to become a soldier like me. It's time for you to begin your training."

Martin felt uneasy. He wasn't sure that he wanted to be a soldier. But since he didn't know exactly what he *did* want, he joined the Roman army as his father wished. Soon he became an officer and was stationed in the country we now call France.

During his off-duty hours, Martin prayed, helped the poor and the sick and told everyone he could about Jesus of Nazareth. He was an unusual soldier! Even more amazing was the fact that Martin wasn't even a Christian. Although he had begun to take instructions in the Christian faith, he had not yet been baptized.

One cold night Martin was riding near the city gates when he noticed a ragged beggar shivering beneath a tree. Everyone was passing by the poor man without doing a thing to help him.

Jesus must want me to help him, thought Martin. But what could he give? He had no money with him. All that he had was his cloak. Martin drew out his sword, cut the cloak in half, and gave one piece to the beggar, wrapping the other piece around his own shoulders. Some people passing by laughed, but others felt ashamed because they had not helped the poor beggar.

That night Martin had a dream. Jesus appeared to him surrounded by a dazzling light. He was wearing the half-cloak that Martin had given to the beggar!

Soon after that, Martin was baptized.

One day, the general ordered his army into battle. Martin approached him and said, "Until today I have served you; from now on I wish to serve only the Lord Jesus."

"You're a coward," retorted the general angrily. "You want to run out on us. Until now I thought you were the bravest of my men, but I see that I was wrong!" And he ordered that Martin be thrown into prison.

Of course, Martin didn't change his mind. After a while he was released from prison and discharged from the army. He became a pilgrim, then a hermit. He even founded a community of monks. Martin's holiness became well known. Soon the people of the city of Tours were demanding to have him for their bishop.

Martin was against the idea. He felt that honors might keep him from being united with God. But the people tricked him into entering the city and took him to the church. Martin was again asked to become a bishop, and he consented, aware that this must be the will of God.

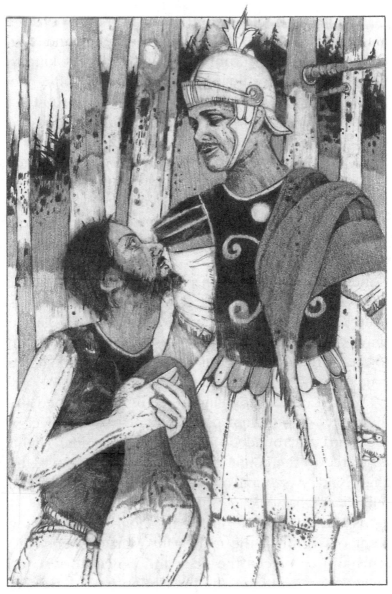

Martin drew out his sword, cut the cloak in half, and gave one piece to the beggar, while he wrapped the other piece about himself.

The honor of being named a bishop didn't change Martin at all. He lived just as simply as before and treated himself just as sternly. He was always very kind to the poor and unfortunate. One day he saw some people mistreating a man with leprosy, and thought, *Charity means not only giving people food and clothing; it also means giving them a smile and a good word.* He went up to the sick man and hugged him, saying, "Jesus is suffering in you, my brother."

Another time, Martin saw a group of men and women, all in chains, in the public square of a village. They were waiting to be beheaded the next day because they couldn't pay taxes to the powerful Count Avitius. Moved with pity, Martin hurried to the count's palace. But it was night, and every gate was shut. Kneeling before the main entrance, he began to pray: "O Lord, send an angel to ask the count to listen to me. Lord, save those innocent people from such a cruel death."

While Count Avitius slumbered in his huge bed and his armed guards slept peacefully nearby, an angel of the Lord, surrounded by a halo of golden light, appeared to the count in a dream. "Arise, Avitius!" the angel said. "A servant of our Lord is waiting for you outside the palace."

Avitius got up and put on his cloak. Trembling, he went out through the main gate. Martin opened his arms and embraced the fiery and powerful warrior, saying, "Come and free the poor people you have sentenced to such a cruel death. Forgive them their trespasses, and God will forgive you yours!"

The count gave in.

Near the end of his life, Martin stopped on one of his journeys to see some monks he knew. He found them arguing. "If the shepherds are not united," Martin scolded, "what will become of the flock? Be at peace, brothers; be at peace."

Truly sorry, the brothers fell on their knees, and Bishop Martin blessed them. Then he said, "My sons, gladden my last days with your good deeds. I am now over eighty years old, and my ears hear the music of heaven. Serve God in joy!"

It was the month of November. The leaves were falling from the trees and clouds hid the sun. Martin was dying, and the monks who attended him wept because they knew how much they would miss his encouragement and guidance.

A strange thing happened when Martin died. All the cold and gloom of November disappeared, and for three days everything was as bright and beautiful as if it had been summer. Of course, no one really needed to see that miracle in order to know that Martin had been a saint; the holiness of his whole life had been proof of that!

When St. Martin was faced with the choice of being called brave and abandoning Jesus, or being called a coward and following Jesus, he chose Jesus. It's the kind of person we are that's important, not what people call us.

St. Monica

(332–387)

AUGUST 27

St. Augustine

(354–430)

AUGUST 28

Although St. Monica lived many years ago, we know a lot about her life because of the writings of her famous son, St. Augustine. In fact, St. Monica is well known for the prayers she offered for her son's conversion.

Monica was born in Tagaste, North Africa, in 332. Her devout Christian parents were careful to teach their children the truths of faith, their prayers, and the Commandments.

When Monica was twenty-two, she married Patricius, who was much older than she. Her friends were worried about the marriage, because Monica was gentle and kind, while Patricius was hot-tempered. He was not a Christian.

"How do you manage to get along so well with such a sharp-tempered husband?" Monica was asked a few years later. She replied that she never argued with Patricius but was always patient and gentle with him. When he was angry, she waited for him to calm down before talking to him.

Monica was a great peacemaker among her friends, too. She always told people the good things that others said about them, never the bad. Her patience and kindness even won over her mother-in-law, who hadn't liked her at first.

Soon Monica and Patricius had two young sons and a daughter—Augustine, Navigius, and Perpetua. Like their parents, the children had the dark skin and handsome features of the Nubians. Monica taught her children to love Jesus. She told them about the Christian martyrs and encouraged them to think often about heaven.

In those days many people waited until they were grown up before being baptized. So Monica carefully taught her children their prayers, hoping that Augustine would be baptized first, since he was the oldest.

Even though Augustine was very smart, he didn't like to study. But both Patricius and Monica were determined that he should learn Latin and Greek, which all educated people knew in those days.

As a teenager Augustine was sent to school in another city, where many of his friends drank and cheated at their studies. By the time he was seventeen he had also begun to drink, cheat, and steal.

Meanwhile Monica's twenty years of prayer and patience with Patricius had changed him into a new person. He became a catechumen (candidate for Baptism). He was baptized and a year later, at peace with God and with his family, Patricius died.

Augustine was now studying in a still larger city—Carthage. Here he learned the teaching of a religious

Even though Augustine was very smart, he didn't like to study. But both Patricius and Monica were determined that he should learn Latin and Greek.

group called the Manichaeans, and soon joined them. Monica felt as if he had died. She stormed heaven with her prayers and tried to convince her son that the Manichaeans didn't believe in the true God. But nothing that she said would convince him.

One night she had a dream in which an angel told her, "Your son is with you."

When she told Augustine about the dream, he said, "Ah, so you're going to join us!"

Monica immediately answered, "No. I was not told that *I* was with *you,* but that *you* were with *me!*" In spite of himself, Augustine was impressed by his mother's quick answer and remembered it often in the years that followed.

At times, Monica asked bishops and priests to speak with her son. They all told her that, one day, he would discover for himself that the teachings of the Manichaeans didn't make sense. When she continued to beg one bishop to speak to Augustine, he said, "It is impossible that the child of so many tears should perish." The bishop knew how much Monica was praying and suffering for her son who was following the wrong road.

When Augustine was twenty-nine, he told his mother that he was moving to Rome to teach public speaking. Monica was determined that he shouldn't go. How could she help him if he was so far away? Finally, Augustine promised her that he would wait a few days before leaving.

But that same night he slipped away and boarded a ship for Rome! Silent with grief, Monica stood on the shore and watched the billowing sails grow small in the clear morning light. She had discovered his plan too late!

From Rome, Augustine went to Milan, where he began to listen to the sermons of St. Ambrose. He wasn't interested in what the bishop was saying, but Ambrose was famous for his style as a speaker. Yet at the same time, Augustine was learning how reasonable the teachings of the Catholic Church were. He thought more seriously about the Manichaean teachings, and decided to abandon them.

Meanwhile, his faithful mother made the dangerous trip to Milan to join him. Monica was convinced that her son would become a Christian before she died. When she learned of St. Ambrose's good influence on him, she prayed even harder.

Little by little, Augustine, helped by St. Ambrose, struggled to understand the Catholic faith. At last his mind accepted the truth. But his will was another story. Augustine knew that to be a Christian means to keep the Ten Commandments—and he felt that this was more than he could do.

One summer day, in his garden, he fought it out within himself. One minute he wanted to give up his sinful habits, but the next minute he didn't think he could. Still, he didn't want to lose God, whom he had found after so much searching. Augustine burst into tears of sorrow. "Help me, God," he begged. "Please help me!" Suddenly he heard a child's voice saying, "Take up and read."

He had left a book of St. Paul's letters lying nearby. He opened it. The first sentence his eyes fell on was, "Put on the Lord Jesus Christ, and make no provision for the flesh, to gratify its desires" (Rm 13:14). This meant, "Be baptized and reject temptation." At last, light and peace flooded his soul. Augustine went into the house and told his mother that he now belonged to God.

Augustine was baptized on Easter Sunday, 387, together with some of his friends. Not long afterward the group traveled to the coast in order to sail for Africa. In the seaport of Ostia, Monica said to her son, "Now I find no joy in anything of this life. All my hopes have been accomplished."

Five days later she came down with a fever. To her sons, Augustine and Navigius, she said, "You will bury your mother here."

"Not here, Mother," protested Navigius. "Not here in a foreign land!"

But Monica, who had often said that she wished to be buried beside Patricius, said, "Put the body anywhere; don't worry about it. I ask only this: that wherever you are, you remember me at Mass."'

Nine days later Monica died.

Augustine didn't cry at the funeral because his mother had died such a holy death. But when he was alone and remembered her loving care for him and her other children, he broke down and wept.

"If I am your child, O my God," he wrote, "it is because you gave me such a mother!"

For the next three years, Augustine lived in Carthage with some of his friends. They lived very simply, prayed every day, and worked to help the poor. In 390, Augustine was ordained a priest, and in 395, he was made the Bishop of Hippo. Augustine never forgot how difficult it had been for him to give up his sinful habits. He spent the rest of his life preaching the Gospel and helping many people learn to love Jesus.

St. Monica is a model for all mothers. No matter what Augustine did, she never stopped loving him and praying for him. Augustine is a great saint who especially helps people who find it hard to be good.

St. Patrick

(389–461)

MARCH 17

In the fourth century, about a hundred years after the Roman Emperor Constantine had stopped the persecutions of Christians, many Romans who lived in Britain were Christian. Most of them were farmers.

Patrick belonged to one of these Christian families. He was born around the year 389, and grew up in the fields and forests. Even though Patrick had been baptized, he had not been well instructed in the Catholic faith. But Patrick loved God, and while he worked out in the fields he often said the prayers his mother had taught him.

One day a fleet of warships raided the British coast. The fierce men who attacked the peaceful villages, burning and killing and carrying off prisoners, were raiders sent by the Irish king, "Niall of the Nine Hostages." They robbed and destroyed the farmers' homes. And they took away everyone they could capture who was young and strong—including Patrick.

The hold of the raider ship was dark and crowded. Patrick lay still, cramped, hungry, and aching from his bruises. He listened to the swish and thump of the waves against the ship's hull and felt the surge and roll of the vessel as it plowed along. Questions kept running through his mind: *Will I ever see my family again? Are my parents alive or dead? Where are these men taking me? Maybe I'm going to Ireland to be sold as a slave!*

"Dear God, be with me and help me!" Patrick prayed.

~~~~~~~~~~~~~~~~~

The slave market was crowded and noisy. The new prisoners stood silently while their captors haggled over prices with the Irish lords and their agents. Their Gaelic phrases sounded strange to Patrick, who spoke Latin. At last a bargain was struck, and Patrick was sold into the service of an Irish lord named Milcho. He set out with his new master toward the northern province.

They journeyed through a land of hills and bogs, where wolves howled in the forests at night. This was a much wilder land than Britain, but its ruggedness appealed to Patrick. He dreamed of escaping and hiding out in the mountains until he could find a ship that would take him home.

Milcho's estate was in the wildest part of the country and was very well fortified against wolves and thieves. But Patrick was not going to sleep within its walls. His duty would be to tend the sheep in the meadows and the swine in the forest, keeping them safe from wolves and making sure that they didn't wander into the cultivated fields and destroy the crops. His home at night was to be a small hut, with a roaring peat fire blazing at the doorway to keep away the wild animals. Patrick's only companions would be the specially trained dogs he was given to help herd the flocks.

That was how Patrick spent the next six years. He became used to all kinds of weather—bronzed by the sun and hardened against the cold. Whenever he met one of the Irish, he tried to learn more of their Gaelic language. After a while, he knew it well.

Patrick grew to love the Irish people. In some ways, they seemed very rough, but in others they were gentler and kinder than any Roman he had known. They worshiped many things in nature, especially the sun. Their priests, who were similar to magicians, were called druids.

"My Lord Jesus," Patrick would pray, "please give them the grace to see that there are not gods in things, but rather that there is one God who made everything. Give me the chance to study about you so that I can someday explain you, the Creator of all, to these people. Please give me a chance to escape!"

Patrick prayed often while he was alone on the slopes of Mount Slemish—in the pastures by day and in his hut beneath the stars at night. Before dawn, he would leave the warmth of his fire and go out to pray in the snow, frost, or rain. Looking back on this period of his life a few years later, he would write, "I could feel the Spirit of God acting within me!"

One night as he slept, he heard a voice say, "Your ship is ready!" Patrick thought it must be his guardian angel. He got up and set out at once for the coast.

How excited he was to see a ship lying at anchor, preparing to sail! Patrick went up to the captain and asked if he could be taken on as a member of the crew. "That's impossible!" retorted the captain. Maybe he could tell that the young man was a runaway slave!

Patrick turned sadly away, but began at once to pray. As he walked slowly down the beach, he heard a sudden shout, "Come back! The sailors are calling you!"

God had touched their hearts. The captain and crew welcomed Patrick aboard their ship and they set sail.

After a long and dangerous journey to other shores, Patrick finally made his way to Britain and rejoined the members of his family who were still living. How happy they were to have him home again! They had thought he was dead! Patrick stayed with them a few years, until the burning desire to bring Jesus to Ireland became too much for him. He decided to go to France, then called Gaul, to learn more about the Catholic faith from St. Martin, the Bishop of Tours.

Sadly, Patrick had spent only a few months with this holy man when the elderly bishop died. Patrick went on to Auxerre and became a monk, joining St.

Martin's friend, St. Germanus. He studied hard and was eventually ordained a priest. Then his guardian angel, speaking for the Irish people, told him in a dream that Ireland was calling him. Patrick heard the voices telling him: "We beg you, holy Patrick, return and walk among us!"

Patrick was no longer young when this sign from God came to him. But many years of preaching lay ahead of him. Most men couldn't have done it, but Patrick still had his youthful enthusiasm.

Germanus gave Patrick a blessing, and so did Pope Celestine. The Pope had already sent a missionary named Palladius to Ireland, but that mission had been unsuccessful. Now Patrick was to take his place. Before he went, he was consecrated the first Bishop of Ireland.

Patrick built the first Christian church in Ireland at a place called Saul—the same spot where he would be buried sixty years later.

He pushed on toward Tara, the palace of the Irish kings. He was in sight of it on Easter Eve, 433, when he and his companions stopped on the hill of Slane to celebrate the Easter vigil. Patrick lit the Paschal fire. It cut the darkness like a knife—the only light that could be seen in the dim, silent night.

Then, from the direction of Tara, angry cries split the darkness. A few moments later, the galloping of hooves and the rumble of chariots could be heard. What was happening? Patrick and his comrades turned to face the horsemen.

What had happened was this: Ireland's pagan lords had been celebrating their biggest feast—the Feis of Tara. The druid priests had proclaimed that on that night no fire should be lit in all of Ireland before the fire of Tara. Without knowing it, Patrick had disobeyed their law!

And so King Laeghaire and his nobles came thundering up to Patrick. The bishop faced them calmly.

"Who are you? How dare you break the law?"

In a ringing voice Patrick began to explain. He told of his purpose in coming to Ireland. He spoke about the great mysteries of the Christian religion, using the three-leafed shamrock to describe the Holy Trinity.

Naturally, the druids challenged Patrick. A terrible struggle followed between the magical powers of the druids and the miracles of the saint. In the end, Patrick won. Laeghaire was not converted, but he gave Patrick permission to preach about Jesus Christ in all of Ireland.

There are many stories about St. Patrick's journeys through Ireland and the many people whom he brought to the Christian faith. Wherever he went, he built chapels and put up crosses as a reminder of our Lord's passion. It is said that he remembered the location of every roadside cross, and paid a visit to each one whenever he had to pass near it—in order to make an act of love for the crucified Savior.

One year, at the beginning of Lent, Patrick was traveling along the western coast of Ireland. Following an inspiration, he climbed the slopes of a rocky crag to spend some time in prayer. For forty days, between

There are many stories about St. Patrick's journeys through Ireland and the many people whom he brought to the Christian faith.

the desolate moorland and the wild sea, Patrick fasted and prayed. He begged God that all the people of Ireland would come to believe in his divine Son, Jesus Christ, and be baptized.

Was it too much to ask for? Not for Patrick. He had always had a way of "taking heaven by storm." He prayed with such faith and love that God never refused him—and so it was this time, too. After many years of preaching and teaching by Patrick and his successors, all of Ireland did become Christian.

On a cold March day in 461, Patrick died. He had converted an entire nation to Christ. That nation has remained Christian for over 1,500 years.

The course of history was changed because Patrick wanted to do good to his enemies. Let's try to see the image of Jesus in those who dislike us. Let's pray for them.

St. Brigid

(d. 525)

Brigid was born during St. Patrick's lifetime—when Ireland was half-pagan and half-Christian. Her father was Duffy, a pagan chieftain, and her mother was Brocessa, a Christian slave. Shortly before Brigid's birth, Duffy sold Brocessa, with the understanding that their child would be returned to him in a few years. Brocessa had Brigid baptized as soon as she could and taught her about Jesus and Mary.

When Brigid returned to serve as a slave in her father's household, she acted differently than the other slaves. If a hungry dog came whining to her while she was cooking, he got a piece of meat. If a poor person came by while she was tending the sheep, Brigid might give away one of the woolly lambs. She seemed to forget that she was Duffy's slave and to remember only that she was his daughter.

One day Duffy called her: "Come here with me in the chariot."

Brigid scrambled in happily and sat next to her stern-faced master. A flick of the whip and off they went.

"I'm not doing this to make you happy," Duffy said abruptly.

Brigid gazed up at him wide-eyed.

"I'm going to sell you to the king. You've been too generous with things that don't belong to you."

Brigid said nothing. How could she explain that it was impossible for her to refuse someone who needed help?

They soon stopped before a grim fortress. "Wait here," growled Duffy, and he went in to speak with the king. Brigid sat quietly in the chariot, watching the horses' tails brushing away the flies. Then she saw a poor man with leprosy walking down the road. He came up to the chariot and Brigid looked down at him. His face was disfigured by the horrible disease. His sad eyes seemed to be pleading.

I have nothing to give him, she thought.

But there on the seat beside her was Duffy's sword—a beautiful jeweled sword with a sharp blade. She took it and handed it to the man. He thanked her and hurried off with the splendid gift.

When Duffy returned to the chariot, he noticed right away that the sword was missing.

"What have you done with it?" he asked, trying to remain calm.

"A man with leprosy came by, and I gave it to him."

Duffy let out a roar like an angry lion. "A leper! You gave my jeweled sword to a leper! That sword was worth a fortune!"

"I know," replied Brigid calmly. "That's why I gave it to God."

Bridget saw God in all who were in need. This was why she was always so generous.

Duffy pulled Brigid down from the chariot and rushed her into the fortress. "There," he sputtered angrily to the king. "There! She's done it again! She's given my famous jeweled sword to a leper. You see now why I will not keep her!"

The king was a Christian. He looked gravely down at Brigid, who stared back with big, round eyes. Suddenly, the king smiled. "She's a Christian," he said, "and a good one. You should be proud of her, Duffy. Take her back home with you, but give her freedom. After all, she is your daughter."

Duffy gulped in dismay. If Brigid were freed, she might give away everything he owned!

As Duffy was driving home with the little girl beside him, he had an idea. Yes, he would free Brigid, for she was as fiery and independent as he. And he was proud of her in a way. Hadn't the king himself praised her? Nevertheless, he would have Brigid marry as soon as possible. That way she would no longer be able to give away his wealth!

~~~~~~~~~~

"Father," said Brigid one day, "I wish to see my mother, Brocessa. May I visit her?"

"No," replied Duffy.

But Brigid went anyway, with Duffy-like stubbornness. Her mother, she knew, was sick and overworked.

Brigid took her mother's place grinding corn, churning butter, and tending cows.

Of course, Brigid's generosity went with her. Even though the butter and milk and cream were not hers, she couldn't help giving them "to God"—to the poor people who came by daily. And God rewarded her by miraculously keeping the dairy stocked with butter and milk! The master of Brigid's mother was so amazed at this that he looked on Brigid as a saint (although he himself was still a pagan), and he offered to give her the whole dairy farm and all the cows.

"Instead, please give my mother her freedom," begged Brigid. And this the good man did. Later he became a Christian.

Brigid brought her mother to live with relatives and then returned to Duffy. She was now in her late teens. She was tall and strong, with rosy cheeks and peaceful eyes. Duffy thought she would make someone a fine wife.

He decided on a poet for her, because poets in those days were educated, wealthy, and highly respected. Brigid would have a high social position if she married a poet.

Naturally, Brigid had other ideas. As soon as she met the poet of her father's choice, she told him where he could find a wonderful girl who would make him a fine wife. She told him she would pray for that intention. And the poet went on his way.

Duffy was furious, but Brigid was stubborn. "I'm going to belong only to Christ," she told him. What could the irritated father do but give in? After all, Brigid had inherited his own hardheadedness.

When Patrick had come to Ireland a few years before, he had started to found monasteries for men right away. But there were not yet any convents for women. Many young women who had become Christians wanted to consecrate their lives to Jesus, and they did. But they continued to live with their parents. They prayed, helped the poor, and did needlework for the new churches Patrick had built. But their own families didn't understand them. Patrick once wrote, "They do this without their fathers' consent, and suffer persecution and misunderstanding from their relatives."

Brigid had seven good friends who wanted to consecrate their lives to God. "Let's live together in community as the monks do," she proposed to them. "Let's go to Bishop Mel. He will receive our vows in Christ's name." And the bishop gladly did so.

By this time, the fiery Duffy had mellowed. He gave Brigid the financial support and political backing she needed to begin several convents all over Ireland. Whether or not he himself became a Christian, we don't know for sure, but because of Brigid's influence he probably did.

Brigid also had acquired the friendship and support of the Irish bishops. Patrick had died a few years before, and they saw in her much of his spirit. They encouraged her missionary labors. From these first Irish bishops, Brigid learned how Patrick had thought and felt about various situations, and she tried to do what Patrick would have done.

Brigid's early convents were little groups of huts, made of poles, branches, and clay, which the young women built themselves. Around the group of huts they would put up a large stone or earthen wall or a hedge of thick bushes. As soon as Brigid had one community set up, she would leave a sister in charge and, taking one or two others with her, she would go to a new spot and build another convent. Like Patrick, she traveled all over Ireland.

Brigid traveled in a little cart, drawn by two horses. It was a dangerous way to travel on the bumpy roads, and at least twice she was thrown out of the cart. Once the horses ran away and stopped at the edge of a cliff!

Brigid certainly had courage, but she was best known for her cheerfulness and generosity. Now that she was a religious sister, she gave even more generously to the poor than she had as a child. On one occasion the sisters were expecting company, and they had carefully put aside milk and butter, bread, and meat for their guests. But who should appear at the convent gates but a group of beggars! Brigid couldn't resist. She gave them all the food she had prepared for the guests.

Another time a wealthy lady brought Brigid a basket of apples. Brigid was delighted. She took all the apples and distributed them to some beggars who were standing hopefully by the entrance to the convent.

"I brought them for you, not for those beggars!" the lady exclaimed.

"What's mine is theirs," said Brigid calmly.

Everyone got a royal welcome in Brigid's convents. Bishops, monks, and young girls from the neighboring farms—all were fed with whatever provisions the sisters had on hand. And somehow they never ran out of food. Brigid was always giving "to God," and God always seemed to match her generosity.

Those early convents were little groups of huts, made of poles, branches, and clay, which the young women built themselves.

Brigid loved to pray and to meditate on the lives of Jesus and Mary. Indeed, she loved our Lady so much and imitated her so well that people began to call her "the Mary of the Gael." Often Brigid prayed and meditated while she milked the convent's cows, churned the butter, or tended the sheep.

Yet Brigid also loved and encouraged studies. In Kildare, the most famous of the convents she founded, women scholars continually studied books of religion and science. Kildare became famous for the beautiful workmanship of its decorated manuscripts, bells, and chalices, which went to churches all over Ireland.

Brigid was known not only for her hard work and prayers. She also liked to play jokes and listen to music. She loved to see people having a good time. And like other Irish saints, she was fond of animals. She saw God in everything around her, and was forever thanking him for the beauties of creation.

When Brigid was born, Ireland was half-pagan and half-Christian. At the time of her death, around the year 525, Ireland was completely Christian, and had begun to send out missionaries to other lands. They went with the same spirit that Brigid had—with enthusiasm, courage, and a love that embraced the world.

Someone once said that a sad saint is no saint at all. Like St. Brigid, we should see God's beauty in everything around us and thank him joyfully, always.

St. Benedict

(circa 480–547)

JULY 11

By the time he was twenty, the young Roman noble Benedict had already become disgusted with the lawlessness and evils of sixth-century Rome. It seemed that whoever had the biggest weapons or fought the hardest ruled the land. Benedict asked his parents' permission to move to the countryside, where he could pray and study. The fresh air and peace he found there were a welcome change from the corruption of the city.

But Benedict felt himself drawn more and more to a life of total seclusion and prayer. A life of prayer, fasting, and penance—this was what the young man felt God was calling him to. He knew that his elderly servant would miss him, but his desire for a new way of life was so strong that one night he left a note and quietly slipped out of the house. He planned to go far into the wild, rugged wilderness that is known today as Subiaco.

Benedict walked on and on. The going became rougher and rougher. At last he found himself in the midst of some rocky mountains. This was just the kind of out-of-the-way place he was looking for! Benedict smiled.

Suddenly a deep, silent valley opened before him. *There will be no people here,* he thought. *No one would want to live in a place like this except someone who wants God alone, someone who wishes to leave everything else behind.* Benedict spotted a cave among the rocks. It looked like a perfect place to make his new home. It seemed to him that God had led him to the cave. "May you be praised, my Lord!" Benedict exclaimed.

"Now and forever!" a voice replied.

Benedict was startled. He frantically looked around. He had thought that he was alone, far from any other human being. Yet a few feet away from him stood an old man—a monk with a very kind face!

"I wanted to live in solitude," Benedict murmured.

"You will easily be able to do that," replied the monk. "My name is Romanus. You're not able to see it from here, but my monastery is at the top of that cliff." The old man pointed upward, then continued. "But tell me, who are you?"

In a few words, Benedict told Romanus where he had come from and how he wanted to leave everything behind and draw close to God. The holy monk understood this very well, for God had inspired him, too, in much the same way. He could see that Benedict sincerely wanted to withdraw from the world, not because he was afraid of the world, but because he wanted to live a life dedicated to prayer. *Yet,* thought Romanus, *he's young, and the life of a hermit is very difficult.*

"Listen," Romanus instructed, "I'll leave a bell here. I'll come by with some food each day. When the bell rings, you'll know that there's something to eat waiting for you outside the cave. That way you won't have to speak or be disturbed by anything."

Benedict was grateful and very happy with this arrangement. He stood at the entrance of the cave and watched as his new friend climbed the rocky slope back toward the monastery. Romanus turned once to wave good-bye, and then he was gone.

Poverty and inconvenience, cold and discomfort, darkness and dampness—these became Benedict's life. But he hardly noticed them because he was so absorbed in prayer, in reading his Bible, and in reflecting on the goodness of God and the beauty of creation. Days and even seasons seemed to fly by.

Three years passed. After a while, food stopped arriving from the old monk. Benedict grew hungrier and hungrier, but no welcome jingle sounded from the bell. *Romanus must be ill,* Benedict thought.

But on Easter Sunday a wonderful event occurred a few miles from Benedict's cave. A priest was preparing his holiday dinner when he heard a voice say, "While you're eating, my servant Benedict is almost dying of starvation in the cave of Subiaco!"

The priest didn't hesitate. He put all his food into a sack, slung the sack over his shoulder, and set out for

Subiaco. "Good health to you, brother!" he greeted Benedict. "I come in the name of the Lord!"

What a happy Easter feast the two men of God had! And how grateful Benedict was for God's goodness to him!

In those days, many people who called themselves monks lived very lazy lives and seemed to have forgotten Jesus' example of poverty and charity. One day, a group of men dressed as monks came to Benedict's cave. He could see that they were not used to climbing up hills. When they reached him, they explained that their own abbot had recently died. They wanted Benedict to come and be their new spiritual father.

Benedict thanked them for the invitation, but shook his head. "I'm afraid that my way of life and yours are too different. We wouldn't be happy with one another." But the monks insisted. Finally Benedict agreed to go with them and become their superior. But after he had lived with them for a while, this group of lazy men began to complain. Benedict was making them work too hard and pray too much. How could they get rid of him? At last they decided to serve him a glass of poisoned wine at the next community meal. With Benedict dead, they would again be free to live as they pleased.

The meal came and the glass of wine was set at Benedict's place. As he always did, Benedict raised his hand over the food and drink to bless it. When he made the Sign of the Cross, the glass of poisoned wine shattered! Benedict realized that the monks had tried to kill him. "I told you that my way of life was different from yours," he quietly said. "Now I'm going to leave you. You can go back to living the way you like." With that, Benedict returned to his cave at Subiaco.

But he wasn't left alone for long. Others who wanted to live only for God had heard of the young hermit's holiness. They began to come to Subiaco, asking to follow Benedict's way of life. Benedict accepted them as brothers and formed them into communities of monks. By the year 520, twelve monasteries dotted the rugged valley. Twelve monks lived in each, with one man appointed to govern each group as Benedict instructed them. From the beginning, Benedict insisted that all his monks not only spend long hours in prayer, but that they also work hard, raising food for themselves. "Pray and work" was Benedict's motto.

Eventually, Benedict moved to a mountain called Monte Cassino. He and his followers demolished a pagan temple there and built a large church and monastery. The men who kept coming to join Benedict were from every group of people who lived in Italy at the time—wealthy Romans, peasant farmers, and strong Gothic warriors. Only a few were priests. Most of them, like Benedict, were ordinary people who had become disillusioned with the violence and immorality of that period. They wanted to live quiet lives of hard work, charity, and prayer.

Monte Cassino and the other monasteries founded by Benedict became centers for worship, learning, farming, and safety from robbers. People from the

Monte Cassino and the other monasteries founded by Benedict became centers for worship, learning, farming, and safety.

countryside would gather at the monasteries for prayer. Besides teaching them about Jesus, the monks also showed them how to raise better crops.

Within the monasteries the monks worked at copying by hand important writings from the Greeks and Romans. These writings are still important today. They would not have been preserved if it hadn't been for Benedict and his monks, who knew the value of these writings and treasured them.

At Monte Cassino, Benedict wrote down a rule for his monks. This rule became the standard way of life for monks and nuns of western Europe. Many religious all over the world still live by it today. "Pray and work" remains a way for many people to find God in everyday life.

One day in 547 (some think it may have been in 543; we are not sure about the exact year), Benedict told his monks, "Brothers, God is calling me!" He came down with a high fever. With great love he received Holy Communion for the last time, and then peacefully died.

Although St. Benedict has been dead for many centuries, the world has not forgotten all that he did and the great example of simplicity and prayer that he left behind.

"Pray and work" is the secret of success. If we want to do well in something, we must work hard at it, but we must also pray for God's help.

St. Columban

(543–615)

NOVEMBER 23

Autumn was at its peak. The elderly monk could feel its twinge in his bones. The trees were still too thick with leaves for him to see what was going on in the valley below, but Columban knew that his monks were there. Today they would be working in the vineyards and olive groves, getting ready for the days of icy winds and swirling snows that would soon be coming. There wouldn't be much food this winter, but the monks fasted so often that their supplies were sure to last until spring.

How are the other monasteries, those beyond Italy, doing? the old man wondered. He thought of each one, hundreds of miles to the northwest, hidden among the forested mountains of Gaul. It had been years since he had seen them. The monk pondered his memories in silence, and then turned back into his cave. During the past two years he had spent many hours at prayer in this retreat. Now he felt he would soon leave the cave for good.

Columban had lived a long and active life. He thought back over the years to his youthful days in distant Ireland, the land of his birth. He remembered how difficult it had been to leave home. In his imagination, he heard again his mother's tearful voice begging him not to go. He relived his journey to the island of Cluain, where he had continued his studies of Latin and Scripture at the monastery. Then he had decided to become a monk himself—a decision that had changed the course of his life.

Columban joined the monastery at Bangor and was ordained a priest. For nearly thirty years he tried as hard as he could to belong only to God. He finally realized that there was one more sacrifice that God was asking him to make. He went to his abbot and begged, "Father, please send me as a missionary to Gaul."

"I would rather have you remain here, Columban," Abbott Comghall replied. "But I'll pray about it. I want you to do God's will."

Soon God did inspire Comghall to let Columban go to Gaul. The abbot even sent twelve monks with him!

The little band of monks packed a few books and sacred vessels for Mass and set sail for the European continent. From Brittany, where more men joined them, they started out for eastern Gaul, trudging along crumbling Roman roads that were almost blocked by thick forests. The forests were dangerous for many reasons. Lurking in them were runaway soldiers and slaves, as well as gangs of thieves—not to mention wild animals. The once glorious Roman Empire had fallen into chaos. Gaul itself was divided among three

Columban had lived a long and active life.

kings who were Christian in name only. There were signs of war and destruction everywhere.

At last, Columban and his companions were welcomed into Burgundy, the territory of King Gunthram. There, in a wild and desolate valley, they converted an abandoned fort into a monastery and an old pagan temple into a chapel.

The monks soon became friends with the peasant farmers in the area. Several young men asked to enter the monastery and become monks.

The monks led a hard life. They spent long hours teaching and instructing the people. It had been many years since there had been any schools in that region. For food, the monks gathered wild plants, berries, and roots. They raised crops and fished in the nearby lakes. They spent hours praying together in the chapel or off alone on the hillsides. As a penance, they would often pray for long periods with their arms stretched out in the form of a cross.

Soon it was time to start another monastery. Columban and some of his monks followed the river downstream until he came to the ruins of Luxeuil, a Roman town that had been destroyed by the Huns. "Here is where we can build," he told his companions.

The monks happily set to work. They cut away underbrush, felled trees, and hauled stones. They rebuilt the town walls and constructed a church, a school, and a number of little one-room houses in which the monks would live. Not long afterward, so many men began to join them that they had to build another monastery a short distance away, in Fontaines.

Soon the three communities in Gaul housed sixty monks and over two hundred students, mostly noblemen's sons. The boys came to the monastery to be educated in the usual subjects, but they also learned self-discipline, honesty, and kindness. People from the surrounding villages would come to spend a few weeks with the monks too. They had the opportunity of receiving the sacrament of Reconciliation and learning more about living the Christian life. It had been many years since some of the peasants had talked to a priest!

Now, almost sixty years after St. Benedict had written his rule for monks, Columban wrote his own rule. Columban's rule stressed the need for frequent fasting and other physical penances that the Irish monks and their disciples had always considered important. But the main purpose of monastic life, Columban wrote, was to learn to love God with all one's mind, heart, and strength, and to love one's neighbor as oneself for the love of God.

"We must think often about God and heaven," Columban taught. "Everything that we have or do should help us to become more like Jesus." Columban was convinced of the truth of his words. It had been a challenge his whole life to keep thinking and acting always more like Jesus. And with his stubbornness and hot temper, it hadn't always been easy!

As abbot, Columban was the spiritual father of all the monks. He corrected them when necessary, just as a good father does. He watched over their spiritual life and their physical health. Above all, he grew to love them very deeply as his brothers in Christ.

About twenty years after Father Columban's arrival in Gaul, he got himself into deep trouble. Until that time, he had been friendly with the kings of Burgundy, even with those who were leading evil lives. Columban had often urged the young King Theodoric to change his sinful ways.

Then one day Columban paid a visit to Queen Brunhilda, Theodoric's grandmother. The two had always been on good terms. But this time Columban said something in his usual honest way that offended Brunhilda deeply. After the abbot left, the queen began to urge the king and the local bishop to drive Columban and his monks out of Gaul!

Not long after that, Theodoric rode to Columban's monastery with a band of soldiers. He had the abbot seized and taken to Besancon, a city forty miles to the south. He permitted only one monk to go with Columban. Although Columban and his companion could to walk freely around the city, the bridge and road leading back to Luxeuil were always guarded.

Then, one Sunday morning, Columban looked out over the river and saw no guards on the bridge. He and his companion quickly set out for home.

Hardly had Father Columban returned to Luxeuil when a band of horsemen thundered up to the monastery gates. They had come for him again. The soldiers searched the monastery, but all the monks looked alike to them. Only the captain recognized Columban, who was sitting by the church door reading a book as if nothing were happening. The captain pretended not to see him. "Let's go," he told his men. "This man is hidden by divine power."

The soldiers got back on their horses and rode off.

A few days later, while they were singing the psalms, Columban and his monks once more heard the clattering of horses' hooves and the clash of steel weapons. Soldiers poured into the church. "Man of God," called one of them, "we beg you to obey the king's command. Leave this land and go back where you came from."

Columban replied slowly, "I don't think it would please the Creator if a man were to return to his homeland once he has left it for the love of Christ."

The soldiers understood. But they knew that Theodoric could have them killed if they didn't obey his orders. "Father, take pity on us," they begged. "We don't want to take you away by force, but if you don't leave Luxeuil, we'll all die!"

Columban was moved with compassion. Turning to his monks, he said, "I'll go with them." He began to walk out of the church, then suddenly stopped and prayed, "O eternal Creator, prepare a place where we, your people, may serve you forever." The monks gathered about him. "Don't lose hope," Columban quietly told them. "Continue to sing the praises of almighty God. The sacrifice we're making will be rewarded by many more young men coming to join us." He paused. "If any of you wish to come with me, you may."

An uproar followed. All the monks wanted to come!

"No," replied the soldiers. "The king has ordered that only the monks from Ireland and Brittany may accompany the abbot."

And so Columban left his beloved Luxeuil with only a few of his monks. The soldiers went with them

all the way down to the River Loire, where they all
boarded a small boat bound toward the sea. It was, in
all, a journey of about 600 miles. In the cities where
they stopped, many people came out to greet the
monks because they had heard about their holiness.
Finally the little group reached Nantes, the port from
which they were to sail for Ireland.

Columban sat down and wrote a long, anxious letter
to his community at Luxeuil and their new abbot. He
urged them to preserve their unity of spirit and their
love for one another. He reminded the monks that their
own sufferings were a share in the passion of Christ.

Confident that they had accomplished their mission, Columban's guards had left him. They weren't
there to witness the fierce storm that blew up and
caught the little ship just before it was to set sail for
Ireland. The winds were so strong that the ship was
lifted right out of the water and set down on dry
ground! The superstitious captain and crew unloaded
the monks and their baggage at once, and immediately the winds died down. The next day the ship sailed
away—without Columban and his men!

To Columban, this was a sign that God didn't want
him to return to Ireland. Almost at once he and his
monks were on the road again, heading northeast
toward the safety of the kingdom of Theodoric's
brother—and enemy—Theodebert. They moved
quickly and secretly. It was a tiring march of hundreds
of miles over rough roads.

In Metz, King Theodebert welcomed Columban
kindly. He was only too happy to help the monks

whom his brother had exiled. He offered them land on which to build a new monastery.

"Since I've decided to journey to Italy, Your Majesty," replied Columban, "I'll look for a suitable place along the route and build there."

After settling down in two different locations and being sent away twice by the non-Christian people of the area, Columban and most of his monks finally moved on to Italy. There, in the city of Bobbio, Columban built his last monastery on land given him by the Lombard king of northern Italy.

Columban had no way of knowing that the monastery of Bobbio would become one of the greatest cultural centers of Europe, preserving for future generations the treasures of the Italian and Irish civilizations. He didn't know that within fifty years his few monasteries would have multiplied into almost a hundred, and that many bishops would receive their early training within those walls. What Columban *did* know was that it was time to meet the Lord whom he had served faithfully for so long. One chilly November day, supported by the prayers of his monks, he peacefully went to his true homeland—heaven.

Sometimes we're faced with a choice between something we know we should do and something we'd like to do. When that happens, let's remember St. Columban and the many sacrifices he made in his life. Let's ask God to give us the courage to do what's right, no matter the cost.

St. Kevin

(d. 618)

JUNE 3

St. Kevin lived in Ireland about a hundred years after the great saints Patrick and Brigid, at a time when his country was called a land of saints and scholars. He was baptized by St. Cronan, and a legend says that angels could be seen around the baptismal font during the ceremony. Because of this, he is often called "Kevin of the Angels."

As a young boy, Kevin was given the duty of watching the family sheep. There is a legend that some poor beggars once came and asked him for part of his flock. Kevin felt sorry for them and gave them four sheep. That night when all the sheep were counted, the original number were still there!

Kevin's parents were wealthy. They could easily have hired a tutor for the boy so that he could grow up among the comforts of home and become a warrior and chieftain. But Kevin's parents knew that a good education is better than comfort, and that learning to serve God is the best kind of wealth. So they sent their son away to study under a wise old monk named Petroc. The boy was seven when he started school and nineteen when he finished. By that time, Kevin was certain about what he wanted to do with his life: he would become a priest.

That meant more time spent in school, but to Kevin it was worth it. He continued to study under the stern guidance of his uncle Eugene, a serious, hard-working priest who expected students to measure up to his standards. Kevin found it difficult at times, but he didn't give up. At last, the great day arrived—he was ordained a priest!

After his ordination, Kevin felt a great need to be alone with God for a while. He wanted time to pray and to think about the many things he had learned during his long years of study. And he still wasn't sure just what type of work he should do now that his studies were finished.

Into the hills of Wicklow he trudged until he reached a wild valley where two lonely lakes mirrored the sky. On one side rose a rocky crag, on the other, a green mountain. The place was called Glendalough, which means "the valley of the two lakes."

For seven years Kevin lived there in a mountain cave so small that he couldn't even stand up in it. He ate berries, nuts, and wild plants, and dressed in animal skins. Kevin spent his time meditating and praying. He sang praises to God accompanied by his harp. He had a great love for nature, and even the wild animals came to him without fear.

Kevin trudged into the hills of Wicklow until he reached a wild valley where two lonely lakes mirrored the sky. On one side rose a rocky crag, on the other, a green mountain.

One day a farmer named Dima came walking through the valley. He was not a Christian, but he had heard that a holy hermit lived at Glendalough, and he was curious. Dima asked Kevin to tell him about the God he prayed to. Of course, Kevin was eager to do so.

Simply and clearly, Kevin told Dima about the one God who made everything from nothing and keeps us all in existence. He told him about Adam and Eve and their sin of pride and disobedience. He told him about Jesus, the Son of God, who became human like us, and who suffered and died out of love for us and the desire to save us from our sins. He told him about the Holy Eucharist and the other sacraments that Jesus gave us. Kevin explained to Dima that God loves us and lives with us, that God gives us his grace, and that God has promised us eternal life with him after death.

Dima listened spellbound. He had never before heard such wonderful things! At last he asked, "Will you come down to my farm and teach my children what you have told me?"

Kevin hesitated. "I'll pray about it," he responded. But almost at once, the answer came to him in his heart. This was what God wanted him to do with his life! The next day Kevin went down to the farm with Dima.

Soon Kevin was teaching not just one family, but dozens of men and boys from the nearby villages and farms.

"We must build a school," he finally decided.

Rocks were plentiful, and the farmers helped Kevin build two stone buildings—a monastery and a school—in the solitude of Glendalough. Soon other men came to join Kevin in his life of prayer and service. Kevin wrote a rule of life and trained them as monks. Together Kevin and his monks taught the children and adults who came to the monastery. At Glendalough the children of farmers and the children of chieftains sat side by side. The rich and the poor lived and worked and studied together. Everyone was treated alike.

More buildings were eventually added to the little settlement, including a sturdy six-story stone bell tower with a cone-shaped top. In those days, such towers were used as landmarks for approaching visitors. They also served as storage areas and places of shelter during enemy attacks. Although so many centuries have passed, that bell tower is still standing today.

Little by little, an entire town grew up around Kevin's monastery. People came from all over Ireland to tell Kevin their problems and ask his help and prayers in solving them. They knew that he was close to God.

Kevin's work was very demanding, and he no longer had long hours for quiet prayer. So, every Lent, Kevin went up to the mountain to live alone in his cave for forty days. There he reflected on his life and work as a priest. He tried to do some penances for those times that he felt he could have done better. And he made strong resolutions for the future. Then he would pray for God's help to become always more like Jesus in order to help others.

Kevin served as abbot of his monastery for several years. Then, once everything had been well established, he built himself a beehive-shaped stone hut where he could continue his life as a hermit, alone with God. Four happy years passed. Then some of his monks came to him with the plea, "Come back with us and lead us as our abbot once more." Kevin unselfishly gave up the life of solitude he loved and went back to the monastery.

The years slipped by. Kevin's hair and beard grew white, but his eyes still sparkled, and his step was as quick and firm as ever. He watched his students grow up. He saw many of them marry. He baptized their babies. He saw many others become monks, priests, or nuns and even travel to foreign lands as missionaries.

Even as he felt himself growing older and tired, Kevin desired to go on a missionary journey himself. "What do you think of the idea?" he asked his good friend Kieran, the Bishop of Clonmacnoise.

Kieran understood Kevin's desire. But he also knew that sometimes it's better for one missionary to train many others than to leave his students and go to the missions himself.

"Birds don't hatch their eggs while they're flying," Bishop Kieran answered.

Kevin realized that Kieran was right. It was a sacrifice, but Kevin would stay at Glendalough, teaching and advising everyone who came to him. Kevin couldn't have known it then, but the monastery he founded would continue to prosper as a center of prayer and learning for nearly two centuries after his death.

On a peaceful June night in 618, the earthly life of this great servant of God came to an end. Kevin's soul sped heavenward to join the angels and saints around God's throne. We can be sure that, from heaven, Kevin continues to pray for missionaries wherever they may be.

St. Kevin knew the importance of speaking to God and listening to him. He also knew how important it is to share our knowledge and faith with others. We can ask St. Kevin to help us to pray well. We can also ask him to help us to answer questions people may ask about our Catholic faith.

St. Margaret of Scotland

(d. 1093)

November 16

"Good-bye, England," sighed Princess Margaret, as she watched the rugged coastline disappear beyond the restless gray waves. "Perhaps I will never see you again."

Margaret, a pretty young woman of twenty, had grown to love England deeply during the ten years she had lived there. Her grandfather, Edmund, had been king of the little island, but Danish invaders had prevented Margaret's own father from wearing the crown. Edgar, Margaret's younger brother, had also tried to claim the crown, but now Norman conquerors were in power. Margaret was sailing to continental Europe with her mother, sister, and brother. The king of Hungary was a relative of theirs and would take them in.

"Margaret, please come below!" her mother called anxiously. "A storm is coming!"

"Yes, Mother," Margaret replied, climbing down to their cramped quarters. As the sailors on deck shouted excitedly to one another, the little ship began to toss wildly. Margaret wedged herself into a corner of the cabin and held on. She smiled at Edgar, who responded with a broad grin. He had never been on a ship before and was enjoying the adventure.

For many hours, the little ship rode the furious storm. When the wind and waves became calm again, the travelers were lost. At last they sighted land to the northwest. "That's the Scottish coast," announced the captain.

"King Malcolm's country," Margaret murmured to her mother. "He was exiled in England before he conquered Scotland and regained his father's throne."

"In that case," replied her mother, "prepare yourself to meet some wild and warlike people. The Scots are not as civilized as the people we have lived among until now."

However, King Malcolm's friendly reception surprised both Margaret and her mother. He was polite and generous, and invited them to stay in his castle for a few months. "My queen has died," King Malcolm explained. "The castle is very gloomy without her. I'd be grateful if you would stay."

Margaret and her mother certainly did brighten up the castle. King Malcolm was impressed by Margaret's beauty and cheerfulness, but most of all by her goodness and kindness. Margaret loved to pray, and her faith in God was strong. It was obvious that she sincerely tried to live according to the example of Jesus.

One day King Malcolm said to Margaret's mother, "Lady Agatha, your daughter Margaret is both beautiful and good. May I have your permission to marry her?"

Margaret's mother hesitated. "I'm happy that the princess has found favor with Your Majesty," she answered. "But Margaret has always intended to become a nun. I must speak to her first."

Margaret was a bit upset by the news. She liked King Malcolm, and she enjoyed the excitement of court life. But she loved God more than anyone and anything else and had dreamed of dedicating her life to him. To solve the problem, she turned to prayer.

One morning, after receiving Holy Communion, Margaret knew what she must do. She felt that Jesus himself had spoken to her, saying, "This is your place. It is here that I wish you to serve me. In this kingdom, you will have many opportunities to do good and to become holy."

Margaret's doubts disappeared, and King Malcolm was overjoyed when she accepted his proposal! Soon, all of Scotland was celebrating its new queen.

Queen Margaret did find many opportunities to do good in Scotland. Most of the people were poor. Unfortunately, those who were richer spent much of their time raiding the English. Queen Margaret found a solution to both the poverty and the raiding. She asked King Malcolm to invite some Benedictine monks from England and continental Europe to settle in Scotland. These monks began to teach the Scots how to raise better crops. They also built churches and monasteries with the help of the warriors who had been attacking the English settlements. Children came to the monasteries to be taught by the monks. There they received an education, which their parents

Princess Margaret liked King Malcolm, and she enjoyed the excitement of court life. But she loved God and wanted to serve him in the best way possible.

had never been given. Many of these children grew up to become priests, monks, and nuns. Some even traveled from Scotland as missionaries to teach the Christian faith to people of the neighboring islands.

Since the Scottish bishops had been out of contact with the Pope for years, Queen Margaret invited some Catholic priests from England to meet with them and talk about the many problems faced by the bishops of Scotland at that time. Margaret herself attended this meeting and took part in the discussions, which were helpful for the Church in Scotland.

Queen Margaret's life was very active. Mass, daily prayer, aid to the poor and sick, and visits to prisoners filled her days. But the energetic queen was never too busy to devote time and attention to her family. She was a loving and attentive wife to Malcolm, for whom she prayed continually. She was a firm but understanding mother to their eight lively children: Edward, Ethelred, Edmund, Edgar, Alexander, David, Matilda, and Mary. "Pray to the Blessed Virgin," she would tell them. "Be kind to the poor; try to avoid all sin. Lead holy lives, and share your belief in Jesus with everyone."

When Queen Margaret was about forty-seven, she became seriously ill. She felt her strength lessening day by day. "I think that I may die soon," she told the priest who served as her chaplain.

At the same time, the English attacked the Scottish castle of Ainwick. King Malcolm said a hasty good-bye to Margaret, gathered his army, and rode off to battle. Their sons Edward and Edgar went with him.

On her deathbed, Margaret prayed anxiously for her husband and sons. She offered her sufferings for their safe return, but more especially for their spiritual well-being.

One day a bruised and battered figure appeared in the doorway of the queen's room. It was Edgar. He was covered with caked blood, and dusty from the long ride. Weakly, with sorrow in his face, he crossed the room and knelt at his mother's bedside.

"Your father?" Margaret asked, already sensing the truth.

"Father and Edward have both been killed, Mother," gulped the boy, burying his face in his hands.

"Few sorrows could have been greater than this," murmured the queen.

After comforting Edgar and calling a servant to treat his wounds, Margaret sent for her chaplain. "I want to ask two things of you," she said. "As long as you live, please remember my husband's soul and my own poor soul in your Masses and prayers. And watch over my children, teaching them to love God and do his will." The chaplain promised, and Margaret, the faithful wife and mother, was at peace. She made her confession, received the sacrament of the Anointing of the Sick, and left her small, war-torn kingdom for the Kingdom of eternal peace.

St. Margaret knew that the people we should spend the most time with and do the most for are our own families. Let's be kind to everyone, but especially to our parents, brothers, and sisters.

St. Francis of Assisi

(1182–1226)

OCTOBER 4

In the city of Assisi in central Italy, over 800 years ago, Pica, the wife of a wealthy cloth merchant named Peter Bernardone, was about to have a baby. There is a legend that a stranger came to the family home and told a servant, "If you want everything to go well, tell Lady Pica to go to the stable at once."

Pica obeyed the strange command. And so her baby boy was born in a stable, just as Jesus had been!

Peter Bernardone was away on a business trip when his son was born. It was Pica who named the baby "John" at his baptism. When Peter returned, he wasn't happy with the name. "My son will be called Francis," he announced, "after the refined and cultured French. I want him to have the best the world can offer."

Peter had great dreams for his son—dreams of great wealth as a merchant. He started to train Francis in business while the boy was still young, even though this meant taking him out of school. Francis soon began to help in his father's store.

Francis became a very good businessman. He was friendly, courteous, and easy to get along with. He even sold expensive cloth to people who hadn't planned to buy anything! Business kept getting better and better.

But Francis wasn't satisfied with making money. He also wanted to spend it. He dressed like a royal prince. His father didn't mind. Peter was happy with the way business was going and glad that his son was the most popular young man in the city. In fact, Francis's friends had nicknamed him "the king of parties"! Singing, dancing, hunting trips—Francis never missed a thing.

Francis did love a good time. But he was also very generous. He liked to see everyone happy, and he often gave his friends expensive gifts.

One day, a poor beggar approached Francis. "In the name of God," the old man said, "please give me some money so that I may eat." Francis pretended not to hear or see the man. But then, as the beggar limped sadly away, Francis felt so sorry that he ran after him and gave him a purse full of coins and some cloth from his father's shop to make up for his unkindness.

When Francis was about seventeen, fighting broke out between Assisi and the nearby city of Perugia. Francis joined the men who were defending Assisi and was taken prisoner. He spent a whole year in prison before finally being released.

Francis wasn't the same young man when he returned home. His health had suffered in prison. His ambitions were also different now. He decided to become a soldier.

After spending some time recuperating, Francis went out and bought the best armor and weapons he could find. His father smiled. If his son wanted to win fame on the battlefield, that was fine with him!

Riding away from Assisi to join the troops, Francis met a knight who had lost everything in the war. Francis generously gave the man his brand new sword and embroidered cloak.

Francis stopped in the city of Spoleto for the night. Almost as soon as he closed his eyes, he began to dream and heard a voice ask, "Francis, is it better to serve the master or the servant?"

"The master, of course," he replied.

"Then why are you leaving the master for the servant?"

Deeply troubled, Francis asked the mysterious voice, "What shall I do?"

"Return to Assisi, and you will find out," came the answer.

As soon as dawn broke, Francis mounted his horse and headed home. His heart was heavy as he imagined what people would say about his return. And sure enough, everyone laughed when they saw him ride back into the city—he who had gone off so full of pride just the day before. "Is this another one of your tricks?" the townspeople asked, shaking their heads.

Francis slipped back into his old habits of going out with his friends, singing loudly, and riding off on hunting parties. He seemed to be his old cheerful self, but in reality his heart was sad and troubled.

As he was coming home from a party one night, Francis lagged behind his friends. He stood still, gazing up at the beautiful stars. Suddenly, light seemed to flood his soul. "My God and my all!" he began to pray over and over again.

When his friends came back to look for him, they found him staring off into space. "Dreaming, Francis?" they teased. "Who's the lucky girl?"

"A great lady," replied Francis slowly. Like every medieval knight, he would have his lady, but she was not a person. Poverty would be his "lady." Poverty, because Jesus had loved it so much and had chosen it for himself.

How was Francis to serve Lady Poverty? At first, he didn't know. But, after a while, he thought of making a pilgrimage to Rome. With some money that his mother gladly gave him, he set out for the Holy City.

In Rome, Francis went to pray at St. Peter's Basilica. Looking around, he saw that the pilgrims were giving small offerings. With a rush of generosity, he put all the money he had into the offering box. His great charity amazed the other pilgrims. He even went a step further, and asked the other pilgrims for donations. Now, to keep from starving, Francis had to depend on the charity of others.

~~~~~~~~~~~

Francis returned from Rome completely taken up with his new ideal, which was becoming clearer every day. It was not enough to give *money* away. He would have to give his own *self* to the Lord. His family couldn't understand him. He often went out into the quiet countryside to think and pray.

One day Francis came across a man who was suffering from leprosy. Francis was turning away in horror when he heard a voice within him ask, "How can you be a knight of Christ if you are afraid?"

Francis remembered the words of Jesus, "Truly I tell you, just as you did it to one of the least of these members of my family, you did it to me" (Mt 25:40). Who could be poorer than that man, sick and abandoned by everyone? Would Francis run away from Jesus? Never! Taking a deep breath, the youth went up to the man. He kissed his face, which was covered with sores. Then he gave the man a generous offering. But his greatest gift was the tender gesture of acceptance he had made. The poor leper stood speechless. It had been a long time since he had experienced such respect. Francis was happy. The experience of reaching out to another had made him realize what true joy was. From that time on, he began to comfort people who were sick with leprosy, caring for their sores, cheering them up, and talking to them about the love of God.

I must begin to live a life like that of Jesus, Francis thought. He went often to pray in a little country church called San Damiano. One day he heard these words coming from the crucifix inside the church: "Go and repair my house, which is falling in ruins."

"Yes! I'll do it!" Francis answered at once. He looked around him. The abandoned church was falling apart. It would take a lot of work to fix it up.

Francis went to pray in a little country church dedicated to San Damiano. There he heard these words from the crucifix: "Go, and repair my house, which is falling in ruins."

Francis returned home and went straight to his father's shop. He loaded some of the most expensive fabric onto his horse and went off to the market. There he sold all the material—and the horse along with it! Taking the money, he rushed back to San Damiano. "Here is money to repair the church," he told the surprised priest, holding out a bag of gold coins.

"I can't accept it, Francis," the old man replied, shaking his head. "What will your father say?"

Francis escaped his father's anger that time, but not for long. Soon Peter Bernardone became so upset with the way his son was acting that he went to the city officials and accused him of being a thief. Francis was summoned to court, but he refused to go. "I should be judged by the bishop, because this is a religious matter," he said. So father and son were called before the bishop's tribunal.

The father was angry and excited; the son remained calm and quiet. Gently the bishop told Francis, "Return to your father what belongs to him. God would not want money for his church obtained this way."

"Your Excellency," replied Francis, "I'll return not only his money, but even his clothes." And right then and there Francis took off all his clothes. Then he told the astonished crowd, "I no longer call Peter Bernardone my father; I give everything back to him. From now on I shall say to God, 'Our Father, who art in heaven!'"

The bishop was deeply moved. He put his arms around Francis and covered him with his own cloak. Peter, meanwhile, was confused and angry. He could tell that the people were on Francis's side. This was not the outcome he had expected! He took his money—and the clothes—and left!

The bishop's gardener had an old tunic, which he gave Francis to wear. Joyfully, the youth put it on while the bishop made a large Sign of the Cross over it to symbolize the young man's consecration to God. Then Francis left the city. Climbing up the slope of the near-by foothills, Francis began to sing. He felt that now he belonged completely to God!

~~~~~~~~~~

"Repair my house!" These words still echoed in Francis's ears. But now he had no money. How could he repair the ruined church? Soon an idea clicked in his mind. He could sing for money, just as the wandering minstrels did. But instead of singing songs about romance or war, he would sing about God! So Francis began to go through the countryside, singing such hymns of praise to God that people crowded about him to listen. They were deeply moved, and willingly gave donations when Francis asked them to help him rebuild the little church.

Soon he had bought enough materials to begin the project. He had learned how to build walls during the war; now he put that knowledge to good use. The priest watched him with kindly interest, and tried to help him in every way he could. Every night he would make supper for Francis, but the young man preferred to go begging from door to door for his food.

A young nobleman named Bernard Quintavalle was very impressed by Francis. He wanted to get to know him better. One day Bernard invited Francis to his home and managed to persuade him to spend the night. They shared a room, and Bernard was able to see that as soon as everything was quiet, Francis slipped out of bed and knelt on the floor. Francis spent the night in prayer, saying over and over, "My God and my All." Bernard pretended to be asleep, but he actually watched Francis all night. In the morning, he told Francis that he had decided to join him.

"Think it over carefully, Bernard," Francis urged. "Poverty isn't easy for someone who has grown up rich and comfortable. Let's pray about this."

After going to Mass at a nearby church, Francis and Bernard asked the priest, Father Peter Cattani, to open the altar missal three times in the name of Jesus. Each time their eyes fell upon passages of the Gospel that spoke of the poverty of Jesus and his disciples.

That was enough for Bernard—and for Father Peter, too. He also admired Francis and had wished for a long time to have the courage to join him. Now Francis knew that God was inspiring him to lead others in the life he had chosen for himself. Together, they would try to imitate Jesus every way they could. "Brothers," said Francis with great enthusiasm, "the poverty of Jesus will be our rule of life. Let us go and preach."

Soon other men joined the group of "little brothers." To all of them Francis said, "God has called us not only for our own sakes, but to save our neighbors, too. We must go out into the world and bring people to do penance and to obey God's commandments."

Francis and his brothers often went to the small shantytown where people with leprosy lived. There they cared for the sick and dying. Because leprosy was so contagious, lepers were forced to live outside of the city, and almost everyone treated them very badly. But Francis and his brothers spoke to them about the great love of God, the death and resurrection of Jesus, and the joys of heaven awaiting those who love God. If their patients had not been living good lives before, many of them changed their ways and prepared for a holy death.

But one man, who was very sick, only cursed and insulted some of the brothers. He was bitter and angry that God was allowing him to suffer so much. The brothers were upset when they heard the man speak this way about God, and they wanted to abandon him. But before taking such a drastic step, they decided to consult Francis.

"Let me see him," Francis said. He went to the hut where the man lived and offered to serve him in whatever way he could. Rudely, the sick man accepted his offer. He told Francis to give him a bath.

The open sores of leprosy had become infected and the odor was terrible. Francis heated some water and added sweet-smelling herbs to it. Taking clean cloths, he gently began to rub the painful sores. Then a miracle happened! Little by little, the man's sores disappeared. But the greatest miracle was the great sense of peace and acceptance that flooded the man's heart. He felt that Francis was not only cleansing his body, but also his soul. As soon as he could, the man dedicated himself to God and spent the rest of his life caring for others.

~~~~~~~~~~~~~~~~~~~~~~

Francis never spared himself in the hard but joyous life to which God had called him. After many years, those who knew him best could see that his health was failing and that he would soon die.

Francis knew it, too. He asked to be taken to the Church of St. Mary of the Angels. On the way, he told his brothers to place him on the ground so that he was facing toward Assisi. Slowly he raised his hand and blessed the city. "May you be blessed by God, holy city, because many souls will be saved through you, and many of God's servants will live in you. They will be among the saints in the kingdom of heaven!"

Francis blessed all his spiritual children and begged them to sing the "Canticle of the Sun," a beautiful hymn he had written to praise God for creation. He raised his weak voice and together they sang.

Death came as the sun set on the evening of October 4, 1226. Francis's soul soared home to heaven to join the choirs of angels in singing the praises of God forever.

Poverty and charity were the special ways in which Francis was called to imitate Jesus. Taking good care of our things, sharing what we have, and telling others about God's love for them are all ways that we can imitate Francis.

St. Anthony of Padua

(1195–1231)

JUNE 13

Young Father Fernando hurried to answer the knock at the priory door. It was late. *Who could be out at this time of night?* he wondered. Opening the heavy door, he was surprised to see five brothers belonging to the new religious community that Francis Bernardone had started in Assisi, Italy. One of the men quickly explained that they were passing through the Portuguese city of Coimbra on their way to Morocco, where they were going to preach the Gospel of Jesus. "May we spend the night here, Father?" he asked.

"Of course, Brothers," Fernando responded. "I'm sure our prior will welcome you. Please come in."

Fernando had heard of these friars who lived such a poor and simple life. It sounded so different from his own calm, predictable life as an Augustinian monk, a life made up of community prayer, study, and teaching.

Two days later, Fernando found himself wishing his new friends well as they continued on their journey to Morocco. They knew that it would be dangerous to preach the Gospel in a land where people were not allowed to practice the Christian faith. But these young friars were full of faith, and they were convinced that knowledge and love of Jesus would be the best way to help others live in peace and justice. In the following months, Father Fernando often prayed for them and their ministry.

Fernando was horrified when, almost a year later, word came that Don Pedro of Portugal would be stopping at the priory with the bones of Franciscan martyrs from Morocco! Fernando was stunned. Tears filled his eyes as he listened to the story of his friends' cruel deaths. At the same time, how proud he was, for they had received the great grace of being killed for their love of Jesus! During the next few weeks, he couldn't get the brothers out of his mind. The thought of martyrdom for the sake of the Gospel strongly attracted Fernando, but he knew that, as an Augustinian, he would have very little chance of becoming a martyr.

Then along came another small group of Franciscan friars. They stopped at Fernando's priory for some rest on their journey. Fernando spent several hours asking them about their life. When they left, they carried with them a letter to their superior. Father Fernando was asking to leave the Augustinian life to become a Franciscan friar.

It wasn't long before the arrangements were made and Fernando exchanged his white linen habit for the rough woolen tunic of the friars of Francis of Assisi. He also took a new name, Anthony, as a symbol that he was taking a new direction in life. With a joyful heart, he joined the next group of friars going to Morocco to preach. Father Anthony hoped that he, too, would be martyred for Jesus. Instead, when he reached Morocco he came down with such a high fever that he couldn't even get out of bed.

Anthony was seriously ill for a whole year. Since he was not getting any better, it was decided that he should return to Portugal. With a heavy heart, Anthony obeyed and boarded a ship for the return journey to Europe. Little did he know what was ahead!

The small ship encountered a terrible storm that lasted several days. When the storm finally ended, the crew realized that they were far off course. The ship had been so damaged that the sailors had to head for the closest land, which turned out to be the coast of Sicily. Once ashore, Friar Anthony found a Franciscan community and went to introduce himself. The friars welcomed him and told him that there would soon be a meeting of all the Franciscans in Assisi. With a new burst of excitement, Anthony joined the Sicilian friars on their journey to Assisi, hoping that he would have a chance to meet Francis himself.

It was 1221, the last year that such a great meeting of all the friars would take place. Although Francis was there, the meeting was run by Brother Elias. Not yet belonging to any particular community, Anthony was quite lost among the three thousand friars. After the meeting ended, when everyone was getting ready to go home, Anthony approached one of the Italian superiors. "Father Gratian," he asked, "would I be able to come with you? I've recently returned from Morocco, and I don't have a new assignment."

"Yes," Father Gratian answered with a smile. "Come with us."

How different was the hard, simple life of a Franciscan friar from the studious routine he had followed with the Augustinians! And how different customs were in Italy from those in Portugal, where Anthony had been raised! None of his new brothers dreamed that Anthony was really a great scholar and teacher of the Bible. For the next few years he was left free to pray in a little hermitage, which he loved very much, and to spend his working hours cooking and chopping wood. All this time, though, he continued to read his Bible and to meditate for hours on the teachings of Jesus and his Church.

One day, at a meeting of priests, Anthony was unexpectedly asked to give a sermon, since no other priest was prepared to do so. Some of the friars were laughing to themselves. *What can he possibly have to say? He's so simple and quiet, and he doesn't have anything prepared.*

But how surprised everyone was! Anthony's words had a power that was hard to explain. They seemed to come straight from his heart and they held his listeners spellbound. All the wonderful truths he had read in Scripture, and prayed over and meditated on, flowed from his lips. The Holy Spirit was inspiring him, and everyone who listened that day was filled with love of God.

Some of the friars were laughing to themselves: simple, quiet Anthony would have to speak unprepared in front of everyone. But how surprised they were by his beautiful words!

After that sermon, Anthony's days of solitude and wood chopping were over. The other friars immediately sent word to Francis about this wonderful new preacher. Francis was overjoyed and sent a message for Anthony to begin at once to go from city to city, teaching theology to the friars wherever he went, and preaching the Gospel and the catechism to the people of every town.

There are many stories about Anthony and his preaching. In one town, where people had been ignoring the teachings of the Church and were no longer living according to their Christian faith, Anthony preached for several days. Instead of listening, the people either ignored him or made fun of him. At last, realizing that his listeners weren't ready to convert and follow Jesus, Anthony turned to his companion. "Friar Albert, let's go down to the river," he suggested. Anthony then began to preach to the fish. To everyone's amazement, the fish in the river surfaced near the shore and remained motionless, bobbing up and down in the waves, as Anthony spoke to them!

"May God be praised!" cried Anthony. "For fish of the water honor God more than the stubborn people of this town!" At the sight of this miracle, the townspeople who had followed him out of curiosity all fell to their knees and repented. Soon they were crowding around Anthony, begging him to hear their confessions.

Wherever Anthony went, people who listened to him preach came to love Jesus and asked to be baptized. Or, if they were already baptized but had not been living a Christian life, they came to Anthony to receive forgiveness and encouragement to start over again. He made many friends all over Italy, but especially in Padua, where he would return after each preaching journey.

One night, Anthony was staying at a friend's house. After supper, he went to his room. Much later, as his friend was going to bed, he noticed a light glowing under Anthony's door. It seemed brighter than candlelight. Curious, he peeked through a knothole and gasped in surprise. There was Anthony, holding the Infant Jesus in his arms! The man watched until the divine Child slowly faded from sight.

Even though he was only thirty-six years old, Anthony felt strangely tired. The fever he had suffered in Morocco had affected his health. The hard life that the friars led and the strain of constant traveling and preaching had also worn him out. Anthony felt certain that he would soon be leaving this earth and going to meet his beloved Jesus face to face. After spending several days lying on his little mat on the floor, he called for another priest, made his final confession, and asked to receive the Holy Eucharist one last time. Then he sang his favorite hymn to Mary, said goodbye to his fellow friars, and softly whispered, "I see Jesus, my Savior!"

Although he had been born and raised in Lisbon, Portugal, Anthony had long made Padua his home. And the city of Padua had adopted him as one of their own. Whenever he was in town, thousands of Paduans had come to hear him preach. When they learned of his death, they insisted that he be buried in their city. This is why, today, Anthony is known as St. Anthony of Padua. He is called the "wonder-worker," because for centuries people have prayed to him, and he has interceded for many with miracles of healing and of grace.

We can learn a lot about how God makes everything work for our good by thinking about the life of Anthony. Even though things didn't always happen as Anthony had hoped or planned, God used the events and circumstances of Anthony's life to bring him peace and joy and to do good to many people. If we let him, God will do the same for us.

St. Elizabeth of Hungary

(1207-1231)

November 17

In the year 1207, in the land of Hungary, a baby girl was born to King Andrew and Queen Gertrude. The child was named Elizabeth, which means, "consecrated to God."

Elizabeth learned her prayers when she was very small. By the time she was three, she was toddling around the palace chanting, "Jesus and Mary, help me to be good. Make me a saint!" Her mother knew that love for God was the beginning of a good education for her daughter.

In those days, marriages of princes and princesses were planned by their parents, often years before the wedding took place. The little princess would go to live with the prince's family until the two were old enough to marry. That was what happened to Elizabeth. When she was four, she went to live with the Duke of Thuringia, so that she could marry the duke's son Hermann when she grew up.

Elizabeth was a good-natured girl and made friends right away with the other children at the castle. Hermann and his father, the duke, were especially fond of her. But it was not so for some of the ladies of the court. "She's too holy," they declared. "She doesn't fit in with the rest of us!"

As she grew older, Elizabeth realized that these women were not her friends. Then two very sad things happened. First came the news that her mother had died. Then, not long after that, Hermann also died. "What shall we do with Elizabeth now?" pondered the duke. Should they send her back to her home in Hungary? Should they place her in a convent? He hesitated. He didn't really want to see her go. She was like a ray of sunshine in his cold castle. The other women spent their time gossiping and buying new clothes and planning parties, but there was something different, something special about Elizabeth.

Finally the duke decided. "She will marry our second son, Ludwig!" he declared. Although the ladies of the court were not happy, Ludwig was very pleased. Elizabeth stayed.

There were many poor people in those days, and hundreds of them would stand outside the castle gates begging for food. Elizabeth gave food to as many as possible, as often as she could. This annoyed many members of the court. "Who does she think she is?" they sneered. They scolded and teased her, but Elizabeth tried to ignore their remarks. She was happy to know that in helping the poor she was doing as Jesus had done. And she was comforted by her love of the duke and of Ludwig.

Then another sorrow came. The beloved duke died. As soon as Ludwig was old enough, he became the new Duke of Thuringia. Shortly after, he and Elizabeth were married. Ludwig was twenty-one, and Elizabeth was fourteen.

Both Ludwig and Elizabeth loved God very much. They were generous and did everything they could to help the poor. Ludwig tried to make fair decisions for all the people who lived on his lands.

When Elizabeth was sixteen, their first child was born. They named him Hermann, after Ludwig's older brother who had died. In the years that followed, two little girls were born. Each child was consecrated to God while still an infant, and Elizabeth taught them their prayers, just as her mother had taught her.

Elizabeth still fed the beggars at the castle gates. She would also go out to visit poor families and the sick in their small huts near the castle. There had been wars and epidemics that left many people without family or strength to provide for themselves. Elizabeth wanted to care for them all.

One day, she met an old man almost dead from leprosy. Elizabeth brought him up to her own room and placed him on her own bed. Soon the old duchess found out, and she was furious. She rushed to Ludwig and told him the horrendous news. Everyone knew that leprosy was contagious!

Even the gentle Ludwig was concerned about this. He was afraid that Elizabeth or their children would catch the disease. He hurried toward their apartment, intending to give Elizabeth a good scolding. "Elizabeth!" he cried as he burst into the room.

One day, she met an old man almost dead from leprosy. Elizabeth brought him up to her own room and placed him on her own bed.

Then Ludwig stopped. Whatever he had intended to say froze in his throat. There, on his very own bed, lay not an old man dying of leprosy, but the body of Christ crucified! Awed and astounded, Ludwig sank to his knees. "Guests like these are welcome, Elizabeth," he managed to say.

Another time Ludwig saw Elizabeth headed out into a snowstorm with her apron bulging. "What are you carrying?" he called out as he hurried to catch up with her. He was thinking, *It must be food for the poor, and she's going to get very sick if she keeps running around in this weather. I'm going to send her back at once.*

Elizabeth turned and smiled as Ludwig came running up to her. She opened her apron, and fragrant red and white roses came tumbling out! *Well,* thought Ludwig to himself, *if God is so pleased with her errands of mercy that he changes bread into roses, who am I to stop her?*

All the people knew that their duke, Ludwig, and his wife, Elizabeth, loved each other faithfully. They saw that Ludwig tried to care for Elizabeth, who often seemed to ignore her own comfort in helping others. And Elizabeth tried to help Ludwig stay calm and happy in the midst of all his responsibilities as ruler of Thuringia. She was sad when he had to go away on trips, and was very happy when she knew he was on the way home. Then she would wear her best dresses and have his favorite meals prepared, making sure the children were there to greet him when he arrived.

How holy and good she is, Ludwig thought whenever he awoke at night and saw Elizabeth kneeling at their bedside, deep in prayer. He had the same thought as he watched her participate at the Mass, return from a visit to the sick, or care for their children. "Never change," he told her, "unless you become even more loving."

Meanwhile, important events were taking place. Many of the knights of Europe were preparing for a crusade. They intended to go and recover Palestine from the Muslims so that Christian pilgrims could visit the holy places where Jesus had lived and walked. Many of the knights who fought in the Crusades were killed in battle. Others caught deadly diseases in foreign lands and died. It was a great sacrifice for Christian wives and mothers to see their loved ones ride off to war. When Elizabeth heard that Ludwig intended to go with the next group of knights, she became frightened. Not only frightened—she was so overcome with the news that she fainted. Sick with sorrow, Ludwig revived her. Elizabeth woke up, pleading, "Don't go. Don't, Ludwig. What if you never return?"

Ludwig tried to help Elizabeth understand that he had to go, painful though it was. Of course it hurt him to leave her and the children. But he felt that it was both his duty and God's will. With tears in her eyes, Elizabeth agreed.

It was a sad but courageous parting. Smiles and tears and shouts of "Long live Ludwig!" came from all the villagers. Ludwig's kind eyes were shining as he waved his good-byes from atop his large stallion, his armor glinting in the morning sun.

Elizabeth raised her hand in a final farewell. A few moments later the band of horsemen had galloped out of sight. Then long months of waiting began. Elizabeth was busy, however, for it was her duty to supervise the castle and the village whenever Ludwig was away.

News traveled slowly in those days. But now and then a letter would arrive, or word about the Holy Land and the war would be brought via a traveler or soldier returning home.

At first the news was good. But then word came that the plague had struck the Christian army. Next came the news Elizabeth had been dreading from the beginning—Ludwig was dead! She had feared it, but she couldn't quite believe it. Ludwig was gone.

"Dear God," she prayed, "give me the strength to bear this sorrow. My worst fears have come true. But I offer you this suffering with my love. May your will be done, O Lord. May Ludwig be with you forever in heaven!"

Elizabeth was a widow at the age of twenty, with three young children to care for. Her son, Hermann, was supposed to become the next duke. Until he was old enough, however, his uncle Heinrich, Ludwig's brother, would rule the land. At least, that was how it was supposed to be. But the power-hungry Heinrich seized the throne for himself, and, on a cold winter day, sent Elizabeth and her three children out of the castle. Only two of her maids were allowed to go with them.

Heinrich was cruel. He had been among those who laughed and teased Elizabeth when they were children. And he had always been jealous of his good brother Ludwig, whom everyone loved. Now he warned the villagers not to take the royal refugees into their homes or give them anything to eat.

Even though Elizabeth had given them so much help, the people were too afraid of the new duke to help her. Eventually Elizabeth found a small shelter where pigs were kept, and there they spent the night. In the morning, Elizabeth woke her family and they made their way to a nearby Franciscan monastery, where she asked the friars for food. She also asked them to sing a hymn of praise and thanks to God for her.

Elizabeth was now one of the poorest of the poor. She had often talked to the orphans and the sick people in her hospital about Jesus, and how he had become a poor man like them when he came to earth. Now she rejoiced in the fact that she was living so much like her beloved Savior. Elizabeth accepted the circumstances in which she found herself. She had been born a princess, and now she was a poor widow. Receiving the bread she needed day by day made her realize how grateful she was to God, who cares for his creatures and meets their needs.

Finally, news of what had happened reached some of Elizabeth's relatives. They immediately sent for her to live with them. Elizabeth soon discovered that because of her husband's death she was entitled to receive a payment of money from her dowry (the money that was given to the duke's family when she married). With this money, she was able to build a hospital to serve the poor and ill of the city, which made her very happy. She also joined the Third Order of St.

Francis, an association of lay people originally established by St. Francis of Assisi. Members of this group dedicated themselves to bringing Jesus to the world through prayer and good works. Elizabeth spent long hours in the hospital caring for the sick.

But overwork soon took its toll, and Elizabeth became very ill. Suffering from a raging fever, she became weaker and weaker. Joyfully, she received the sacrament of the Anointing of the Sick. After a life filled with good works, happiness, and times of great sorrow, Elizabeth was going home to heaven. On November 17, 1231, she died. So many miracles were worked through her intercession that, in less than four years, Elizabeth was canonized a saint of the church.

Generosity is a virtue that God loves very much. We can practice it as Elizabeth did, by sharing our things with our brothers and sisters and friends, and by helping to take care of our home.

St. Clare

(1193–1253)

AUGUST 11

By the year 1211, Brother Francis Bernardone, who was later to become St. Francis of Assisi, had a small group of followers—men who were trying to live lives of poverty and penance, the way Jesus of Nazareth lived. Like Jesus, they went through the cities and towns preaching the Gospel. This particular year, Francis was invited to the parish church of San Giorgio, in Assisi, to preach the Lenten sermons. It was a time when a few people were becoming very rich, but also a time of violence, injustice, and poverty for many. The simple sermons Francis preached were attractive to his listeners. He called people to be sorry for their sins and challenged them to live according to the teachings of Jesus. Every day the little church of San Giorgio was full.

In the congregation was a young woman named Clare. Clare was the oldest daughter of a wealthy man named Faverone Offreducio. She and her two sisters had grown up in Assisi and learned all the things that rich girls learned in those days—music, fine embroidery, and the art of entertaining guests. Their mother, Ortolana, was very religious and taught her daughters all about Jesus. Together they would go to Mass each Sunday, and this particular year they went every day to listen to the Lenten sermons.

Clare's father was happy to see how gentle and religious his daughters were. But he wanted to make sure that they each married a wealthy young man who could continue his business and make even more money for the family. He had already picked out a husband for Clare, who was seventeen.

Clare was very popular at the parties held for the wealthy young people in Assisi. She had probably met Francis once or twice at such events before he left everything to follow Jesus. Now as she listened to his enthusiastic preaching and saw how much he loved Jesus, she began to think about her own life. It wasn't very challenging, and lately Clare had felt her conscience bothering her as she saw more and more beggars and homeless children filling the city streets while her own family was becoming richer. She enjoyed her friends and the comforts of her home, but she didn't feel satisfied. Comparing the peace in the faces of Francis and his companions with the tension and anxiety that often lined the faces of her father and uncles, Clare began to wonder, *Could there be something more for me than a life of parties?*

After Lent and Easter had passed, Clare couldn't get the words of Francis out of her mind. How had he been able to give up so much? At last she sent a trusted servant to the chapel of St. Mary of the Angels, outside the city walls, to find Francis. The servant asked Francis if he could meet with Clare in secret.

For several months Francis and Clare met privately. They talked about Jesus, about the great freedom and beauty of poverty, and about the need to care for the poor and the sick as Jesus had done. By the following Lent, Clare knew what she wanted to do.

That year, 1212, she again attended the Lenten sermons with her mother and sisters. On Palm Sunday, she wore her finest dress and favorite jewelry. No one else knew, but she was preparing to "elope" with Jesus that night! After returning home, she called the same servant, who had been her teacher since she was a small child, and together they went out into the black night and through the quiet city gates. At last they reached the chapel of Our Lady of the Angels. Inside, Francis and the friars were waiting, holding lighted candles and singing psalms.

Clare knelt in prayer before the altar. Then, in a little hut outside the chapel, she removed her jewelry and the beautiful velvet gown she was wearing. She slipped on a rough, gray robe and tied a knotted cord around her waist. She exchanged her fashionable shoes for a pair of wooden sandals.

When Clare returned to the chapel, Francis quickly cut off her long, golden hair. A black veil was placed on her head. Radiant with joy, Clare promised to follow Jesus in the same way as Francis and the friars— poor, chaste, and obedient. Clare was no longer a rich young lady, but a humble nun with her heart set on the infinite treasures of heaven.

Right after this simple ceremony, the brothers took Clare to a nearby Benedictine monastery, where she would live with the nuns and learn about religious life. Later, she would be able to start her own monastery.

It seems that Clare's father may have died by the time Clare left home to give her life to God, because historical records don't mention him anymore. But how surprised and angry Clare's uncle and other relatives were when they found out what she had done! In an armed band, all of Clare's male relatives stormed the Benedictine monastery. The young nun saw them coming and ran into the church, thinking that she would be safe there. She went right up to the altar and held on to it. As her relatives crowded around her angrily, she calmly showed them her shaven head. "From now on, I belong to God alone!" she said. Defeated by her firmness—and by the grace of God— the relatives retreated and left her in peace.

Just over two weeks later, Catherine, Clare's younger sister, left home to join her. In a burst of anger, Uncle Monaldo rounded up his men, and off they thundered to the peaceful monastery. Pulling up sharply in the open courtyard, the men swung off their horses and rushed into the nuns' cloister, searching for Catherine. "Here she is!" came the shout. In an instant they had surrounded the girl. Monaldo seized her by her hair and started to drag her away, cursing all the while.

Radiant with joy, Clare promised to follow Jesus in the same way as Francis and the friars—poor, chaste, and obedient.

"Clare! Help me!" cried out Catherine.

Clare heard her, but she didn't come out into the open. Instead, she sank to her knees and prayed. God would be their strength. As she prayed, the attackers felt themselves growing weaker and weaker, and Catherine growing heavier and heavier. And it wasn't because Catherine was putting up a struggle, because she had already fainted! The men trembled in fear.

Furious, Monaldo drew out his sword and raised it. If he couldn't move the girl, he would kill her! But Monaldo couldn't lower his arm to bring the sword down on Catherine's neck. He stood frozen, as if he were paralyzed.

Clare arose from her prayer and walked toward the men. She scolded them with such fiery words that they turned and quietly walked away.

Word of what had happened reached Francis, who came hurrying to the monastery. His words comforted and encouraged Clare and her sister. Then he said, "This was your 'novitiate,' Catherine! We'll consecrate you to God right now!" That day, Catherine received a new name—Agnes. She also received a rough robe with a cord around her waist, just like Clare's, and promised to live in chastity, poverty, and obedience.

As time passed, the anger of Clare's relatives cooled. Other wealthy women came to join Clare and Agnes, and Francis appointed Clare to be their superior. The women came to be known as the Order of Poor Ladies, or Poor Clares, and they lived in a small monastery at the Church of San Damiano.

The nuns were always busy. They grew their own food, sewed altar linens, and provided clothes for the poor. They wore no shoes, fasted often, and slept on the hard wooden floor. In their desire to live as simply and poorly as Jesus, nothing was too difficult for them.

Clare spent many hours each night in prayer before Jesus in the tabernacle. Yet she was always the first one up in the morning, the first to call her companions, the first to light the lamps and prepare everything for Mass, the first to think of little things to help her sisters spiritually and materially.

Once when Clare was ill, an army of Saracens, who had invaded Italy, passed near Assisi. Seeing the monastery, they came to attack it. Their shrieks and battle cries terrified the nuns, who went running frantically to Clare's bedside. Clare stood up and went to the chapel. She took the monstrance holding a consecrated Host, praying all the while with ardent faith, and carried it out into the courtyard where the soldiers—who were climbing over the monastery wall—could see it. Then Clare heard the voice of Jesus say, "I shall always be your salvation."

The Saracens stopped where they were, shocked. Then, gripped by a mysterious terror, they turned and ran away! What had they seen in that gentle woman whose only weapons were the Holy Eucharist and a strong faith? Only God knows the answer. After the danger was over, the sisters joined Clare in singing a hymn of gratitude and praise to God.

Many years passed, and so many women had come to join Clare and her nuns that several other monasteries had been opened. The reputation of the Poor Clares spread so far, in fact, that Agnes, daughter of the King of Bohemia, wrote to Clare asking permission to live as a Poor Clare nun in Prague. Clare and Princess Agnes were never able to live in the same monastery, and perhaps they never even saw each other in person. But through their letters to one another they became the best of friends, and Clare called Agnes the "other half" of her soul. Soon more women joined Agnes, and the Poor Clares spread out across all of Europe.

Many years after Francis's death, Clare felt that her own time had come to leave this earth. Three of the first friars, who had been present on that night so many years before when Clare had left her family to follow Jesus, came to be with her as she was dying. They read out loud the story of Jesus' own death from the Gospel of St. John, just as they had done for Francis as he was dying. Clare was so well known for her holiness that even Pope Innocent IV and several bishops and cardinals came to see her one last time.

On a beautiful morning, as the nuns and the three friars were gathered around her bed, Clare said, as if talking to her soul, "Go forth in peace, for you have chosen and followed the good road. Go forth without fear, for the good God who created you has also made you holy, and will always protect you as a mother would. Blessed may you be, my God, for having created me." Then she spoke a moment to her sisters, encouraging them to follow carefully the rule of life she and Francis had given to them, and to always be kind to one another. As she lay back, she peacefully died. The next day she was buried. Barely two years later, Pope Alexander IV proclaimed her a saint.

To this day there are convents of Poor Clare nuns all over the world. They dress much the same as Clare and her first sisters did. Like them, they spend their entire lives loving Jesus and his people in a special way. They pray continually for the needs of the world. Let us, too, pray for the needs of the world, especially for all the people who are poor.

St. Peregrine

(1260–1345)

May 4

Peregrine Laziosi was born in the city of Forli, in northern Italy, around the year 1260. He was an only child, and his parents, like most people in Forli at that time, were strongly against the Pope and the Catholic Church, and were unwilling to live by the teachings of Jesus.

By the time Peregrine was eighteen, he was a leader in the "Anti-Papal" party. This political group was so violently against the Catholic Church that the Pope put the whole city of Forli under the penalty of interdict. This meant that Mass and the sacraments could not be celebrated there. Because of this, most churches had closed and most of the priests had left. This made it very difficult for the people who still wanted to practice their Catholic faith.

Pope Martin IV tried everything he could to bring about a reconciliation between the city and the Church. Finally he thought of the right person to send:

Father Philip Benizi. He was an excellent preacher and a holy priest. Father Benizi agreed to travel to Forli, sending word ahead that he would preach in the town square when he arrived.

It was about mid-morning when Father Benizi approached the city gates. He could see a large crowd gathering. "Blessed Mother," he fervently prayed, "help me to speak words of peace and reconciliation to these people. Open their hearts to hear the Good News of Jesus, and let them be willing to turn away from the sinful lifestyles that many of them are following." He also prayed for his own safety, because several of the priests who had already been sent to Forli had been killed!

As he entered the town square, the crowd parted, and he could see a large platform that had been built for him. Father Benizi slowly made his way to the platform, wondering if the crowds' sudden silence was a sign of their desire for reconciliation. As he reached the top of the platform, it seemed that this elderly, humble priest already had some sort of power over the crowd. A great calm met his clear gaze. Many people—probably the Catholics—had crowded onto the balconies and roofs to hear him speak. *No doubt,* he thought, *they feel safer there than down in the square.*

Father Philip held a crucifix in his right hand. He raised it toward heaven, while his lips moved in a quick, silent prayer. Then he began to speak, gently inviting the people to repent. The holy priest's heart was pounding. Was God really converting all these people?

Suddenly a disturbance began at the far end of the square. A young voice hurled an insult, and the spell was broken. From every point in the square new voices rang out, shouting new insults. While some people fled, others rushed toward the preacher. Leading them was a young man.

Father Philip stood tall and straight, holding the crucifix and looking up toward heaven. The leader of the young men bounded up the steps of the platform and insulted the holy priest. Father Philip remained silent. The youth raised his fist and hit him on the cheek!

The square was in an uproar. Insult after insult rained on Father Benizi as people mounted the platform and shoved him around. He kept the crucifix clutched tightly in his hand and repeated over and over the prayer of Jesus, "Father, forgive them, they don't know what they're doing."

Relentlessly, the crowd half-pushed, half-carried the priest to the city gates and its drawbridge. After he crossed it, the drawbridge was lifted behind him, and the walled city of Forli retreated within itself.

Father Philip walked painfully along a little brook that wound through the countryside. The soft murmur of the waters soothed his pounding head, and formed a perfect background for his prayer. Battered and beaten as his body was, the old priest's soul was as calm as ever.

"Father, forgive them," he prayed. "They are blind!"

He thought of the young man who had struck the first blow, recalling the face hardened by anger and bad living; he saw again the raised hand...and still he prayed.

"Lord, bring him close to you. He's a poor and ignorant boy."

He walked on in the stillness as evening fell.

And then Father Philip heard running footsteps. Could someone else be coming to attack him? Perhaps it was only his imagination.

But no. Now he heard the footsteps clearly. A voice was calling, "Father! Father!"

The elderly priest turned and saw a young man running toward him. His arms were outstretched, as if in desperation, and he threw himself to the ground at Father Philip's feet. Kissing the hem of his robe again and again, he begged, "Forgive me, Father, forgive me!"

Father Philip understood everything. He bent down and raised the young man to his feet, hugging him as a father would his child.

The face of this teenager who had struck him that morning was now softened and covered with tears of repentance. His eyes were now glowing with a clear, new light.

"Pardon, pardon!" he repeated. "I'm so sorry for my terrible sins!"

"I know it; I can see it," replied Father Philip gently.

"I want to change my life. I want to leave this craziness behind and spend my life doing good to others," the young man blurted out. "God is calling me, but I know that a great change must take place in me. I don't know where or what God wants of me...but I do know that everything that I found so much pleasure in, until today, now makes me sick."

Father Philip consoled him and gave him some important advice. "Return home and begin to practice honesty, purity, and humility. Listen to the voice of your conscience, and do what God will lead you to. It won't be easy, but pray. The Lord is with you. Perhaps someday you will do a great work for him." He paused. "What's your name, my son?"

"Peregrine Laziosi, Father."

Surely God had planned this meeting between the great saint, Philip Benizi, and young Peregrine, who would one day also become a saint!

Peregrine finally said good-bye and walked slowly back to the city. He knew that he must abandon his former companions. At first it seemed that this would be hard. But as he devoted himself to prayer and meditation, he realized that his old friends and amusements—the drinking, the partying, the political debates—repelled him now. The new joy that had taken possession of Peregrine's heart was to please Jesus and his mother, Mary. Nothing else mattered.

Peregrine's old friends and family were amazed at the change. But they thought that it wouldn't last and tried to win him back. After all, hadn't he been one of the most daring of them all?

"Come back to life!" they urged. But Peregrine wouldn't listen to them. He had found life, he told them, but it was the true life that Father Philip had come to preach about. And it seemed that he could actually feel the life of God's grace flowing into his soul.

The days passed, and Peregrine felt himself growing closer and closer to God. As the holy priest had urged him to do, he was developing a trusting, childlike confidence in the Blessed Mother. He prayed to Mary often, and with great love read and reread the Gospel stories telling about the birth and childhood of Jesus. Then, one day, while praying in the shadows of the darkened cathedral, Peregrine actually saw his heavenly Mother, surrounded by angels.

Peregrine felt a trembling in his heart. His whole being was caught up in admiration of the heavenly vision. Then Mary spoke to him.

"I am the Mother of Jesus, the one whom you adore on the cross. In Siena there is a monastery of my servants, the Servites; go to Siena, for that is where you belong."

The vision disappeared, and Peregrine hurried home, with only one thought in mind—to obey the wonderful invitation of the Queen of Heaven. In the silence of the night, he slipped out of the darkened house and set out toward Siena.

At last he was knocking nervously at the monastery door. When he had been let in, he told the monks of his great desire to join them, confessed his past sins publicly, and asked to be accepted into the community. Smiling joyfully, the superior, who was none other than Father Philip Benizi, received him into the Servites.

In the years that followed, Peregrine studied hard as he prepared for the priesthood. He showed great humility, prayerfulness, apostolic zeal, and a spirit of penance and self-sacrifice. After his ordination, he strongly desired to return to Forli, where he had spent the wild days of his youth. He wanted to dedicate himself to doing good in that city, so filled with darkness and sin.

Permission was granted, and the young priest retraced his steps across the mountains to the city of his birth.

The rebellious city welcomed its holy son, opening wide to him the doors of homes filled with misery. The people brought him to their sick, and Father Peregrine cured them. They told him their needs, their troubles, their hopes and desires, and he listened and encouraged them. His favorite places were the hospitals, the prisons, and the homes of those who had not yet returned to the Christian faith and way of life. He walked through the city continually, seeking to visit, comfort, and instruct, by his presence, words, and deeds, all those who needed help.

At night he prayed, and if he fell asleep through exhaustion and toppled to the floor, he picked himself up and began to pray again. Very early in the morning he celebrated Mass. He went to confession almost every day!

Once a band of thieves was roaming through the countryside, attacking and robbing everyone they found traveling on the lonely roads. The city officials and police could find no way of stopping them. Father Peregrine decided to act.

Armed with only a crucifix, the holy priest entered the forest where the gang was known to hide out. In a short time he found himself face to face with them. They were heavily armed. If they had wished, they could have killed him right there, but something held them back. The priest was calling many of them by name, and their thoughts turned back to the days of their youth, when they had been Peregrine's companions! Now he was looking at them with a gaze that touched their hearts. They didn't raise a hand against him, but let him speak.

Perhaps he spoke to them about heaven, or maybe he told them the story of the prodigal son or the lost sheep. At any rate, from that day on the country roads were free from those robbers. And the story goes that most of the members of that once-violent gang entered monasteries and spent the rest of their lives in prayer and penance.

Father Peregrine's hard life of poverty and penances was leaving its mark. Long hours of being continuously on his feet caused an ugly sore to form on one of his legs. When the sore turned cancerous, the doctors said that the leg must be amputated.

In the solitude of the night, Father Peregrine prayed before a large crucifix. "How can I serve you, my Lord, if I can no longer walk? How will I be able to reach all those people who are waiting for me, expecting me to tell them about you and about your infinite goodness? Yet not my will, but your will be done."

Armed with only a crucifix, the holy priest entered the forest where the gang was known to hide out. In a short time he found himself face to face with them.

His heart was full of fear. Suddenly, the figure of Jesus on the crucifix came down, touched the painful sore, and disappeared. Father Peregrine wondered whether or not he was dreaming. Dazed, he struggled to his feet and discovered that his leg was completely healed! Overcome with joy, he flung himself down in front of the crucifix to pour out his gratitude. The next morning, the doctors found no trace of the cancer or the infection.

The years passed and Peregrine continued his work in Forli. But he knew that the beautiful Queen of Heaven was waiting for him as a mother waits for her dearly loved child. After his eightieth birthday, his soul left this world with complete calm and serenity.

At the funeral a great crowd of people who had known and loved him gathered around his body to mourn their loss. They knew that Peregrine had been a saint. And just as they had brought all difficulties to him in life, they now prayed for him to help them from heaven.

It was hard for Peregrine to break his bad habits and form good ones. But his love for the Blessed Mother helped him make the change. We, too, should pray to Mary, especially when we have a hard time giving up bad habits.

St. Catherine of Siena

(1347–1380)

Stephen turned around to see what his six-year-old sister, Catherine, had stopped for. Always happy and curious, she sometimes forgot her mother's directions to come straight home from her older sister's house. "Catherine!" Stephen shouted. He frowned as he saw her staring up at the sky. Looking up himself and seeing nothing, he thought she was playing a joke on him. But he had to get home and finish his chores! He ran back to her and grabbed her arm playfully. Catherine suddenly jumped and pulled away from Stephen.

"Why did you do that?" she demanded. "I was seeing the most beautiful thing! Jesus was there, and he was reaching out to take my hand!"

Stephen looked at his sister. *What a wild story,* he thought. But Catherine was too serious to be making it up. Later that night, Mrs. Benincasa, Catherine's mother, noticed that Catherine took an extra-long time to say her night prayers. In fact, after that day it seemed as though praying was the only thing that interested her. She still played with her friends, but there was nothing she liked more than praying or learning about Jesus and the saints. By the time she was twelve, Catherine had told everyone—her parents and her many brothers and sisters—that she never wanted to marry. She wanted to be a nun.

Catherine's father was very upset. Catherine was beautiful, and he could see no reason why she should go to the convent. To encourage her to forget her dream, her parents held many parties at their house. They invited many young men to come and visit their youngest daughter. Finally, Catherine couldn't take it any longer. Not knowing how else to convince her father that she was serious, Catherine had all her beautiful long, brown hair cut off. Since no women in the town of Siena had short hair except the nuns, her parents were horrified. At last they gave in—but they would only allow sixteen-year-old Catherine to be a Third Order Dominican. That meant that she could make the promises to live poorly, never to marry, and to be obedient to their bishop, but she would stay at home instead of going away to the convent. The Third Order Dominicans were also permitted to wear the white and black religious habit of the community. Catherine was eighteen when she received the habit.

Catherine spent most of her time in a little room at the family's big house. Her father gave her part of the family's income to give to the poor people she met on the way to church. During this time, Catherine learned how to read. But she spent much of her time praying and thinking about the sermons she heard at church.

When she was twenty-one, Catherine had another vision of Jesus. This time she saw him with his mother, Mary. Together, they placed a ring on her finger, just like a wedding band. It was a beautiful experience, and Catherine knew that now she belonged entirely to Jesus forever. Jesus also told her that instead of staying in her parents' home, he wanted her to go out and help others know how much he loved them.

Immediately, Catherine started to join some of the other Third Order Dominicans in Siena to care for the sick in the hospitals. Many people were in the hospital because they were dying and had no money or families to take care of them. Catherine became well known for choosing the sickest and poorest patients. She especially liked to care for people who were going to die soon. She talked to them about God's love for them and about heaven. She also went to visit prisoners, including men who had been condemned to death. Some of these men were real criminals, but others were innocent people who had been unjustly accused. She talked to all of them, no matter what they had done or how much they were suffering.

One young man from another city had gotten into a fight while in Siena and had been put in jail. The judge had condemned him to die. The young man was angry and bitter at this unfair sentence, and felt that God had abandoned him. Catherine spent long hours talking to him and praying with him. She tried to convince the judge that this man shouldn't die, but the judge wouldn't listen. Finally the young man realized that no matter how mean or unjust human beings might be toward one another, God is always merciful and just. He listened as Catherine explained how Jesus, too, had been condemned unjustly and had accepted crucifixion in order to free us from our sins. The young man began to pray with Catherine and even looked forward to being in heaven with Jesus, where there would be no more suffering. On the day he died, Catherine was right there beside him.

Even though Catherine had not gone to school, she was very wise. She was good at settling arguments between people and even wars between cities. Soon, business people, mayors, and bishops were calling Catherine to help them settle their disagreements. In this way, more and more people came to know her. Always a friendly person, Catherine formed many close friendships. In fact, a whole group of people began to spend time with her, helping her to write her many letters. They also wrote down the things she said about God and prayer. But often Catherine didn't feel very successful in her work. And for a long time she felt that God was far away from her. She kept praying, but it didn't seem as if anyone was listening. She was even tempted to give up her life as a Third Order Dominican!

One day, as Catherine was alone in the chapel, she had an overwhelming sense of God's presence. She cried out to him, "Where have you been, Lord? I've been having terrible thoughts and feelings!"

And then she heard God answer. "Catherine, I have been in your heart all this time. It was I who gave you the courage and strength to keep going each day!"

Suddenly Catherine understood. God is not to be confused with good feelings or success. God is always present with each person, always helping in every situation. But in order to keep close to God and remain aware of his divine presence, we must make a quiet place in our hearts for God—a place where we can stop at anytime to talk to him and love him. Catherine told many of her friends about this experience. They were happy to listen to her, because many of them were busy working and caring for their families. They didn't have much time to go to church and pray. They began to take a few minutes of quiet time each day just to speak heart-to-heart with God and to think about his great love for them.

Catherine also knew that in order to keep that quiet place for God, a person has to live a good life. That means being honest in business deals, being faithful to one's husband or wife, treating others justly—in other words, to know God within them, people have to try to act like Jesus. Many of the people who listened to Catherine understood this. They desired so strongly to know God that they went to confession and returned to Mass, desiring to do their best to live as good Christians.

Catherine's reputation finally reached Pope Gregory XI, who was having a very difficult time leading the Church. Some of his difficulties were his own fault. Instead of remaining in Rome and taking care of the affairs of the whole Church, he had spent several years in France, where he had gotten involved in local affairs of the French bishops and royalty, causing confusion and hard feelings in the Church. Pope Gregory wanted to return to Rome, but he needed some encouragement, which Catherine energetically gave him. At her urging, he finally packed his belongings and set out for Rome.

By now Catherine was in her early thirties. She looked much older, though, because she fasted often and had done much traveling in all kinds of weather. Her difficult journeys had taken her on missions of peace to cities that were at war with one another.

One day Catherine had a vision. Jesus was on the cross, and Catherine could see how much he was suffering. Suddenly, bright red rays came from his hands, feet, and heart. Catherine felt his pain. It was as if she, like Jesus, had nails in her hands and feet. Other people very close to Jesus have experienced this same thing. It is called the "stigmata." In Catherine's case, people could not see the wounds, but they could see that she was often in great pain.

At last, when she was thirty-three, Catherine had one more vision of Jesus. This one was also painful. Jesus seemed to be taking her own heart and blood and pouring it out over his Church. Catherine understood. She offered all her last sufferings and prayers to God for reconciliation within the Church that Jesus had started. She died not very long after this, and from heaven she helped the Pope and the other bishops settle their differences. In the year 1461, she was declared a saint.

Pope Gregory wanted to return to Rome, but he needed some encouragement, which Catherine energetically gave him.

Right after Catherine died, Father Raymond of Capua, a Dominican priest who often heard Catherine's confessions, started to write the story of her life. He also helped her friends to collect the many letters she had written and the thoughts and meditations that she had shared with them. We have many of these writings today. Catherine of Siena is known as one of the "Doctors of the Church." This is a special title given to saints whose writings have helped other Christians live as Jesus did. Catherine is also called a mystic, because of the many special visions that she had of Jesus.

Following Catherine's example, we can try to keep a "quiet place" for God in our hearts. We can take a few minutes each day to talk heart-to-heart with him and thank him for his help in every situation. If we sin by choosing to do the wrong thing, we can tell God that we are sorry, go to confession as soon as possible, and promise to try harder to be like Jesus.

St. Joan of Arc

(1412–1431)

MAY 30

Thirteen-year-old Joan put down her heavy bundle and stared. There was the house she and her family had left just last week, but almost everything around it was ruined or burned. She could see wisps of smoke still blowing off her father's field of rye. Looking up at her father, she started to cry. Her mother shifted Joan's younger sister from one hip to the other and said calmly, "Well, let's thank God it wasn't worse. At least we're safe. The house is fine. And," continued the patient and faith-filled mother, "it doesn't look as if they found our underground cellar. We'll have enough food until spring."

"Yes, Papa," added Joan's older brother. "Mama is right. Thank God we're all safe. And if we plant tomorrow, maybe a new crop can still ripen before the winter comes."

It was the year 1425, and the Hundred Years' War was raging violently near the village of Domremy,

France, where Joan's family lived. The Burgundians, who were fighting with England against France, often raided the border villages in the area of Lorraine. This time, the people of Domremy had received warning in time and had fled to the neighboring village of Neufchatel.

Those were years of fear and anxiety. Often, wounded men or homeless families would stumble into Domremy for shelter. Joan's family was among the first to offer aid, and Joan frequently gave up her own bed to the refugees.

But in spite of the war, the children of Domremy found time for games and dancing, and even occasional picnics in the nearby hills. As Joan grew older, young men frequently came to call at her house. Like other young women in the town, Joan hadn't been taught to read or write, but everyone knew about her talents for cooking and spinning. Her future as a bride and mother seemed pretty well set, until an extraordinary event took place.

Joan was calmly tending the garden one afternoon when a strange voice caused her to look up. A bright light was hovering between her and the village church. What could it be? Joan remained frozen to the spot.

"Joan, daughter of God, go to church often. Be good and pure. God wants you to do this."

The light disappeared. In spite of the hot summer sun, Joan shivered. What was this all about? *Maybe I should rest in the shade a minute,* she thought. But, no, she was sure that she hadn't imagined the voice. Perhaps God wanted something special of her. Surely he wanted her to be virtuous! "My God," she whispered, "I promise you I'll go to church often, and I'll remain only yours, in body and soul, for as long as it pleases you!"

Soon after, the voice spoke to her again. And again on another day. This time, in the bright light, she saw a splendid being whom she knew was the Archangel Michael! Around him were many other angels. They were so beautiful! When they disappeared, Joan started to cry. She wanted so much to go with them!

Over the next three years, the girl had more heavenly visits from St. Michael, as well as from St. Catherine of Alexandria and St. Margaret of Antioch. Both of them had been martyrs, and were often prayed to by people of Joan's village. St. Michael was a patron saint of the French royal family.

"Joan the maiden, daughter of God," the saints began to say to her, "you must leave this village. You must lead the dauphin to Rheims, where he will be crowned." The "dauphin" was a prince who was supposed to become king of France. Because of the war, he had not yet been officially crowned king. The saints also told Joan that she would go into battle for the sake of France.

All of this was frightening to Joan. "I'm only a poor girl!" she protested. "I don't know how to ride a horse or make war!"

"Go, daughter of God!" was the reply. But Joan didn't even know where to begin.

The voices spoke to her often. And at last a way opened for her.

Durand Loxart, the husband of one of Joan's relatives, lived in a village some distance from Domremy. He and his wife invited Joan to visit for a few weeks. Joan agreed, because she saw that this might be the opportunity she needed to obey her "voices." She gathered her belongings, said a few quick good-byes, and left with Durand.

Until then, Joan had told no one about her voices—neither family nor friends nor even her pastor. But she needed help, and Uncle Durand seemed to be the person who could give it. She told him what she had been asked to do.

Durand was amazed. At first, he didn't know whether to believe Joan or not. But Joan was so sincere that at last he promised to help her in whatever way he could. They decided that Joan should present herself to the dauphin, and that Robert de Baudricourt might provide the escort.

Robert de Baudricourt was a well-known noble who fought on the dauphin's side. He knew that until the young Prince Charles could go to Rheims and receive the crown, there would be no peace in France. People in every part of the country were suffering from the war.

When Joan and Durand arrived at Robert's castle, they had a difficult time convincing the guards to let them in. Once inside, Joan began speaking. "Your Lordship, I have a message for you. The dauphin must remain ready to fight. But he should not enter the battle himself. This kingdom does not belong to the dauphin, but my Lord wishes him to become king in spite of his enemies, and I myself will lead him to be anointed and crowned."

As Joan spoke, the guards around them began to laugh. How could this young country maiden lead the dauphin to the crown?

"Who is this Lord you speak of, and what right has he to give orders to the king?" growled Sir Robert.

"He is the Lord of heaven," Joan replied.

The onlookers burst into laughter. De Baudricourt turned to Durand. "Take this little girl and her stories home. And tell her father that she needs a good spanking!"

Joan and Durand returned home. *I won't stop trying, God,* she vowed. *Use me to answer the prayers of your faithful people!*

Several months later, Joan was at home in Domremy when Uncle Durand again asked Joan to come and stay with them. Her aunt was expecting a child, and they needed Joan to help. She knew this was her chance to once again approach Robert de Baudricourt.

This time de Baudricourt was willing to listen. The French had been suffering serious defeats. After Joan declared that the French army had just been defeated near Orleans and a messenger confirmed this a few days later, de Baudricourt relented. Naming four of his most trustworthy soldiers to escort Joan, he sent her to the dauphin, a journey that took eleven days. Joan was dressed like a boy and had her hair cut short like a soldier's. She rode a high-spirited stallion.

Word was sent ahead that Joan was coming, and so the dauphin was waiting for her arrival. But he wasn't dressed as the prince! He wanted to test Joan and make sure that she really came from God, so he stood among the nobles, trying to look like just another one of them. Joan went straight up to him and introduced herself, then whispered to him a secret that only he could have known. With that, he was convinced that she had truly been sent by God.

Dauphin Charles had a suit of armor made for Joan. In a vision, St. Margaret and St. Catherine described to Joan what her flag should look like: it pictured the King of heaven with angels on either side of him, and bore the names of Jesus and Mary. After receiving the sacraments of Reconciliation and Holy Eucharist, she was ready to drive the English from the city of Orleans.

Orleans had been under siege for months. The English had built forts around it and cut off the flow of food and other supplies. One dark night, Joan and a few soldiers slipped past the enemy forts and entered the city. How eagerly the people greeted her! They waved and cheered, while their torches flickered wildly.

A few days later, Joan rode into battle. Some of her soldiers went out first and attacked one of the English forts. The fort put up a good defense, however, and no progress was made until Joan thundered up on her big war-horse. The banner she carried was whipping in the wind and was a signal for the French to attack. Her troops sprang into action at once. They had heard the ring of authority in her voice and were certain that she was being led by God. They stormed the fort and took it that night.

*Some of her soldiers went out first and attacked one of the forts.
The fort put up a good defense, however, and no progress was
made until Joan thundered up on her big war-horse.*

The next day was Ascension Day, and Joan gave orders that there should be no fighting. She spent the day in prayer and attended Mass, receiving the Holy Eucharist. The next day, she and a band of fighting men stormed another English fort. Again, the French were successful!

The following day they attacked a larger English fort. While arrows rained down upon them, the French placed ladders against the strong wall and started to climb. Then an arrow came whistling down from the battlement and drove into Joan's shoulder.

Breathlessly, the soldiers crowded around her. Would she be all right? Joan wrenched the arrow free, and said, "The wound is not deep, but I should like to go to confession before risking another one. Please call the chaplain." After receiving absolution, she returned to the battle.

They fought on until evening. "We may as well retreat," said the French commander at last. "We're getting nowhere."

"No," Joan replied. "It won't be long before we take the fort." And sure enough, that same evening the French soldiers fought their way up the walls to victory.

On the following day, the English army retreated and left Orleans in peace. This battle completed the first part of Joan's mission. In the years to come, the English would be driven back to the coast from which they had come. Now they were fighting a nation that knew that God was with them. Soon, France would again be whole and free.

Joan returned to the dauphin and urged him to go to Rheims to receive his crown. But Charles was not a very brave prince. He was afraid to travel, thinking that the English (or even one of the opposing French nobles!) would capture him. "We shall clear the way for you," Joan promised. She and the army set out with hopeful hearts and drove the enemy away from the route to Rheims so that Charles could travel in safety.

On July 17, 1429, Charles and Joan marched down the broad aisle of the Rheims cathedral. The archbishop anointed the dauphin with great solemnity and proclaimed him king. Joan, who stood nearby holding her beautiful banner, now knelt at the king's feet, weeping for joy.

Joan's main mission had been accomplished. What should she do next? "Continue to fight," her voices told her. "But, daughter of God, be prepared, for you will be taken by the enemy!"

And so it happened. About ten months later, late at night, Joan was cut off from her men during a small battle with the Burgundians. Someone grabbed the bridle of her horse, and she was taken prisoner. The Burgundians quickly sold her to the English as a prisoner of war.

Joan was put on trial. For several weeks, she was questioned for hours at a time. The English clergy who were interrogating her asked confusing questions about theology and philosophy. Their purpose was to show that Joan had not been sent by God at all, but that she was a witch. If they could prove that, then the French would again lose confidence, and the English would win the war once and for all.

At the end of the long trial, which lasted for several weeks, the judge declared that Joan's voices had been from the devil. He handed her over to the civil court, which declared that she was indeed a witch—and witches must burn at the stake! She was sentenced to die on Wednesday, May 30, 1431.

On the morning she was to be burned, Joan was led out to stand before the people. She said to them, "I beg all of you here to forgive any harm I have done, as I forgive you the harm you have done to me." She fell silent and remained in an attitude of prayer for some time. Then she asked, "Does anyone have a cross?" An English soldier quickly tied two pieces of wood together and handed them to her. Joan slipped the cross inside her dress, next to her heart.

Then they led her to the stake and bound her to it with heavy chains. Someone held up a crucifix so she could gaze at it. "St. Michael," Joan whispered, "help me die a good death." The wood had caught on fire now, and the flames were beginning to lick around her ankles. She could hear the snapping and crackling, and soon she felt the heat. Orange tongues of flame surrounded her. Thick smoke filled her nostrils and a wave of terror ran through her. Then, as the flames caught her clothing and hair, she felt hot and searing pain.

"Jesus," Joan called softly. She continued to call his name until she died.

At the moment of Joan's death, many of those who had condemned her realized that they had burned a saint. Until then, their eyes had been blinded, but now they knew.

Twenty-five years later, Joan's family succeeded in having her trial reviewed. Many of her relatives and friends came to testify on her behalf. Finally, on June 7, 1456, Joan was declared completely innocent. Her voices had been not from the devil; Joan had not been a witch.

Many years later, Joan was canonized—not because she had won battles or because she had been burned, but because she had remained faithful to what she knew God was asking of her.

Once Joan understood that the voices she heard were from God, she bravely obeyed them. We often learn God's will for us from the voices of our parents and guardians and through faithful daily prayer. Like Joan, let's always try to do the right thing, even when it's difficult.

St. Bernardine of Siena

(1380–1444)

MAY 20

It had been an important day for Bernardine, but he was glad it was over. He said good-night to his aunt and uncle, and to the many guests who had come to the reception at their house.

The young man wanted some time alone to think about his mother and father. How much he missed them! They had died when he was a child, and Bernardine had moved to Siena to live with his relatives. Now he was sixteen, and today, on the eve of the feast of the Assumption, he had offered his candle to the Blessed Mother. This was the custom for all young men of his day. For most, the candle ceremony was simply a reason for having a party afterward. For Bernardine, the ceremony expressed his love and devotion to Mary, the Mother of God.

Fourteenth-century Siena was a rough place to live. Not even twenty years had passed since the great Catherine of Siena had died, but already the renewed fervor for Christian living and virtue was waning. Street gangs again ruled sections of the city, and drunkenness and sinfulness were widespread even among the young. Bernardine had never followed that lifestyle. When he prayed and read the lives of Jesus and the saints, something within him seemed to burst into flame. It was so obvious that Bernardine had chosen to remain chaste and sober that his friends avoided swearing or telling rude stories in his presence. They knew that Bernardine was a good fighter and not afraid to stand up for what was right!

That night, as Bernardine was dozing off, he heard screaming in the distance. *Another street brawl,* he thought disgustedly. But then the screaming grew louder, and Bernardine recognized the voice of Robert, one of the boys who often joined him to pray or to visit the sick. He jumped up and ran out the gate of his home. Heading through a narrow alley, he raced toward the increasingly frantic screams. Seeing a large crowd of boys from the next neighborhood beating his friend, Bernardine rushed into the midst of the fight. He quickly realized, however, that he and his friend were far outnumbered, and a sick feeling settled in his stomach as he struggled to stay on his feet.

The drunken gang members were yelling loudly. "Hit the sissy! Knock him down! He thinks he's so good! Kick him!"

Suddenly, some of Bernardine's friends came rushing to the rescue. The invading gang quickly disappeared into the night. They would attack one or two boys, but would never stand up to a whole group!

"Thank you," he murmured to his friends. "You came just in time."Wiping the blood from his face and pulling Robert to his feet, he added, "We've got to unite! The young men of Siena should be the city's glory, not its disgrace!"

~~~~~~~~~~~

In 1400, at the age of twenty, Bernardine joined the "Company of the Disciplined of Mary." This group of men worked in the hospitals, caring for the poor and the sick. One afternoon, as Bernardine was outside for some fresh air, he saw someone walking slowly up the street. Thinking that it was an elderly pilgrim, he ran to offer food and shelter. As Bernardine reached him, the man fell. Bernardine stooped to help him, but the man pushed Bernardine back roughly with his walking stick. "Go away! Go away!" he gasped. His hood fell back, and Bernardine grew pale with fright. He saw that the man was dying of the plague.

The plague, a dreadfully painful and contagious disease, had not been around for some time. But recently, the people of Siena had heard rumors that it was again spreading in Rome. *And now,* thought Bernardine somberly, *the plague has come to Siena.*

Without thinking of the danger to himself, Bernardine picked the man up and carried him to the hospital. Within a week, hundreds of people of every age and class were sick. Terror-stricken, the wealthier people of Siena packed up what food they could and left the city, hoping that the fresh air of the country would prevent them from getting sick.

But Bernardine and his companions remained in Siena. They were everywhere, from morning until late at night, caring for the sick and comforting the mourning. They set up large bonfires outside the city to burn the dead, for the disease was so contagious that normal burial was impossible. One day, when it seemed that all hope was gone, Bernardine told his tired companions, "In the Gospel, it says that God will not fail to reward us for all the good we do. Will you stay and continue to care for the sick?"

"We're with you!" they answered. After praying together and offering their own health and lives to the mercy of God, they went back to their work with a new enthusiasm. The sick continued to arrive. Bernardine did all he could for them, even leading those who still had strength in singing hymns to Mary.

Finally, the terrible plague was over, and people began to return to the city. Many had lost not only their families, but most of their belongings as well, because widespread looting and fires had broken out in the chaos.

Worn out and exhausted, Bernardine became very ill. On the edge of death for days, he was tended by his cousins in the house where he had grown up.

At last the fever broke, and the danger of death passed. But Bernardine was so weak that it took several months for him to regain his strength. During that time, he was doing some serious thinking and praying. One day, as his aunt brought in his dinner tray, he told her, "You've been a true mother to me. Now I must tell you before anyone else that I think the Lord is calling me; I must spend the rest of my life for him in a special way."

As soon as he could get up, Bernardine began giving away everything he owned. He asked to enter the Franciscans, and the friars were only too happy to receive this twenty-two-year-old man into their community. Bernardine was assigned to a small monastery.

"We have only a little bread and some cooked vegetables," the friars told him when he arrived. "We're very poor here." They were afraid that this young man would expect something elegant or fancy.

"No, brothers, we're rich!" replied Bernardine. He meant that anyone close to God is rich.

Bernardine fell easily into the friars' routine of prayer and work. In the evenings he continued his studies for ordination, because his superiors had invited him to become a priest.

Bernardine was incredibly happy, but some of his relatives were not so pleased. He had been one of the brightest and most handsome young men in the city. They didn't understand how he could throw every worldly thing away and choose to live in such poverty. When they met him on the streets of Siena they were embarrassed, and said to him scornfully, "You're nothing but a crazy beggar! We're ashamed to be related to you."

"Time will tell if I'm crazy or not," replied Bernardine calmly. But he was concerned. So many of his own family and friends thought very little of God. It seemed that they were ruled only by their greed and ambition, and knew nothing about the great love that the Lord and his Blessed Mother were ready to shower on each of them. Bernardine longed to preach sermons that would convince them of that divine love, but his sickness had left his voice hoarse and weak. Even after he became a priest, it didn't seem that the Lord wanted him to preach.

~~~~~~~~~~~~~~~~

Years passed, and the cities and countryside grew more and more violent. Wealthy landowners hired foreign soldiers to fight their battles against one another. As the small villages were destroyed one by one, the poor peasants were left without homes or work. Bernardine's heart ached, until one day he could keep silent no longer. With two other friars, he set out on a mission to bring peace throughout Italy.

Bernardine's long hours of prayer and meditation on the words of Jesus helped him to know what to say. He grew more and more confident as he realized that his once weak voice was now strong and clear. He attributed this miraculous cure to Mary. Who more than she desired that the life and teachings of her Son be made known to these poor, suffering people?

From city to city Bernardine and his companions went. Bernardine instructed group after group of men and women in the Gospel. Gently, he heard their confessions and gave absolution. Everywhere he encouraged devotion to Mary, the Mother of Mercy, and to Jesus, our Savior and Redeemer.

Not everyone was pleased with Bernardine's great success. His opposition to drunkenness and other sins was costing some businessmen their profits. They watched Bernardine carefully, hoping to catch him doing something wrong so they could destroy his reputation. At last they thought they had it. They noticed that everywhere in the towns where gangs had marked their boundaries, Bernardine would go and cover over the marks with the initials "IHS." He would also hold up a large banner with the same insignia and ask the people to venerate it. "Do you see that weird emblem the friar holds up after he preaches? It must be a symbol of something that's against the Catholic faith!" they exclaimed to one another.

While Bernardine was preaching at Viterbo, a very important envoy arrived at the monastery where he was staying, bringing him a message from His Holiness, the Pope! Why would the Pope bother to send such an important delegation to a poor friar? *It must be something important,* thought Bernardine, as he went to meet them.

It was a call to Rome, and Bernardine realized that his enemies had probably made a serious accusation against him. Yet when he prepared to leave for Rome, he was completely calm. He had no idea what the charge could be, but he knew he had done no deliberate evil. Trusting as always in the care of Mary, Bernardine went to meet the Pope.

Soon the two men of God were laughing together like old friends. They spent a long time discussing the serious needs of the Church and of society. When Bernardine left, only one demand had been placed on him by the Holy Father: he was to spend several

In every town where gangs had marked their boundaries, Bernardine would go and cover the marks with the initials "IHS."

weeks preaching in Rome! It was Bernardine's hour of triumph, and everywhere he displayed the "IHS" insignia, which was really a symbol for the Holy Name of Jesus! In fact, to put a stop to the overwhelming amount of cursing with the name of God, Bernardine had been spreading devotion to the Holy Names of Jesus and Mary. Now his "new devotion" had full approval of the Pope! To the warring factions and gangs, Bernardine preached peace, and he urged them to unite under the standard of the Holy Name of Jesus. "Put his Holy Name on your banners and on the flags of your ships. Write it everywhere!" he encouraged.

By now tremendous crowds gathered wherever Bernardine went. And as the Lord began to work miracles through his intercession, people were even more ready to listen to him and change their lives. Many young people were so filled with love for Jesus as they listened to Bernardine's words that they decided to give their lives totally to God, just as he had done. The group of friars that he had joined had numbered only 130 when he was a novice. Now there were over 4,000! And so many young women were becoming nuns that new convents were being built all over Italy.

Reaching Milan, however, Bernardine ran into trouble. Duke Philip Visconte had held a grudge against Bernardine ever since the friar had reproached him publicly for his sinful lifestyle. Now the duke called Bernardine to his castle and warned him, "Brother, if you don't stop preaching, I'll have you tortured!"

"I'll be happy to suffer for the love of Christ," replied Bernardine. The duke was about to insult him for this answer when one of his courtiers whispered something in his ear. Then the wicked duke said in a smooth voice, "Pardon me if I've offended you. Please accept this money for your monastery." And he held out a bag heavy with gold coins.

But Bernardine knew that if he took the money, people would be confused. Everyone knew that Bernardine preached against wealth. And there was no doubt that this money had come to the duke through dishonest means. So Bernardine answered the duke, "We don't need money. But if you force me to accept it, then allow me to use it where I want."

Followed by the duke's curious men, Bernardine took the bag and went directly to the prison. There he used the gold coins to buy the freedom of poor political prisoners. To each one he said, "Go home. You are free, in the name of Jesus Christ!"

The duke's men returned, grumbling, to the castle, and Bernardine continued his travels, always on foot. He journeyed to distant places and in the worst weather.

Wherever he went, Bernardine was like a flame of love that purified souls and brought peace to all. Those who had quarreled with their friends or relatives went in search of them to tell them, "Come back home! Let's give each other the hand of friendship." Those who had stolen property returned it with interest, and those who had enslaved others or failed to pay employees now paid their workers in full. As the warring family groups were reconciled to one another, the whole land once again grew peaceful and everyone prospered.

But there was still work to be done, so Bernardine, now old and worn out, continued to travel. One day in 1444, he and a group of friars were on their way to Aquila. The people were expecting them, and there was to be a whole week of preaching and praying. They stopped to rest as they approached the city, and one of the friars asked Bernardine, "Do you remember, Father, the time you preached in this same area on Assumption Day?"

"Yes," Bernardine replied. "I do remember." And he seemed to be living again that moment when he had said in his sermon, "Clear, precious, and beautiful as a star is our most pure Virgin Mary!" Then the crowd had suddenly begun to shout, "Look up at the sky! The star!" Sure enough, in broad daylight, a brilliant star had appeared in the sky.

The memory of that soul-stirring moment was too much for the poor heart of God's weary traveler, and Bernardine sank to the ground murmuring, "Most Holy Virgin, my sweet Mother...." Frightened, his brothers tried to help him.

The people of Aquila, who had come out to meet their beloved preacher, carried him into the city in a sorrowful procession. For three days they waited in suspense, hoping he would regain his strength.

But on Ascension Day, the bells announced Bernardine's last great journey. From everywhere, people gathered to honor the great Franciscan preacher who had just passed on to his heavenly reward.

Many miracles occurred after Bernardine's death. He was canonized in 1450, and is remembered for his great devotion to the Holy Name of Jesus and for his mission as "Messenger of Peace."

Like Bernardine, we can give good example to others by always respecting and honoring the Holy Name of Jesus. We can also imitate St. Bernardine by being peacemakers in our family and at school.

St. Juan Diego

(1474–1548)

December 9

Icy wind swept down Tepeyac Hill in what is now Mexico, howling like distant voices through the bleak winter landscape. Here the Aztec Indians had once offered human sacrifices to their mother goddess. Then, in 1519, the Spanish conquistador Hernando Cortes had arrived.

Angered by the practice of human sacrifice and greedy for the Aztecs' gold, Cortes and his men destroyed Tenochtitlan, the great Aztec city. They killed many of the native people and captured the rest, placing them under the care of Bishop Zumarraga and the other Franciscan friars who had come from Spain.

"As brokenhearted as we are over what has taken place," Bishop Zumarraga told his missionaries, "we must act with generous love to all. This way we may change the hearts of our Spanish soldiers and help to heal the poor Aztecs, who have lost everything."

Bishop Zumarraga and the friars prayed fervently to the Blessed Virgin Mary for help. *Mary, give me a sign that you are with us,* the bishop silently pleaded. *The native people are resisting our teaching. And who can blame them, after everything that has happened? Lord, have mercy on your Aztec children!*

Bishop Zumarraga could not have known that his prayer would one day be answered with a great miracle.

It was Saturday, December 9, 1531. As the sun was beginning to rise, a short, middle-aged Indian walked briskly down the road toward Mexico City, nine miles away. Juan Diego was on his way to morning Mass and a catechism lesson that would follow.

Juan was fifty-seven, but a life of hard work had given his skin a weathered look, making him appear older. His wife had died two years earlier. Juan now lived with his uncle, Juan Bernardino, who had raised him. Juan didn't mind the long walk. He loved attending religion lessons.

It was cold, and Juan pulled his *tilma* tightly around him. The *tilma* was a kind of cloak, often made from the fibers of a cactus plant. It did very little to keep out the winter chill. But it was all the protection that Juan Diego had.

As Juan Diego rounded Tepeyac Hill, he suddenly heard music. But it was no ordinary music. It was as if every bird in the world had joined in one harmonious song. Juan spun around in confusion. *What are birds doing out in December? What is happening?*

As suddenly as the music had begun, it abruptly stopped. Then Juan heard a young girl's voice calling his name in his *Nahuatl* (NAH-wat) language, "Juantzin! Juantzin!" "Little Juan! Little Juan!" In Juan's native tongue, the addition of *tzin* to a person's name was a sign of love and respect reserved only for family members and close friends.

Juan raced up the hill in the direction of the young girl's voice. He suddenly found himself before the most beautiful Aztec maiden he had ever seen! She was about fourteen years old, but she possessed the great dignity of an emperor's daughter. The light that radiated from her fantastically colored the rocks and bushes on the bare hill. Juan spontaneously fell to his knees.

"Juantzin, my little son, where are you going?" the Lady asked.

"My Holy One, my Little Lady, I am on my way to Tlatelolco!" Juan Diego answered. "I am going to my religion lesson."

The Lady smiled, and Juan's heart felt as if it would burst with joy.

"You must know, and be certain, littlest of my sons," she said, "that I am truly the ever-Virgin Mary, holy Mother of the true God."

Can this really be happening? Juan wondered. *Can the Mother of God be visiting a poor Indian?*

The young Lady continued, "I wish very much to have my church built on this hill. Here I will show everyone my love, my help, and my protection. I am truly your merciful Mother. I am a Mother to you and to all the people dear to me—to those who call upon me, and to those who look for me and trust in me.

"I am the Mother of all who live in this land, and of all people. I am the Mother of all who are devoted to me and of those who come to me for help. Here I will listen to their weeping and their sorrows. I will cure them and make things better for them.

"Go to the bishop of Mexico City and tell him that I sent you and that I wish to have a church built here on Tepeyac Hill. Tell him everything that you have seen and heard."

"My holy Lady," Juan answered reverently, "I am your servant. I will go and do as you have said. Wait a while for me. I will return to you."

With Mary's words in mind, Juan hurried to Mexico City. He found Bishop Zumarraga's house and knocked on the door, but the servants wouldn't let him in. Although they kept him waiting outside for a long time, Juan wouldn't leave. He had promised the Blessed Virgin that he would bring her message to the bishop, and he was going to keep his word! Finally, Juan was admitted into the bishop's presence. He told the bishop everything.

Bishop Zumarraga asked many questions. Juan Diego certainly sounded sincere, but the bishop needed more proof. "Thank you for bringing me the message, Juan," he said kindly. "You may go now. We will speak about these things again another time."

Juan hurried back to Tepeyac Hill. The young Aztec maiden was still there, waiting for him! Juan knelt down. He had failed in his mission for the Lady.

"My very dear Daughter! My Queen, my Lady," Juan stammered, "I did what you asked. I gave His Excellency your message, but I don't think he believed me. Please, my Lady, send some important person with your message. Then the bishop will know it's true. I am only a poor villager."

"My well-beloved son," Mary gently replied, "I have many others whom I could send if I wished, but I want to send you. I want you to go back to the bishop tomorrow, and tell him to build the church that I ask for. Tell him that the one who sends you is the Virgin Mary, the Mother of God."

Juan Diego looked up at Mary's radiant smile. "I will do everything you ask," he replied.

The next morning, after Mass, Juan returned to the bishop's house. After another long wait he was allowed inside. He faithfully reported everything that the Blessed Mother had told him. The bishop asked more questions. "Go back and ask the Lady for a sign," he finally said.

Juan left the bishop's residence feeling like a failure once more. What he didn't realize was that two of the bishop's servants were following him. Once he reached Tepeyac Hill, Juan suddenly disappeared! The confused servants had to return to the bishop and report that they had lost him.

Mary was waiting for Juan on the hill. He quickly told her all about his second meeting with Bishop Zumarraga.

"So be it, my little son," she answered. "Come here tomorrow and I will give you a sign. Once you show it to the bishop, he will believe you."

That same night, Juan Diego's uncle came down with a terrible fever. In the morning, Juan realized that his uncle was dying. "Please...call...a priest...Juan," the older man choked. "I want...to receive...the sacraments."

Juan raced out of the house. He didn't want to miss his meeting with the Lady, but he had to bring back a priest for his uncle. *I must avoid seeing her,* Juan thought anxiously. *I must go around Tepeyac Hill.*

A gentle voice broke the silence. "Juantzin! Juantzin!" The Blessed Virgin, whom he had been trying to avoid, was coming toward him! Juan froze in embarrassment.

"Where are you going, my little son?" Mary asked.

"Please don't be angry with me," he said. "My uncle is dying. I'm hurrying to call a priest for him. As soon as I've done this, I will come back to see you, my Little Lady."

Mary listened with great kindness. "Listen, my son," she replied. "Don't be troubled or disturbed. Don't you know that I will protect you? Don't you remember that I am your Mother? Do you need anything else? Don't worry. Your uncle is already cured."

Juan smiled in relief. He was sure that the heavenly Lady only told the truth. "Then I will carry out your errand right away, my Lady," he responded.

"Go to the top of the hill where you first saw me, my son," the Blessed Virgin directed. "There you will find many flowers. Collect them and bring them to me."

Juan obediently scrambled up the hillside. What he discovered at the summit astounded him. There, blooming in the cracked soil, were the loveliest roses he had ever seen!

Quickly, he took up the front corners of his *tilma* and began filling the cloak with the fragrant flowers. He eagerly carried them back to Mary. She rearranged them, explaining as she worked, "My little son, these roses are the sign that you are to take to the bishop. Tell him you have come in my name and that he must do what I ask."

With that, Juan hurried off once more to Bishop Zumarraga's residence. The servants were irritated. "When will this Indian stop bothering His Excellency?" one muttered. "And what's that he's carrying?" the other asked. When Juan showed them a few of the roses, they grasped at them but were unable to touch them. Nervous and confused, they quickly ushered Juan into the house.

"I have the Lady's sign!" Juan exclaimed to the surprised bishop. Lowering the corners of his *tilma*, Juan let the roses spill onto the floor. Bishop Zumarraga stared in disbelief. *Castilian roses don't grow here!* Suddenly the bishop sank to his knees. He was no longer looking at the scattered roses. His gaze was fixed on Juan Diego's *tilma*.

Perhaps my tilma is not good enough for the Lady's flowers! Juan thought for a moment. Then he looked down and gasped in amazement. There, on his *tilma*, was a beautiful picture of the Blessed Virgin Mary—exactly as she had appeared on Tepeyac Hill!

"Juan," the bishop whispered with emotion, "may I keep your *tilma* in my chapel until a church is built for the Blessed Virgin Mary?"

"Of course, Your Excellency!" Juan happily answered.

Juan spent that night at the bishop's residence. The next day he led Bishop Zumarraga to Tepeyac Hill and showed him just where Mary had appeared. A crowd of people went along with them. To everyone's surprise, the hilltop was brown and bare. No sign of the roses remained. Juan then returned to his home. He found his uncle in good health. "After you left to call a priest, the Blessed Virgin Mary appeared to me," Juan's uncle explained. "She cured me right away! She wants a church built on the hill where you saw her. The Virgin said that the bishop would call her by the name 'Ever-Virgin Holy Mary of Guadalupe.'"

News of Mary's visits to Juan Diego spread quickly. Men and women from all over Mexico worked enthusiastically to build the church that the Virgin Mary had requested.

On December 26, Juan Diego's *tilma* was carried in solemn procession from the bishop's chapel to the new adobe church on Tepeyac Hill.

"Will you serve as guardian of the Virgin's shrine, Juan?" Bishop Zumarraga asked. "You will have to tell the story of the Blessed Mother's apparitions to everyone who comes to visit and pray here."

"I will repeat it gladly as long as I live!" Juan exclaimed.

Juan Diego lived in a small house by the shrine for about seventeen years. He told the story of Our Lady of Guadalupe and of her apparitions to everyone who visited. Juan always considered himself Mary's humble servant. He never took any credit for the part he had played in bringing Mary's message to the bishop. Juan Diego died in 1548 at the age of seventy-four. He was declared a saint by Pope John Paul II in Mexico on July 31, 2002.

We celebrate the memorial of St. Juan Diego each year on December 9. On December 12, three days later, we celebrate the feast of Our Lady of Guadalupe.

St. Juan Diego, who was not born into a Christian family, but was baptized as an adult, never took his Catholic faith for granted. It became a very real and important part of his everyday life. Juan was always eager to learn more about God and the Blessed Mother. He was just as eager to do whatever they asked of him—like trying to convince the bishop that Mary had appeared to him and wanted a church built on Tepeyac Hill—even when it wasn't easy. Let's ask St. Juan to help us to be strong in our faith and open to God's will in our lives.

St. Francis Xavier

(1506–1552)

DECEMBER 3

Francis Xavier was the son of a noble Spanish family. Although he was quick, lively, and athletic, he didn't choose a military career as most young nobles did at that time. Instead, in his late teens, Francis went to Paris to study at the College of Sainte-Barbe.

Students in Paris led a carefree and active life, and Francis was always in the middle of the good times. He kept up his studies, too, because he saw a university diploma as a way to reach fame and fortune. Even though he had no definite plans for the future, Francis knew he wanted to do something great.

Peter Favre, who became a good friend of Francis's, was his roommate. Peter was from France. One day Peter said to Francis, "Have you seen the new student? He's Spanish, just like you. His name is Ignatius Loyola."

The name didn't mean much to Francis. And he wasn't impressed by Ignatius's appearance either. Ignatius was an older man, and he dressed very poorly. Francis prided himself on his fine clothes, which obviously marked him as the son of a noble. But there was something unusual about Ignatius, and word quickly spread that he had once been a famous soldier. *What's he doing here?* Francis wondered. *And why does he spend so much time praying in the chapel?*

Little by little, Francis learned Ignatius's story. During a war in Spain, Ignatius had been seriously injured. For months he'd had to lie in bed, waiting for the infection in his leg to go away and the bones to heal. To pass the time, he asked his cousin, with whom he was staying, to give him some novels to read. This cousin was a very religious woman, and the only books she had were lives of the saints! "These stories are exciting," she explained, "and besides, they're true! I know you'll enjoy them." Since nothing else was available, Ignatius agreed to try them.

Months passed, and Ignatius became more and more impressed by the courage and devotion of the saints. *These saints are true soldiers of the great King in heaven,* he thought. *I want to know and serve that King, too. But where can I start?*

When Ignatius's leg was healed, he didn't return to the army. His mind was full of thoughts of St. Augustine, St. Francis of Assisi, and St. Dominic, and he began walking from monastery to monastery and shrine to shrine as a pilgrim. He begged for his food and did small jobs to earn a place to sleep. He journeyed from Spain to Italy, where he boarded a ship for the Holy Land.

Ignatius remained many months in the land where Jesus had lived and walked. At last, feeling that God was leading him to a special mission of his own, Ignatius returned to Spain to study. He wanted to become a priest.

There were many things he had to learn. First came Latin, which all priests in those days had to know. Sitting with schoolboys, thirty-three-year-old Ignatius stumbled over Latin grammar, trying not to take the boys' laughter at his mistakes too seriously.

To study logic and theology, Ignatius next traveled to Paris, where he met Peter Favre, Francis Xavier, and their friends at the College of Sainte-Barbe. Peter began tutoring Ignatius, and Francis teased his friend about this. He didn't mind the tutoring so much. What bothered him was the fact that Ignatius spent so much time talking with his friends about God that it seemed they never had time for going out anymore. One day, Francis was making fun of them at the dinner table, when Ignatius asked with a smile, "Tell me, Francis, 'what good is it for a man to gain the whole world but lose his soul?'"

"I didn't ask you to preach to me," retorted Francis.

Even though Francis wouldn't admit it, God was working in his soul. He knew that many of the other students had been going to talk to Ignatius privately, and he could see that their lives were changing. Little by little, Francis also felt attracted to prayer and the spiritual life—but he would fight it all the way!

Finally, the Lord took matters a step further. Francis's friend, Peter, went home to see his family. Everyone knew that Francis was the best choice to replace Peter as Ignatius's tutor. Reluctantly, Francis agreed.

But he soon found that he was more of a student than a teacher. He went with Ignatius as he visited the hospitals and was impressed with the gentleness and love with which Ignatius treated the patients. He walked with him through the filthiest sections of the city, where misery was stamped on every face, and watched the older man ease the sufferings of the poor, the sick, and the starving. Ignatius thirsted for sacrifice, while Francis had become almost bored with his own comfortable and lazy life. Feeling challenged to match the enthusiasm for life that his older pupil had, Francis at last gave in to God's call. He asked Ignatius to permit him to join the community of religious that Ignatius was forming.

The little group of men who gathered around Ignatius made their first vows on the feast of the Assumption, 1534. In 1537, Francis, Ignatius, and four others were ordained priests. Three years later, their way of life was approved by Pope Paul III, and they settled in Rome. They called themselves the Company of Jesus. They also became known as the Society of Jesus, or the Jesuits.

Father Francis Xavier and Father Ignatius had become as close as son and father. Now Ignatius asked Francis to go to India as a missionary. He was to join the few priests already there, instructing the people in the Christian way of life, baptizing, and celebrating the sacraments. It was hard for Francis to leave Ignatius, but he wanted to serve God and this was clearly God's will.

The ship bound for India plowed through the blue Atlantic, rounded the tip of Africa, anchored at Mozambique, and then sailed across the Arabian Sea to Goa, on India's southwest coast. It was a year-long voyage through unhealthy climates. The food aboard ship was very different from what Father Xavier and the other Europeans were accustomed to, and, as always happened on those long voyages, many of the passengers became ill. Some even died. Although often seasick himself, Father Xavier was always among the passengers and crew, washing and feeding the sick, giving them medicine, preaching sermons, and preparing the dying for a holy death. Even the rough sailors, whose confidence he won with his sincere friendliness and gentle ways, stopped using bad language out of respect for the priest.

Everyone who met Father Xavier noticed how friendly and cheerful he was. He seemed to attract people like a magnet. And having drawn them to himself, he turned their thoughts to Jesus, who loved them with such infinite love that he had shed his last drop of blood for them. Many people became kind and considerate of others because of Father Xavier's kindness to them!

Goa was an Indian seaport that the Portuguese had conquered not long before. Many of the Indian people had been killed or mistreated, and the Portuguese

Catholic settlers were leading lives of cruelty, sin, and greed. Father Xavier found conditions so bad that he once wrote, "It would be far better for me to be massacred by those who hate our holy religion, than it would be for me to live on as a powerless onlooker to all the outrages that are committed daily against God, despite all our efforts to prevent them. Nothing saddens me so much as my inability to end the terrible scandals being given by certain important persons."

Yet the poor were not beyond his reach. It was to the poorer Portuguese and the Indians that Father Xavier finally directed his efforts in Goa.

Each morning he walked through the streets, ringing a bell, calling out, "Faithful Christians, friends of Jesus Christ, send your sons, your daughters, and your slaves to Christian doctrine classes, for the love of God!" People crowded around the black-robed priest and followed him to church.

Father Xavier's teaching method was simple. He recited each catechism lesson in rhyme and encouraged the people to sing it. In this way, the Creed, the commandments, and lessons on the sacraments were soon being sung by people everywhere—in the streets, on the ships, in the fields. Other priests began to follow Father Xavier's example.

It was difficult to convince the Indians that God loved each person equally. In their culture, everyone was born into a certain social class, or "caste." People of one caste were not permitted to associate with those of another caste. And it was impossible to move out of a caste. Because they believed that it was a person's fate to be born into a certain caste, the rich people had no sympathy for those who were poor. Those who had power used it to dominate those who did not. Goa was a challenging place for a Christian missionary!

Even with all the work to do in Goa, Father Xavier was eager to visit the poor fishermen who lived along India's southeastern coast. As soon as possible, he traveled to the coastal villages above Cape Comorin at the southern tip of India, to teach the people there the truths of the Catholic faith.

From the Cape he walked northeast, from village to village, bringing the Gospel of Jesus to the Paravas, who were pearl divers. These people had been baptized many years before, but because there was no one left to continue their religious instruction, they had returned to their former non-Christian beliefs. When they understood why Father Xavier had come to them, they welcomed him warmly. Those who were most eager to learn more about Jesus came for extra classes. Father Xavier appointed official catechists who would spend their time instructing the people after he moved on.

Father Xavier soon became a familiar figure. The people called him "Black Man," because of the long black robe he always wore. He helped the villagers build chapels out of sticks and mud. People would bring him all those who were sick, asking him to cure or bless them before they died. Within five years, Father Xavier was reported to have baptized over 10,000 persons!

Later, Father Xavier traveled north to the village called St. Thomas of Meliapor, where, according to legend, the Apostle Thomas had been buried. A priest and a small community of Christians received him happily, and the missionary set about preaching and baptizing.

One day Father Xavier sought out a rich man whom he knew had been avoiding him for some time. The man's name was Jacinto, and he was the object of gossip for miles around because of the sinful life he led.

"Good evening, Jacinto," Father Xavier greeted him. "I trust you'll forgive me for calling upon you at this hour!"

Here it comes! thought Jacinto. *He's going to preach to me!* But there was no getting out of it. It was time for the evening meal. It would be very rude not to invite the priest to eat with him. Glumly, Jacinto ushered Father Xavier into the dining room.

The two men sat and chatted. Father Xavier joked a good deal, and Jacinto found himself becoming more at ease as they talked and laughed together. But he was still waiting for the sermon.

At last Father Xavier said, "Thank you very much for your kindness, Jacinto. It's been an enjoyable evening. I should be going now."

"It was a pleasure having you, Father. Please come again," the rich man mumbled. He watched the slim figure of the priest stride away into the dusk. *Not a word about changing my ways,* he thought. *Has he decided that I'm a hopeless case?*

Jacinto did a lot of thinking that night. He paced from one room of his fine house to another, pausing now and then to stare out into the velvety tropical darkness. *I guess I've gone so far that Father Xavier won't even bother to talk to me about changing my ways—yet he has converted really great sinners!*

Father Xavier wasn't at all surprised when Jacinto approached him the next day and blurted out, "Father, I have something to tell you!" Jacinto made a full confession of his sins, and promised to perform all the penances and follow the good advice that Father Xavier gave him. From that day on, he was a new man!

At the tomb of St. Thomas the Apostle, Father Xavier prayed earnestly, "My Lord, please show me your divine will, to which, with the help of your grace, I will be faithful no matter what!" And God, who had given Francis the desire to serve him, now gave him the answer to his question. Suddenly, deep in his heart, Father Xavier knew that he must go to Malacca, a Malaysian seaport where merchants from Arabia, Persia, and India traded with the people of the Far East.

The missionary's fame traveled ahead of him. As he stepped ashore, he was greeted by a large crowd, especially children, eager to see the famous priest who loved people so much. Father Xavier greeted them warmly, then started right away to teach them about Jesus. He took up residence in the hospital, where he cared for the sick by day and prayed by night, allowing himself only two or three hours of sleep. Many times he fasted and prayed for the conversion of the greedy Europeans who had conquered this beautiful land and people. He often went into the soldiers' barracks, into the prisons, into the homes of the poor and destitute, becoming a friend and an inspiration to everyone. Little by little, Malacca became a more humane and just place to live and lost its reputation as a wicked city.

After meeting the challenges of Malacca, Father Xavier sailed to the Spice Islands located along the equator near New Guinea. This was a steamy region of jungles, volcanoes, and geysers. What challenging mission territory! But the priest loved the time he spent there, and the people came to know and love him, too. Through his example and teaching, many came to believe in Jesus' love for them.

But there was another land that Father Xavier had always dreamed of: Japan. Although not much was known about the "Land of the Rising Sun," Father Xavier had met a young Japanese man in Malacca. Through him, he learned about the religion and customs of Japan. It seemed to Father Xavier that these people were ready to learn about Jesus!

Although the priest's friends were concerned about the dangers, Father Xavier was determined to bring the Gospel of Jesus to the Japanese. With three others, he bravely set off on the long journey.

In spite of many difficulties, Father Xavier spent over two and a half years in Japan on the islands of Kyushu and Nippon. Even though there were not very

After meeting the challenges of Malacca, Father Xavier sailed to the Spice Islands located along the equator near New Guinea.

many Japanese converts, the people who did come to believe in Jesus were strong as steel in their new faith, and fervent in their prayers. Years later, even in the face of bloody persecutions, Japanese Catholics remained steadfast.

After this, Father Xavier planned to leave the Japanese mission in the care of another priest, and return to India. However, he unexpectedly had an opportunity to travel to China. In those days, very few Westerners had ever entered that enormous country, and no Catholic missions had been established. It would be risky, but Father Xavier knew he had to try. Imagine all those millions of people who had never heard of Jesus!

It was illegal for a foreign missionary to openly enter China. Father Xavier would have to be smuggled onto the mainland. Such a move would be terribly dangerous.

Finally, Father Xavier and two laymen boarded a small ship and sailed to an island called Sancian, off the China coast, where they dropped anchor and waited.

For two months the ship lay at anchor while Father Xavier awaited his chance. At last it came. A Chinese trader asked for a huge sum of money to smuggle them ashore. Father Xavier had powerful friends; he knew he could borrow the cash. The deal was soon set.

But when the appointed day came, the Chinese trader didn't appear. He didn't come that day, or the day after. As the hours slipped away, the missionary who had labored so tirelessly for years felt his strength ebbing away, too. Such a fever seized him that his companions took him to the shore and placed him on a rough pallet in one of the traders' huts. Through its doorway, Father Xavier could see the China coast.

The fever made the priest's mind wander, but he prayed almost continually, "Jesus, Son of God, have mercy on me! Mother of God, remember me."

There was no priest to hear his confession, to give him the sacrament of Anointing or bring him the Holy Eucharist. Except for his companions, Anthony and Christopher, Father Xavier was all alone. What a strange end to his heroic labors for Jesus! But what did it matter as long as all had been done for God? "In you, O Lord, have I hoped," he exclaimed with some of his old joy. "I shall never be put to shame!"

In the early hours of December, Father Xavier raised his eyes to a crucifix. "Jesus," he whispered— and his soul passed peacefully into eternity.

Word of the holy missionary's death spread quickly throughout the East. It passed from ship captains to cabin boys, from merchants to townsmen, from missionaries to Indian villagers. From the far-flung Spice Islands to the coast of the Paravas, from Malacca to Goa, the people of the East mourned the passage of their greatest benefactor.

In Goa, where Father Xavier's body was brought, crowds packed the beach to meet the ship. For days, people filed past the body, which showed no sign of decay in spite of the heat. Father Xavier had passed in and out of those people's lives in a few short years, but not even centuries would erase his memory from their hearts.

One burning desire filled St. Francis Xavier's soul—to do something for Christ, who had suffered so willingly for him. We can show God our love, too. We can do so by being kind and loving to others, as Jesus wants us to be.

St. Stanislaus Kostka

(1550–1568)

November 13

"Paul, pay attention to me. You're sixteen now, and your brother Stanislaus is only fourteen. I want you and Mr. Bilinsky to keep an eye on him in Vienna. You know how much I love your younger brother." Count John Kostka's voice softened a bit with this last statement. It wasn't easy to send his two sons all the way to Austria, but there was no college near the family castle in Poland where they could receive a good education. As much as he disliked the Jesuits, the count knew they were the best teachers in Europe.

Paul felt his throat tighten and his fists clench, but he knew better than to interrupt or contradict his father. His ears burned as he listened. Why was Stanislaus always the favorite? After all, he, Paul, was the oldest son. Just because he knew how to have a good time, while his dull little brother...oh, what good was it all?

Startled, Paul broke out of his angry daydream as his father grabbed his arm. "Paul, are you listening?

Here's some more money. I want you to use it on Stanislaus. Bring him out with you at night and teach him how to enjoy life. I don't want him spending more time than necessary with those priests."

Paul smiled as he felt the bag of coins. *Well,* he thought, *now Father is talking my language!* "Yes, Father," he replied. "You know Mr. Bilinsky and I can teach Stanislaus how to have a good time!"

Early the next morning, Paul, Stanislaus, and Mr. Bilinsky set out on the journey to Vienna. Their horses were frisky and ready to run. Paul and the stout middle-aged tutor, Mr. Bilinsky, traveled together, a bit ahead of Stanislaus. They laughed coarsely as Bilinsky told Paul crude stories about his own days as a teenager away at school. Stanislaus was happy to lag behind. Ever since his early childhood, he had felt such a great love for the Blessed Mother and for Jesus, that any sort of impurity or bad language actually caused him physical pain. Once he had become so upset by the stories told by some of his father's friends that he had fainted! How angry and embarrassed Paul had been that day! Stanislaus bit his lip as he thought about his "secret desire." He was inwardly excited to be going to Vienna. There he would surely have a chance to tell the Jesuits that he wanted to join them.

That night the three travelers stopped at a roadside tavern to rest. It had been a long day, and Stanislaus was tired. He slipped quietly upstairs as Paul and Bilinsky ordered another round of drinks for everyone. *They're certainly free with Father's money,* thought Stanislaus. *I wish they had given at least a little to that poor family we met on the road.* Stanislaus knelt beside his bed and began his Rosary. At least he would have a chance to say all his prayers in peace tonight.

On the third day, they arrived in Vienna. Stanislaus marveled at the magnificent buildings and churches. Everywhere there seemed to be crowds of people armed with shopping baskets, and venders with carts full of flowers, fruit, and fresh vegetables. By the time the three companions had found the college and settled into their apartment, Stanislaus's head was spinning. As usual, Paul and Bilinsky had wasted no time in scouting out the nearest tavern. Stanislaus rested his head on the pillow. Before he had time to worry about the future, he fell sound sleep.

The days at school went by quickly. Stanislaus rarely saw Paul and Bilinsky, since they had no classes together. But he was embarrassed to hear how soon word got around that "for a good party" all one had to do was contact Paul. And Paul, for his part, was equally embarrassed by the reputation his younger brother was achieving. Several of the boys had noted his piety and dedication to studies. Most nights, in fact, there would be a small group gathered in Stanislaus's room to study—and, most embarrassing, they would end their evening by praying the Rosary!

No wonder the priests here can't praise him enough, Paul thought bitterly. *The way he acts, you'd think he wanted to be one of them. Wouldn't that upset Father!*

Eight months into the school year brought an unexpected turn of events for the Kostka brothers.

Many nights a small group of boys gathered in Stanislaus's room to study; they would end their evening by praying the Rosary together.

The emperor of Austria, Ferdinand, died. His successor, Maximilian II, asked the Jesuits to give him the building that served as the students' living quarters. That meant that the students would have to find their own lodgings in the city. Bilinsky and Paul set off to find suitable quarters. Since the boys' father was a wealthy and important count of Poland, their lodging had to be in keeping with their social position.

At last they came across a gentleman who had an entire apartment for rent, complete with a cook and individual rooms for the boys. When they returned to pack their things and told Stanislaus about the arrangements, they neglected to mention that their new landlord was not Catholic, had a strong dislike for the Church, and insisted that no priests be allowed in his house.

While living on campus, surrounded by Jesuit priests and other students, Stanislaus had enjoyed his own small circle of friends. He had also been near the chapel, where he could go early each morning to attend Mass and spend time in spiritual reading and meditation. Their new quarters did not allow for this. Now Stanislaus had to follow Paul's schedule and ride with him each morning in the carriage. Often they were late for the morning prayer service, which annoyed Stanislaus. Once he brought up the matter with Paul, but his brother became very angry—so angry, in fact, that he hit Stanislaus hard on the side of his head.

As the weeks passed, Stanislaus became more and more worried. Paul and Bilinsky were out drinking almost every night. When they were home, Paul was often violent and insulting toward Stanislaus. But Stanislaus only kept silent and tried to avoid annoying his older brother. The trouble was, it seemed that just his presence bothered Paul.

That winter, the situation between the brothers grew worse than ever. Paul would often insist that they eat out at one of the local bars. Stanislaus would refuse to go, for several reasons. For one, he knew that Paul would never come home in time to finish his homework. Stanislaus often ended up with a piece of bread left over from his lunch and a bottle of water. Frequently Paul would come into his brother's room late in the evening and heckle him.

Three weeks before Christmas, Stanislaus developed a high fever. The doctors were called in, and, much to Paul's annoyance, they said that Stanislaus was seriously ill. *I won't tell our father,* thought Paul. *He'll probably be fine.*

Three days before Christmas, Stanislaus woke up feeling worse than ever. He called Bilinsky and Paul. "Please," he begged, "get one of the priests for me. I think I'm dying. I want to go to confession and receive Communion one more time." The boy's eyes were glazed and his forehead hot and dry, but he saw no pity on Paul's face. Tears slipped silently down his cheeks as the other two turned and left the room.

"Paul," Bilinsky hesitatingly suggested, "maybe we should call a priest."

"No!" exclaimed Paul. "You know the landlord made us promise never to bring a priest here. Besides,

I should be so lucky that Stanislaus would die." The bitterness in the young man's voice shocked even Bilinsky, but fearing Paul's temper, he said nothing.

The two companions avoided Stanislaus's room for the next two days, sending up the housemaid with a bit of broth each evening. But the Lord was keeping his own watch over the boy. On Christmas Eve, when Stanislaus was certain he wouldn't live until morning, an extraordinary thing happened. Just after the bit of candle stub had burned out, a soft light filled the room. Too weak to sit up, Stanislaus opened his eyes and was startled to see a lovely woman standing at the foot of his bed. As he saw the beautiful Infant she was holding, he realized this was the Blessed Virgin. He held out his arms, and she laid the Child Jesus on his chest.

"Stanislaus," said the Holy Mother of God, "you will not die from this illness. You will soon be well. God wishes you to become a Jesuit, but you must go to join them soon." With that, the Infant was taken up from his arms and the vision disappeared. Stanislaus felt health and peace flood his entire being. Sure enough, the next morning he woke up completely cured!

That week, Stanislaus approached one of the priests at the college and told him about his desire to join the Jesuits. The rector of the college had been expecting this, since Stanislaus's piety and goodness were apparent to everyone who knew him. Equally well known, however, was Count Kostka's opposition to almost anything related to the Catholic Church. What would he do if his son were to join the Jesuits?

Having thought out the matter carefully, the rector advised Stanislaus to travel to their German province and ask admittance there. Father Peter Canisius was the provincial of the German Jesuits, and he was a priest of good judgment and some influence.

That night, Stanislaus put on his oldest set of clothes, took a few coins from his purse, and left a note for Paul. He didn't say where he was going, but asked him to say good-bye to their dear father and not to worry.

"'Don't worry!'" exclaimed Bilinsky the next morning. "The boy is only sixteen, and the favorite child of his father—and he asks us not to worry now that he's run off! Hurry, Paul, we have to catch up with him and bring him back at once!"

The two set out, asking the stableman which way Stanislaus had gone. For two days they traveled up and down the roads leading out of Vienna, but with no luck. At last they gave up their search. With a trembling heart, Bilinsky wrote a note to the count. It was obvious that young Stanislaus had gone off to join the Jesuits.

Meanwhile, Stanislaus traveled 450 miles to the German town in which Father Peter Canisius lived, and gave him a note from the rector in Vienna. Father Peter read it and looked thoughtfully at the tired but happy young man sitting before him. "Stanislaus," he said at last, "stay with us a few weeks and rest. Then, if you still wish to join us, I'll send you on to our house in Rome. Father Francis Borgia, our Father General, is there. He'll accept you, I'm sure. And Rome is so far away that perhaps your father won't follow you."

Stanislaus nodded. The thought of his angry father only seemed to strengthen his resolve to obey the inner voice telling him that to become a Jesuit was not only his own will, but also God's. The next three weeks flew by. Stanislaus was asked to help the cook and to clean the rooms of the Jesuit novices. Everyone was impressed by the quiet kindness and prayerfulness of this young man from Poland. As he set off for Rome with two companions, they followed him with their prayers.

In Rome, Stanislaus lost no time in finding the Jesuit novitiate and contacting Father Borgia, who had been expecting him. Everyone in Europe knew the power and wealth of Count Kostka. Receiving his son into the Jesuit novitiate wasn't a decision for the priests to make lightly. But after their first interview, Father Borgia was convinced that Stanislaus was certainly gifted with a vocation. He would enter the novitiate immediately, and together they would face the count's opposition.

Within weeks, a letter arrived from Poland with the count's seal on the envelope. Stanislaus opened it and read it slowly. He had expected this. His father was demanding that he return immediately, or he would see to it that the Jesuits would be expelled from Poland forever! It wasn't a threat to ignore, but Father Borgia only said, "God has brought you here, Stanislaus. Let's have faith and pray for your father."

Relieved and with great peace in his heart, Stanislaus fell easily into the routine of the novitiate. At last he could pray and study to his heart's content without being bullied. In fact, the Jesuit community was so fervent under the leadership of Father Borgia that there was almost a holy competition to see who could become a saint first! But if a vote were taken, Stanislaus would probably have come out in first place. He did his duties well and was kind to everyone; he was so obviously happy to be a religious that just his presence in a room was enough to inspire good thoughts and desires in his fellow novices. He was soon a favorite companion of young and old alike.

But the years of stress and abuse from Paul and the long trip to Rome had taken their toll on Stanislaus's health. Now, in the hot, humid summer of Rome, he again developed a high fever. He had only been there for nine months, but Stanislaus knew that Rome would be his last home on this earth. He told his novice director, Father Fazio, that he felt ready to die and go to heaven. The energetic priest laughed and gave him a pat on the back. "Stanislaus," he said, "don't joke like that! This is just a typical 'Roman fever' that you have. As soon as the cooler weather comes, you'll be as healthy as ever." But that evening Father Fazio went to speak with the infirmarian, Father Ruiz. They both knew that their favorite novice was gravely ill, and decided to move him at once into the infirmary.

In the early hours of August 15, 1568, Stanislaus suddenly woke up. Father Ruiz was by his bed, as he had been for several nights, placing cool towels on the boy's head. Now he grew worried as he saw Stanislaus sit up with a supernatural glow on his face. The priest heard him quietly say, "I see the Blessed Virgin Mary! And she's surrounded by beautiful angels!"

Then Stanislaus lay back down and died. Father Ruiz rang the bell to let the other priests and novices know that the young novice was dead. Sadly, they gathered around his bed to recite the Office of the Dead and to prepare his body for burial. Even though he had been in Rome for only a short time, many people had come to know and esteem this holy novice from Poland. The Jesuits' chapel was filled for the funeral, and many of the people were speaking of the "new saint."

It was no surprise to Father Borgia when, a few days later, he was told that Stanislaus's brother, Paul, and Mr. Bilinsky were in the parlor to see him.

Father Borgia opened the parlor door and held out his hand to greet Paul. But Paul ignored the gesture and asked roughly, "Where is Stanislaus? I demand that you bring him to me at once!"

Shocked, Father Borgia realized that the news of Stanislaus's death had not yet reached Paul. "I'm very sorry," he said quietly. "Your brother Stanislaus died this very week."

After a long moment of silence, Paul let out an agonized scream and dropped to the floor. "My brother, my brother!" he cried. "My brother was a saint, and I've killed him with my jealousy, abuse, and meanness!" As the young man continued to sob, Father Borgia looked up at Bilinsky and was surprised to see that he, too, was crying shamelessly.

"What do you mean?" asked the priest. "You didn't kill Stanislaus. He was very happy here. He died of a prolonged fever." But soon the story came pouring out of Paul and Bilinsky. They told Father Borgia about their hatred for the gentle and pure young Stanislaus, their jealousy of his good reputation and self-control, the many times they had left him hungry and alone at night, and the nights they had come home and bullied the boy as he was sleeping or trying to study. Slowly, Father Borgia realized that Stanislaus had been more than just a "good novice." In fact, the young man had practiced heroic virtue and patience for many years. He really was a saint.

Father Borgia explained to Paul and Bilinsky that Stanislaus had always spoken well of his parents and family. Certainly, the priest was aware of how much Paul's father disliked the Church and opposed Stanislaus's vocation. But Stanislaus had prayed fervently that the Lord would grant his family the grace to accept his choice. He had never talked about having been mistreated by Paul.

Within a short time, Father Borgia petitioned the Vatican to open the canonization process for Stanislaus Kostka. His parents, Paul, and Bilinsky were among the people who testified to the boy's innocence, love for purity, and goodness with everyone. Paul himself spent many years struggling to reform his life, and at the age of sixty he entered the Jesuits as a novice.

Stanislaus always longed for heaven. In spite of suffering, persecution, and abuse because of his desire to remain pure and close to Jesus and Mary, he didn't become bitter or give in to peer pressure. We can pray to St. Stanislaus Kostka to help us when others make fun of us or mistreat us because we're trying to do what is right.

St. Benedict the Moor

(1526–1589)

APRIL 4

"Good night, Benedict! Sleep well, my son!" Diana Manasseri blew out the candle and lay down beside her husband, Christopher. They were Ethiopian Christians who had been captured years before by slave traders and brought to the island of Sicily. As slaves, they led a hard life, but they were grateful that their master treated his workers well. In fact, he had been so pleased with the work that Christopher and Diana did that he had made Christopher his foreman and promised that their firstborn child would be freed when he turned eighteen. That child was their son, Benedict.

Benedict grew up knowing that he would be free, just as his parents had been in Ethiopia. Once he was eighteen, he was given his own hut outside the slave quarters. Working for his former master as a free man, he eventually saved enough money to buy his own team of oxen, and soon he began to plow fields for good pay, which he shared with his parents and the other slaves. For the next three years, Benedict worked every day as a hired plowman. Every farmer knew that for the straightest furrows and cleanest fields, Benedict was the man to hire.

But this made other young men jealous, since they were less likely to be hired than Benedict. They also laughed at and insulted Benedict because of the color of his skin. One day some of these jealous youths picked up clods of hardened dirt and stones to throw at Benedict. But just as they were about to hurl their weapons, a strong voice rang out, "Stop that! Stop, I command you!"

The men froze. They recognized Brother Jerome Lanzi, once one of the wealthiest noblemen in the country. He had become a well-respected Franciscan hermit. "You're making fun of this man now," said Jerome, "but I tell you, before long, all the country will be saying great things about him!"

The seriousness of Brother Jerome's tone, as well as his reputation, warned the men to say nothing. Looking once more at Benedict, who was as surprised as they were, they turned around and went on their way. "Thank you, Brother Jerome," stammered Benedict. "What did you mean by that?"

"Come with me, Benedict. The Lord wants you to join us in the hermit's life. You're already very much like our gentle father, St. Francis. Come." Brother Jerome held out his hand and smiled. Benedict had never considered the life of a religious for himself. He wasn't educated; he didn't know anyone of African descent who was a priest or a friar. Yet something in Brother Jerome's eyes and voice attracted him.

"Yes, yes, I'll come," Benedict replied. "What should I do?"

"Sell your oxen," advised Brother Jerome. "Give the money to your poor family. Then come join us in the forest. We'll be expecting you."

As Brother Jerome turned and walked quickly back into the woods, Benedict felt his heart leaping. What had happened? He had never felt such joy, such excitement! He turned the oxen around and prodded them back to the village. The man he had bought them from would surely buy them back. With that money, his parents would be able to care for his younger brothers and sisters.

The next evening, he walked into the forest where the small band of hermits lived, and found a little hut ready and waiting just for him.

The life of the hermitage suited Benedict well, and the years passed quickly. He was an excellent cook, and the other hermits were happy to assign him that duty. Besides, he always managed to have some extra food to give the beggars who came by.

Brother Jerome Lanzi was a good leader and a holy man. These hermits were not attached to any large community of Franciscans, but lived the Franciscan rule as an independent group. Often they would be forced to move on as new farmers came in and cleared the forests where they lived. Eventually they ended up near the city of Palermo. Just when they were settled, however, their beloved leader, Brother Jerome, died.

Sadly, the brothers buried their spiritual father. The next day they gathered to decide who should take his place. Benedict had been deep in thought all night. Who should it be? Brother Giacomo was wise and had studied theology. Father Tommaso was the community's priest; surely he would be a good choice.

Benedict was startled out of his thinking by the voice of Brother Salvatore. "We have elected you, Benedict. You were the most faithful son of Brother Jerome. Now you will take his place as our spiritual father."

"What? Me?" Benedict was shocked. Perhaps the brothers were teasing him. Racing to the clearing where they had gathered, he began to protest. But Father Tommaso came up to him and gently motioned for him to kneel for the blessing. Benedict humbly obeyed. The hermits had made a good choice. In spite of never having studied, Benedict had a keen mind and an excellent memory. He could quote Scripture better than anyone, and he knew the rule of St. Francis as well as his own name. Most important of all, Benedict was a man of great prayer and compassion.

Life for the little group was not to continue in peace for long, however. It was 1562, and because there were so many independent groups of friars roaming around Europe—some holy and some not so holy—Pope Pius IV had ordered that they all disband. Their members could freely join any of the already established and approved religious orders, of which there were plenty! Saddened by the news, but maybe not entirely surprised, the hermits said their good-byes. Each friar went where the Spirit led him. Benedict headed for the nearby Franciscan community of St. Mary of the Angels.

The community of St. Mary welcomed him at once, for already his reputation for holiness and wisdom had spread throughout the region. They asked him if he would be their cook, a job that he readily accepted. This involved not only cooking for the friars, but also distributing food to the poor who came each day to the convent gate. The friars relied totally upon what food they could grow in their garden and what the neighboring farmers and bakers donated. The community soon noticed that even though more and more people were coming to the gate, they never ran out of food. It was no surprise to anyone but Benedict when he was elected their next superior!

As superior of St. Mary of the Angels community, Benedict had the added responsibility of guiding the other Franciscan groups in the area. The friars had chosen St. Mary of the Angels to be a model community for reform, and recognized Benedict as the man to lead them. The next three years saw dozens and dozens of Franciscans coming through St. Mary of the Angels to talk and pray with Benedict. No one even noticed that he was "uneducated," so great was his wisdom and knowledge of Scripture. By the end of his three-year term, all of the friars realized that a good and holy novice master was needed to train the youngest and newest members. No one had any doubt that Benedict was the man for the job.

As superior of St. Mary of the Angels community, Benedict had the added responsibility of guiding all the other Franciscan groups in the area.

Always ready to do the simplest and the most difficult task; always kind and generous in helping the poor; always on time for the community prayers— Benedict was a good model for the younger men aspiring to the hard life of the friars. At that time there were many periods of fasting throughout the year. During those times the friars would eat only one small meal a day. In addition to their long hours of daily prayer, they also worked in the fields and preached in the nearby churches. The life of a friar required not only physical strength, but a lot of self-control and generosity!

Benedict was a wise guide for the novices. Often he was able to understand what was bothering them even before they told him! As his reputation continued to spread, more and more people came to seek his advice. Princes, bishops, the wealthy, and the poor—all came to Benedict. And he treated everyone with equal dignity and respect. When his term as novice master ended, the community asked him to be their cook again. Joyfully he accepted. This time, though, an assistant was necessary. So many people continued to come to speak with him that Benedict had little time left for lettuce and herbs!

Benedict was now over sixty years old. His many years of hard work and responsibilities had caused his shoulders to stoop a bit, and his fingers were bent from arthritis. But he had become such a part of the life of the friars that no one even noticed these things. Instead, people noticed the miracles that resulted from his blessings, and the reconciliations that occurred through his mediation.

It was a surprise for everyone when they gathered for Mass early one morning and Benedict's place was empty. Hurrying to his room, they found him lying there in great pain. All the brothers soon realized that this would be his final day with them.

Kneeling beside him and around him, the friars prayed with their brother, who was also their mentor and their friend. With tears in their eyes, they heard him ask forgiveness for any wrongs he had committed. He looked fondly into each face that he knew so well. At last, his gaze turned upward, and he smiled and said, "Father, into your hands I commend my spirit." And Benedict, son of slaves, superior and friend, passed into eternal life. He became known as Benedict the Moor, because in Italian he was called *il moro santo,* which means "the black saint."

People loved Benedict because of his humility and kindness. Benedict loved people because in each one he saw the image and likeness of God, the Creator of all. He saw the beauty of each person whom Jesus had died for. We, too, can see Jesus in each person, regardless of social position, race, or the religion that individual practices.

St. Aloysius Gonzaga

(1568–1591)

JUNE 21

Five-year-old Aloysius was sleeping next to his younger brother, Ridolfo. Their father, Marquis Ferdinand Gonzaga of Castiglione, was already dreaming of an exciting future for his oldest son.

"We'll make a great soldier of him!" he proudly said to his wife, Marta. As the oldest son, Aloysius would someday inherit his father's fortune and carry on the Gonzaga name. The marquis was certain that Aloysius would be one of the bravest fighters in all of Italy.

Aloysius's mother, Marta, was of a very different character than his father. She was a gentle, religious person who made sure that her sons learned their prayers before anything else.

Even when Aloysius was still a toddler, his mother had noticed that he was more like her than like the marquis. Little Aloysius was bright and full of mischief, but he was also gentle and sensitive. At night he said his prayers with so much attention and fervor that she often wondered whether he was destined for the army of the king or the army of God. But since Aloysius loved playing toy soldiers with his little brother and friends, and because of her husband's dreams for their oldest child, Marta didn't bring up the subject of her own hopes for a priest in the family.

When Aloysius was almost six, his father decided to take him along on an inspection tour of the troops camping across the Italian countryside. The young boy felt proud to be with his famous father. He soon became the mascot of the soldiers, and from them he learned bad language and habits that made them laugh. But when he learned that these words and actions were offensive to God, he gave them up immediately.

One afternoon, while the soldiers were resting, little Aloysius went to look more closely at the cannon they had fired that morning during their drill. All the equipment was still sitting beside it. Aloysius was a strong boy, but he could barely lift the cannon ball to push it into the barrel. Once it was in, he had to stop and think what the soldiers had done next. Spying the fresh wick sticking up from the barrel, Aloysius quickly found a branch, lit it at the nearby cook's fire, and ignited the wick. He ran back and covered his ears, just as he had seen the soldiers do that morning.

The big gun jerked backward, and there was an enormous *boom!* The force of the jolt sent the boy spinning away, and his father and a soldier who came running were afraid that he was seriously hurt—even dead. They ran up to Aloysius, only to be met by a big grin. The boy was as calm as if he had been playing with a toy!

Of course, his father was delighted. "What a fine soldier we'll make of him!"

As Aloysius grew, his father's hopes grew more and more. One night, when the boy was twelve, a candle toppled over and set fire to his bed curtains. The brightness of the flames awakened Aloysius, who jumped up and found something to throw on top of the blaze to smother it. The entire household was impressed by his calm, quick thinking.

"Ah, yes," exclaimed Marquis Gonzaga, "my son will make a splendid soldier indeed! Certainly he will be a captain someday!"

In order to educate his sons properly for their future lives at court and in the service of the king, the marquis sent Aloysius and Ridolfo to study in Florence. Even though they were only nine and eight, they had lessons in languages, mathematics, fencing, and dancing. Dancing was very important, because as sons of a marquis they were required to attend all kinds of parties. Both boys soon became favorites at the court. In those days, marriages were arranged by the parents while the children were quite young, so many mothers at the court parties were keeping a close eye on Aloysius and Ridolfo.

Although both boys were popular, there was something about Aloysius that set him apart. He took his studies much more seriously than the other students. And everyone noticed how attentive he was to the sermons given at the Sunday Mass. When it was time for the boys to receive First Communion, the famous preacher Father Charles Borromeo, a future saint, was chosen to instruct Aloysius and Ridolfo for the sacrament. One lovely morning in May, Aloysius knelt in complete adoration after receiving Jesus in Holy Communion. For him, the Lord was so truly present that he wanted to stay and talk to him in his heart for as long as he possibly could. "I am yours—completely yours. And I always will be," he whispered over and over. It was about the same time that his confessor permitted him to consecrate himself entirely to God. The boy asked the Blessed Virgin to protect him. He knew there would be many temptations, but he was determined to keep his promise to the Lord.

~~~~~~~~~~

When Aloysius was thirteen, his father decided to send him to the Spanish court of Philip II. There he would learn more about the art of warfare. Even though Aloysius felt attracted to the life of a priest, perhaps even a monk, he knew that until he was older he had to obey his father's commands. So he went to Spain, again accompanied by Ridolfo.

Intelligent, good-looking, and polite, young Aloysius was soon the talk of the Spanish court. But he also made enemies among those young men who liked excessive drinking, cursing, and other kinds of immoral behavior. Aloysius wouldn't stand for any talk that offended God, and he would say so openly. This led to many verbal exchanges, which annoyed the more easy-going Ridolfo. The younger boy couldn't understand why his brother had to be that way. Nor could he understand why Aloysius refused to eat the best food or wear the best clothes. But his older brother seemed happy, so Ridolfo concentrated on his own friends and interests.

At about this time, Aloysius came across the writings of some of the first Jesuit missionaries who were bringing the Christian faith to India and Japan. Filled with admiration for their courage and great learning, he felt in his heart that this was what he also wanted to do. But how? He had already been through the first of many ceremonies that would make him heir to his father's fortune and titles.

When Aloysius was fifteen, however, he had an experience in prayer that confirmed his longing to join the Jesuits. He told his confessor, who said he would have to get his family's permission to enter the Order.

His father was furious to hear that Aloysius wanted to give up his birthright. The marquis decided to send Aloysius and Ridolfo on a tour of the courts of Italy, hoping that these worldly experiences would change his son's mind. Aloysius was determined, however, and his father finally gave in. In 1585, Aloysius renounced his inheritance in favor of his brother Ridolfo and traveled to Rome, where he was admitted to the novitiate of Sant'Andrea.

How happy the young man was as he forever put aside the fine clothes of his noble rank and put on the plain habit of a Jesuit novice! Now he was truly poor, and he looked like any other novice in the community. No one could tell that he came from a wealthy and noble background! In fact, Aloysius was careful to ask to be given the lowest and most annoying duties—

Ridolfo didn't understand why Aloysius refused to eat the best food or wear the best clothes. But his older brother seemed happy, so Ridolfo concentrated on his own friends and interests.

anything at all that would make him forget the comfort and wealth of his boyhood. For the rest of his life, he was determined to be as poor and humble as Jesus.

Aloysius settled into the routine of classes, prayers, and work. His spiritual director in Rome was a holy priest, Father Robert Bellarmine, who would someday be canonized as a great saint.

Because Aloysius was not very strong, the Jesuit superiors would not allow him to continue his frequent fasting. They made sure he went every day for some fresh air and exercise with the rest of the novices. If he wanted to go to the missions, Aloysius would have to build up his strength. He was so prayerful and generous that everyone fully expected him to be accepted as a missionary.

But, in 1591, a chance for a different kind of heroism came unexpectedly, as the plague broke out in the city. Within a matter of days, thousands of people were sick and dying. The hospitals and doctors were unable to care for all the sick. The Jesuits decided to open a hospital of their own. All the priests, brothers, and novices were allowed to choose between leaving for the country and staying to care for the sick. The plague was so contagious that anyone caring for the sick usually caught it, too. But most of the men, including Aloysius, stayed. Day after long day he joined the others in cleaning, cooking, feeding, and burying. All night, the wails of people mourning the dead and cries of pain from the dying split the silence. One by one, many of the Jesuits also became sick and died.

Not until the plague had almost run its course did Aloysius become ill. For a few days it seemed that he, too, would be among the victims. Instead, he pulled through, and the immediate danger passed. But he was left with a low fever that continued to eat his strength.

Spring was quickly turning into a warm summer, and Aloysius's superiors decided to send him to one of their country houses to recover his strength. The night before he was to leave, though, he asked to speak with Father Bellarmine. Aloysius knew that he was dying, and he asked to receive the sacrament of the Anointing of the Sick. Father Bellarmine knew how serious and fervent a religious Aloysius was; if Aloysius felt that he was dying, the experienced priest believed it must be true.

Aloysius stayed in Rome, and his brother Jesuits took turns sitting at his bedside. Another few weeks passed, and Aloysius seemed to be in no immediate danger. Again, however, he asked to receive the sacrament of Anointing. That night, after midnight, Aloysius became restless, and within a short while he breathed his last breath, the name of Jesus on his lips.

Aloysius Gonzaga understood how difficult it can be to remain good and pure when our society tells us that God's laws are not important. He understood what courage it takes to attend Mass on Sunday and receive the sacraments regularly even when other members of our family may not. For that reason and others, Aloysius was canonized a saint of the Church in 1726. In 1926, Pope Pius XI declared him the patron saint of young people.

St. Philip Neri

(1515–1595)

MAY 26

In the early 1500s, Florence, Italy, was an exciting and sometimes dangerous place to live. The period of history called the Renaissance was at its peak, and Florence—as well as Rome—was one of its main centers. The arts, music, architecture, and learning seemed to occupy almost everyone's attention. The Church, too, seemed to be more intent on the affairs of this world than on preparing people for eternal life.

Young Philip Neri's family was no exception. Though he was not wealthy, Francis Neri had great plans for his four children, especially Philip, whom everyone affectionately called "Pippo Buono" (Good Philip).

Philip was educated by the Dominicans until he was sixteen, and then was sent to live with a wealthy uncle on his estate. Philip was so cheerful and generous that his relatives liked him right away and treated him as if he were their own son. They put him in charge of the men who worked in the fields. Philip enjoyed long hours beneath the wide blue sky, supervising the planting and harvesting. The countryside was beautiful, and he lived in a fine house—yet Philip felt that something was missing from his life.

He didn't have to look far for it. Against the skyline loomed the great Benedictine monastery of Monte Cassino. It called him, gently but irresistibly. Philip began to visit the monks in the evening, after the day's work was done.

"Why don't you join us, Philip?" the monks started asking after they had known him for a while. "Come here, and you'll know true peace."

Philip wished he could say yes, but deep down he knew that his call was to another type of life. God wanted him, yes, but not as a monk meditating in his room or as an overseer of farm workers. God wanted him to go to the poor, to the sick, to prisoners, to confused teenagers—to all who were suffering—and bring them food, clothing, tenderness, and mercy. Philip said a grateful farewell to his uncle and aunt and, at the age of eighteen, set out for Rome.

Rome was a city in trouble. A few years before, in 1527, it had been attacked by the powerful armies of the German emperor, Charles V. In only eight days, thousands of churches, buildings, and homes had been destroyed. Once a center of Renaissance learning and culture, the city was now trying to rebuild and recover.

Philip found himself a small room where he could live in exchange for tutoring the two young children of some friends of his father. At night, he studied philosophy and theology and spent long hours in prayer.

Several years went by. Philip began to show God's love in action by caring for the sick, the homeless, and especially the many gangs of teenagers who roamed the streets day and night. Each morning, he went out and talked about Jesus Christ to anyone who would listen. He explained that after dying for our sins, Jesus rose again so we might have eternal life. In the afternoons, he rang the church bells and invited everyone to join him in prayer.

Little by little, many people came to pray with Philip. After the prayers, Philip taught his listeners about the Scriptures, history, and the lives of the saints. He was also instrumental in popularizing the Forty Hours' Devotion to the Blessed Sacrament, in which people take turns praying before the Blessed Sacrament for forty hours.

Often he would gather people to do some good work for the poor, or they would go off together to the mountains for a picnic. Philip especially attracted teenagers, whom he would often greet with the words, "Well, my friends, when shall we begin to do good?"

It was while Philip was praying on the feast of Pentecost in 1544 that the Holy Spirit descended on him as a ball of fire and lodged in his heart. From this time on, Philip always felt his heart to be enlarged and filled with heat—a "fire of love."

Philip encouraged people to go to confession and receive the Eucharist often. But Philip himself wasn't a priest! He had such a great respect for the priesthood that he had felt unworthy to be ordained. Eventually, however, he allowed his confessor to persuade him to receive the sacrament of Holy Orders. He immediately began to study and was ordained at the age of thirty-five.

Within a few years, some of his penitents were also ordained. Desiring to follow the example of Father Philip's life and ministry, they went to him for direction. He had them promise to live together, sharing everything in common and supporting one another in prayer and by good example. Soon this little group grew, and the Pope gave them an abandoned church to be their home. They became known as the Congregation of the Oratory. Like Father Philip, they went about among the working class and teenagers, to preach, to teach, and to care for spiritual and material needs.

They gathered people together for prayer daily. So many people came to Father Philip for confession and spiritual direction that he often spent the whole day and most of the night in the confessional!

One day Father Philip was approached by a teenager who had sinned so much that he didn't have the courage to admit it to anyone.

"Come on," Father Philip urged him. "You'll feel better soon."

"Father, I've made so many mistakes and hurt so many people...."

"All your sins will be forgiven."

"Maybe, but I'm afraid of the penance I might have to do!"

Father Philip Neri went about among the teenagers to preach, to teach, and to care for spiritual and material needs.

"Nothing exceptional!" Father Philip assured him. "Only this: every time you sin, come back right away and put yourself in the state of grace."

The young man promised. He confessed, received absolution, and went on his way happy.

But he returned the next day, head down, humiliated and discouraged.

Father Philip Neri comforted and encouraged him many, many times. Every time he returned with bowed head, weary and dejected.

But eventually the young man began coming less frequently. Father Philip's smile, which had never faded, now grew brighter as he saw that the boy, aided by God and his desire to live as a Christian, was becoming a virtuous and holy person.

Father Philip also had the gift of prophecy. One day, one of his young friends told him that he planned to take a trip to Naples.

"It would be best for you not to go," the priest advised at once.

"But, why not, Father? It's a pilgrimage, and Naples is a beautiful city. I don't see anything wrong with going."

"Listen to me: don't be stubborn."

"Father, I really want to go."

"All right, do so if you wish. But you'll be ambushed by the Turks and almost drowned."

The youth decided to go anyway, and set sail for Naples with the other pilgrims.

Turkish pirates attacked the ship. Not knowing what else to do, the boy flung himself over the side and struggled to keep himself afloat in the water. He went down once, and then again.

"Father Philip!" he screamed. "Father, save me!"

Father Philip Neri, who was miles away in Rome, appeared before his eyes, got hold of him, and carried him to safety. What a miracle! Father Philip was one of the saints who had the gift of bilocation, the ability to be in two places at the same time.

Father Philip always acted according to the needs of the people who came to him. He was gentle with one person, stern with another, playful with yet another. In everything, he tried to follow the lead of the Holy Spirit, who helped him see what each person needed most.

Father Philip continually prayed for guidance, relying on God's grace. "Lord, watch over me this day," he would pray. "Without your help, I could betray you!"

No matter how distinguished Father Philip's visitors were, they found him doing ordinary tasks. He would frequently greet them with an apron on and his sleeves rolled up. He was careful not to let his fame make him proud.

Often, when he was to meet with very important people, he would dress in a fantastic costume, or turn his clothes inside out and wear long white shoes. Sometimes he would walk through the streets carrying a huge bunch of weeds in his hand. He would hold them like a bouquet of roses, stopping every now and then to sniff them. This not only hid his holiness, but it also made people laugh—and that was important to him.

Father Philip Neri felt that people couldn't make progress in the spiritual life or conquer sin unless they were cheerful. "Never commit sin, and always be cheerful" was his favorite advice. "A cheerful soul becomes holy more quickly." He was convinced that a happy heart is a sign of purity and innocence.

When boys and young men played games in the courtyard, the other priests would complain about the noise. "Don't listen to them," Father Philip would tell the young people. "Go on playing."

"How can you put up with that racket?" a visitor asked once.

"They could chop wood on my back and I wouldn't mind," answered Father Philip, "as long as they keep out of sin."

~~~~~~~~~~~~~~~~~

The celebration of the Eucharist became an almost continuous ecstasy for Father Philip. Often he was seen suspended in the air, as if he wished to go up to heaven. At other times he would become as still as a statue, his gaze directed upward.

When he was nearly eighty, Father Philip became sick. Cardinal Frederick Borromeo, brother of Charles Borromeo, came to anoint him and bring him Holy Communion. Father Philip received the Eucharist with great joy, saying, "Anyone who wants anything but

Jesus doesn't know what he wants. Everything else is emptiness."

On May 25, 1595, the feast of Corpus Christi, he went to confession and celebrated Mass. Then he spent the day praying, reading the lives of saints, and hearing confessions. But by six o'clock that evening, he was dying.

"If you don't have any more medicines," he joked with his friends, "don't worry about it. I can't use them anymore."

With tears in his eyes, one friend asked, "Father, will you leave us without saying anything? At least give us your blessing."

Father Philip Neri opened his eyes, raised his gaze to heaven, and then looked around. He lifted a hand and weakly blessed everyone gathered in his room.

This was his last act. When his hand fell, his great heart stopped beating. That heart had known heavenly joys even on earth—so much so, that at times Father Philip had cried out: "No more, Lord, no more; I can't bear so much joy!" Now that same Lord drew near to lead him to a place where happiness never ends.

True joy comes from avoiding sin and doing good deeds. Joy is the mark of a Christian. We will find joy if we try to imitate Jesus in the way we treat others and pray to our Father in heaven.

St. Germaine

(1579–1601)

June 15

Laurent Cousin rubbed the shoulders of his young wife, Marie. Here, in the small house they had shared for the past year, they were now preparing for the birth of their first child. "How do you feel, Marie? Is this helping?"

Marie looked up at her husband's anxious face and smiled. "Don't worry, Laurent," she said. "I love this baby so much that no amount of discomfort is too great. Maybe you should go call your sister now. I think the baby may come tonight."

Laurent ran to the neighboring farmhouse where his sister Monique lived. He thought his heart would burst with excitement. As he ran up the path he cried, "Monique, come home with me. Marie thinks the baby will be born tonight!"

"Calm down, Laurent." Monique was laughing at her brother. "Everything will be fine!" When they arrived back at the house, Monique realized that the baby would soon be born.

But as the hours passed, Monique began to worry. Marie was not well and seemed to be growing weaker by the minute. At last a baby girl was born. As Monique picked up the infant, she gasped. Besides being far smaller than usual, the tiny girl clearly had a crippled right hand. There were also two large lumps on either side of her neck. Monique sadly handed the infant to her mother.

Marie hardly noticed the deformity of her tiny daughter. Nothing could lessen the love she felt for her baby. Marie smiled. Then, laughing and crying all at the same time, she called Laurent to come and welcome their first child into the world. Laurent couldn't hide his disappointment when he saw the child. His baby was sickly and deformed! He felt as though he couldn't breathe.

"Laurent, what's wrong?" Marie asked. "So what if her hand is misshapen? I can see already that this little girl will be beautiful and kind. Come, let us thank God for her. What shall we name her at the Baptism tomorrow? How about Germaine, after my mother?"

And so the baby was named Germaine the very next day. The neighbors came, bringing gifts of food and small blankets woven from the fine wool for which their village of Pibrac was famous. But after that day, they all whispered the same thing: "Too bad. That child will not survive long. And Marie looked terrible. Do you think she'll live?"

Laurent anxiously cared for his wife. Never a very religious person, he now found himself begging God not to let her die. But day by day, Marie grew weaker. While Germaine was still very young, Marie died.

During the next few months, little Germaine was shuttled from one relative's house to another. The glands on her neck often swelled, and, even though she was only a year old, her joints were already growing deformed because of a disease called scrofula. Many of the people of the village claimed that the child must have "evil spirits" in her to be so sick so young. It was the year 1580, and people then didn't know very much about sickness or birth defects. Germaine's father didn't want anything to do with her. He wanted to marry again and was afraid that no woman would marry him with a sick child to care for. Eventually, though, he did find a new wife, and Germaine went to live with her father and Hortense, her stepmother.

In the years to come, Germaine became a favorite of the parish priest in Pibrac. He had never known a child so quick to learn her prayers and so eager to know about God. Germaine wasn't yet ten years old, but she knew her catechism well enough to teach the younger children! One day the priest went to pay a visit to Germaine's parents. "Laurent," he began, "I wanted to tell you how well Germaine is doing with her catechism. Why don't you allow her to come to the school and learn to read and write with the other children?"

"Never!" growled Laurent.

"Never!" snapped the stepmother, who by now had two young children of her own.

"Where is Germaine?" the priest asked. "She is too small, surely, to be out working in the fields, isn't she?"

"Her size has nothing to do with it! She's a naturally lazy child. It's all I can do to get her to watch the sheep in the field!" insisted the stepmother. "In fact, she should be grateful that I allow her to sleep with the sheep. With her sickness, I live in fear that she will contaminate the flock!"

"Sleep with the sheep!" exclaimed Father. "Surely not! Why, Germaine's sickness is not contagious...and you have plenty of room in the house, don't you?"

"And risk having my own two dear children get sick? She will never sleep in my house!" By now Hortense was furious. Just the sight of Germaine was often enough to send her into a rage, and almost daily she hit and kicked the frail girl for one thing or another.

"Calm down, my dear," purred Laurent. Then, turning to the priest, he said roughly, "I don't come to the church and tell you how to mind your affairs. I would appreciate it if you don't tell me how to mind mine!"

"Maybe you should consider coming to church, my friend," said Father. "In any case, I beg you, be kind to the child. I can see from her eyes and gentle manners that the Lord has a special place in her life. Good-day."

That night, as Germaine finished herding the sheep into the stable, she thought of the children whom she had taught that day. There was a regular group of almost a dozen village children who came to her after their school classes to learn about God. Though Germaine wasn't pretty, and her neck was sometimes swollen so badly that she could hardly speak, there was something about her that made the villagers realize that she was special in many ways. When she spoke about God and his love for each and every person, it was with such conviction that every listener went away encouraged and peaceful. It seemed everyone loved Germaine except her own father and stepmother.

~~~~~~~~~~~~~~

"Germaine!" shrieked Hortense. "Stop dawdling and get over here. Did you finish spinning the wool I gave you this morning?"

"Yes, Mother," said Germaine. "I finished it, and here it is." As she handed the large woman the bundle of wool, Germaine couldn't help but cringe. Her stepmother's violent moods were so unpredictable. Every morning and evening Germaine said special prayers that God would soften this woman's heart, and that her father would love her as his daughter. But so far, her prayers seemed to go unheard.

This night proved to be no different. As Germaine was walking down the back steps with her supper of bread crusts, her stepmother said softly, "Germaine, turn around. Let me see the face that the priest likes so much."

As Germaine turned she could just see the broomstick coming at her, but didn't quite duck in time.

Falling down the steps, she dropped her bread in the muddy path. "That will teach you to show off in front of the villagers!" her stepmother cried. "You might act holy for them, but I know what a wicked child you are! Now get away from my house and my children!"

Germaine limped away to the barn. Later, as she lay gazing up at the stars, she prayed, "Dearest Father in heaven, dearest Mother Mary, I am your child. You give us every good blessing, and I thank you. Please change the hearts of my father and stepmother. They are so unhappy, and they don't even realize it! Let them recognize the love you have for them through my patience and goodness. I offer my whole self to you; I wait for every good thing from you." Praying the Rosary on a string of knots, Germaine fell sound asleep.

Years passed. Germaine was now over twenty years old, but because of her small build, she didn't look more than twelve. Although she still slept in the barn, her stepmother never beat her anymore. She didn't dare!

This is the reason: One afternoon when Germaine had come home from the fields, she had met an old beggar. Knowing that her supper crusts of bread would be on the kitchen table, Germaine had crept quietly into the house to take them and give them to the old man. Just as she was closing the door, her stepmother appeared. "Germaine! What do you have in your apron, you thief?" Hortense picked up the large wooden stick used for rolling the bread dough and began chasing Germaine into the village, shouting,

"Thief! Thief! I have been raising a thief, and now everyone will see the truth of what I say!"

And indeed, almost the whole village came out to see what Madame Cousin's latest rage was about. Seeing Germaine trying to outrun the angry woman, they gasped. "She'll kill that poor child someday!" some exclaimed.

By now they had reached the village square and Germaine could go no farther. *Well,* she thought, *if I let go of my apron and let the bread spill out, I'll be beaten for taking it. If I refuse, I'll get a beating anyway.* With that, she stood facing her stepmother and calmly let the apron drop. Immediately she heard the crowd of peasant women gasp. Many fell to their knees. In amazement, Germaine looked down. Instead of crusts of old bread, beautiful flowers of a kind they had never seen were lying in a pile at her feet.

"A saint!" she heard someone say. "She's a saint!" another agreed. One by one the crowd came up to gather some of the miraculous flowers to bring home. At last, only Germaine and her stepmother were left. With a shamed look on her face, Hortense could only say, "Well, I never. Well, it's late, Germaine. Come home; let's begin the evening's work." The lady was too proud to apologize, but she realized that never again could she beat the girl who was so clearly blessed by God.

Even though Germaine was now welcome to live in the house, she preferred to sleep out in the stable with the sheep. There she could lie on her straw mattress and gaze up at the star-filled sky, thinking of God who had made so many wonderful things. And there she was also free to pray, as she often did, into the early hours of the morning. Her joints were always stiff and painful now, and she could no longer stand up straight. But dozens of children still came to her in the fields to learn their catechism and prayers. And she still left her flock of sheep in the care of her guardian angel each day as she went to Mass and Communion in the village church. Although the field was at the edge of a forest known to be inhabited by wolves, her sheep were never harmed!

One evening, two monks who were traveling through Pibrac on their way to Toulouse saw bright lights and what looked like angels hovering over the farmhouse of Laurent Cousin. Stopping to watch, they stayed there until morning. When Hortense got up and saw that the sheep were still in the stable, she ran out, calling, "Germaine! Germaine, are you sick?" As she entered the stable, she gasped and tears ran down her face as she picked up the small body of her stepdaughter. Germaine had died peacefully during the night.

The two monks told everyone in the village about the lights and the angels they had seen.

At Germaine's funeral, the villagers were convinced that they were burying a saint. From that day, people have prayed to Germaine and received many miraculous cures and graces. From heaven, the little shepherdess of Pibrac continues to love and assist all who come to her in their need.

Although the field was at the edge of a forest known to be inhabited by wolves, Germaine's sheep were never harmed!

Even though she was sick all her life and was born with physical disabilities, Germaine allowed God's love to shine through her and touch the lives of hundreds of people. No matter what we look like or how healthy or sickly we may be, we are all children who are greatly loved by our heavenly Father.

St. Camillus de Lellis

(1550–1614)

July 18

John and Camilla de Lellis had been married for almost forty years, and as much as they had hoped to have a large family, Camilla had never had a child. Now, long after most of their friends and relatives had given up hope for them, Camilla realized she was expecting a baby! Early one spring day in 1550, when the hills of central Italy were bursting with flowers and green grass, she gave birth to a healthy little son. The couple decided to call the baby Camillus in honor of Camilla. Everyone said that he would be the blessing of his parents' old age.

Soon, however, most of the small town was wondering if Camillus would ever be a blessing to anyone! He wasn't sickly—far from it. In fact, even before he was a teenager, the boy was almost six feet tall and solid muscle. He was also uncontrollable—rebellious, quarrelsome, and impulsive.

When Camillus was thirteen, his mother died. Camillus's behavior became even worse. His father had soon had enough. John de Lellis was a captain in the army, and he would not tolerate disobedience. "If this is the way you're going to act," exclaimed the father, "you'll not live here any longer!" At the age of sixteen, Camillus made the choice to leave home.

Free at last! he thought. He went immediately to the part of town where there were many bars, dance halls, and gamblers. Everyone knew he was a teenager, but Camillus was so big and strong that no one questioned his right to be in such places.

Camillus soon learned the thrill of winning a bet, and before he knew it he was an addicted gambler. He quickly learned that all he had to do when in debt was to challenge some unsuspecting stranger to a fight. His friends would place their bets, and Camillus would come up with money to spare. That is, until his luck—and his friends—ran out. Camillus was so proud and quarrelsome that after a while no one wanted to be around him anymore. At eighteen, Camillus found himself alone. He decided to join the army.

There was a war going on with the Turks, and strong soldiers were needed. Camillus enlisted and quickly moved up in the ranks because of his size, strength, and courage. But he developed a foot infection that soon became so bad that he couldn't walk. He was sent to St. James's Hospital in Rome.

St. James's was a hospital for people with "incurable" diseases, and many of its patients were very poor. Camillus was accepted as a patient, but was also required to work part-time in the wards. For a few months, all went well, and the infection began to clear up. But the longer Camillus was there, the more fights he got into with the other workers and patients. For Camillus there was only one way to do anything—his way. And when others didn't agree, there was trouble! At the end of nine months, Camillus found himself discharged from the hospital and once again out on the streets.

He went back to gambling and drinking, and ended up in trouble in one town after another. Camillus moved farther and farther south until he was in the lively port city of Naples. For several weeks he was the talk of the taverns as he won fight after fight, bet after bet. The more he won, the more he would risk on the next game. One day he lost everything he owned!

He awoke lying in a gutter. Realizing that he couldn't stay in Naples, he headed east, and didn't stop until he reached the town of Manfredonia on the shore of the Adriatic Sea. In the clear fresh sea air he felt himself coming back to life. Tired of begging for scraps of food, Camillus decided to look for a temporary job.

At that time, a community of Capuchin friars were enlarging their monastery on the outskirts of Manfredonia and needed construction workers. Camillus was hired right away, and as his pay he accepted room and board with the friars. Humbled by his circumstances and ashamed of himself for having reached such a miserable state, Camillus became a loner. He didn't join the other hired workers for drinks after work, and he was careful to avoid card games on his lunch break. His reputation had not spread this far, so everyone assumed that he was just a quiet, sad young man.

The Lord, however, knew Camillus's heart. And, slowly, grace began to break through the hardened crust of his soul. As so often happens, grace was working through ordinary human events. Whenever the friars were in the chapel chanting their prayers, Camillus felt irresistibly attracted. He would move closer to the chapel walls and sit beneath the window so he could hear better. "O God, come to my assistance," one group of friars would sing. And then came the response, "O Lord, make haste to help me."

"Lord, make haste to help me." The ancient prayer echoed in his head morning and night. He also noticed the great peace with which these friars went about their daily duties. He especially noticed the kindness and wisdom of Father Angelo, the community "guardian," or superior. It was Father Angelo who assigned the work each day and distributed the week's wages to the workers. Father Angelo could see the sorrow on Camillus's face, and his heart ached for the giant of the construction crew. Day after day, Father Angelo patiently waited for the moment of conversion to come. He didn't approach Camillus, but waited for Camillus to approach him. And, eventually, the day came.

"Father Angelo," stammered Camillus, "may I talk to you, please?"

"Camillus, isn't it? Yes, I've been waiting for you." Father Angelo stood up from his desk and gently took

Camillus's arm. Looking up at the young man's red face, realizing how difficult this must be, he said, "Let's go out into the garden. We'll be alone and able to talk freely."

Three hours later, Camillus felt like a new man. He began joining the friars for prayer. No one was surprised when, a few weeks later, he appeared dressed as a Capuchin novice. Camillus felt that he had to make up for all the pain and hurt he had inflicted on his family, on his friends, and on the Lord. There was no novice so devoted as he to performing the most humble tasks and to keeping the many fast days of the Capuchin rule so strictly. Camillus had never in his life known such joy.

One afternoon, Camillus received a message to go at once to Father Angelo's office. There was a sinking feeling in the pit of his stomach as he limped toward the main house. Was Father calling him to tell him he would soon be able to profess his vows? Or was he calling him because the sore had reappeared on his foot? Before he reached the guardian's office, he felt sure that he already knew what he was about to hear.

"I'm truly sorry, Brother Camillus," Father Angelo said. "There's nothing at all wrong with your behavior, far from it. But we cannot admit someone to profession who will not be able to keep our strict way of life. And with that foot of yours, well...let's pray that another stay at St. James's will cure you for good. If so, you may return."

Sadly, Camillus took off his religious habit and accepted the offer of a ride to St. James's. He was so big and strong—why should such a small thing as a foot infection keep him from fulfilling the only dream he had in life? Yet he was forced to leave the monastery three times to be treated at the hospital.

At last, Father Angelo had to tell him that it seemed the Lord was leading him to another way of life. Not knowing what else to do, Camillus returned once again to St. James's and began to help care for the patients. But it was not the same Camillus who had been expelled from the hospital so many years before! Indeed, everyone was talking about the way Camillus was acting. He treated everyone with such kindness and respect that several of the "incurables" had recovered and gone on to live normal lives! What was the gentle giant's secret?

Camillus had come to think of each patient as being Christ himself. After all, Jesus said, "'Truly I tell you, just as you did it to one of the least of these who are members of my family, you did it to me'" (Mt 25:40). And to govern his own attitudes and behavior, he reflected often on the words, "'Truly I tell you, unless you change and become like children, you will never enter the kingdom of heaven. Whoever becomes humble like this child is the greatest in the kingdom of heaven'" (Mt 18:3-4).

But while he was trying his best to treat each patient with kindness and respect, he couldn't help but notice that many of the attendants were unkind to the sick and poor.

Gradually, Camillus began to recognize which of the attendants were concerned about the patients and

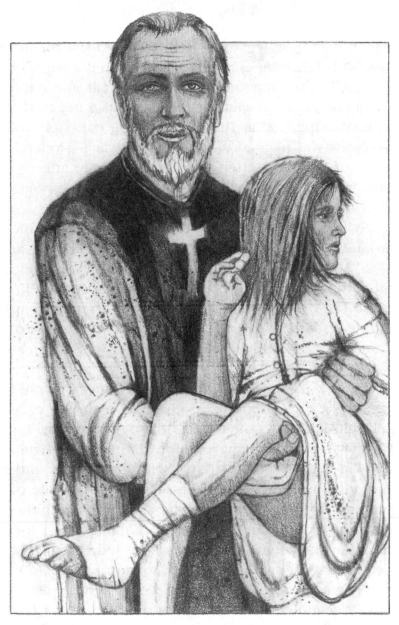

Camillus treated each patient with such kindness and respect that several of the "incurables" had recovered and gone on to live normal lives! What was the gentle giant's secret?

which were not. For those who were caring for the sick with Christian compassion, he started a support group. They met together to pray and to talk about the particular needs of each patient. They also began the custom of praying at the side of dying patients. Not everyone was pleased with Camillus's ideas—indeed, some of the other attendants became quite angry—but many took notice, and soon Camillus was appointed administrator of the hospital.

By this time, Camillus had organized his daily life around regular periods of prayer and attendance at Mass. His confessor and spiritual director was none other than the famous Father Philip Neri. Father Philip could see God working in Camillus, and guided him into considering priestly ordination. At thirty-two, Camillus began studying, and in 1584 he was ordained a priest.

As an ordination gift, one of his relatives granted Camillus a large annuity. This guaranteed him a steady and substantial income for life. It also set the stage for Camillus's dream of the religious life to come true. Camillus left his administrative role at St. James's, and, gathering his closest followers, began to live a life of prayer and service of the sick. He and his companions went out to the ships that had been quarantined and cared for the plague victims. They visited colonies of people with leprosy, and went to the poor shanty-towns where no other doctors would venture. They called themselves the Servants of the Sick.

When a war broke out between the Venetians and the Croatians, Camillus sent his best men to care for the wounded soldiers. This was the first time that there was a medical corps for the battlefield! In 1591, Pope Gregory XIV officially recognized the group as a religious community. Camillus was seen everywhere, accepting new members, encouraging and instructing the older members, and always caring for the sick wherever he was.

His brothers all knew, however, that Camillus himself was in need of medical care. The sore on his foot never healed completely, and there were times when the infection was so bad that he was confined to bed. As he grew older, his health declined in other ways as well. But Camillus never allowed his physical ailments to be an excuse for special treatment. He shared everything with his community, and was always available to give advice and settle the inevitable disagreements. This once reckless and quarrelsome youth had become so patient and gentle that no one feared to approach him.

Soon his community numbered in the hundreds, and the burden of leading them all was clearly too demanding for the ailing Camillus. He knew it was time to step down and turn the duty of authority over to another. In 1607, a new superior was appointed. Camillus was free to serve his beloved sick. In 1613, he attended the general chapter of the community, and after a new superior general was appointed, the two men set out for a tour of all the communities. They went slowly, for Camillus's health had again taken a turn for the worse.

By the time they reached Genoa, he was seriously ill. They stopped for a few weeks of rest, but then Camillus insisted that they continue. At the end of the tour he collapsed, and everyone knew the end had come. At sixty-four, the gentle giant and servant of the sick received his last Communion, gave a final sermon to the brothers gathered around his bed, and passed into eternal life. From heaven he prays and intercedes for everyone who cares for the sick, especially the members of his community, who continue his work even today.

Camillus was good to the sick because in them he served the suffering Christ. We can pray to St. Camillus to help us see Jesus in every person— especially in those who are disabled or suffering in any way.

St. John Berchmans

(1599–1621)

November 26

"If I don't become a saint while I'm young," John Berchmans once remarked, "I'll never become one." This wish to become a saint was a force that motivated him, from childhood, to live a life filled with holiness, hard work, and concern for others.

John was born in Diest, Belgium, in March of 1599, the oldest son of a shoemaker. He was a lively boy, kind and cheerful, always ready to help his many friends settle any differences and keep peace among them. In spite of his high spirits, he was very religious, and could often be found off in a corner, praying the Rosary. By the time he was seven, he was getting up early every morning and hurrying off to serve two or three Masses in the parish church of Notre Dame. When he returned home, he did what he could to help his mother with the younger children before leaving for school.

When John was nine, his mother became ill. As the oldest of the five children, John took care of her, leaving her bedside only to attend school and to run errands. He was very patient and considerate toward his mother, whom he loved very much.

The following year, John went to live at the rectory of his parish church, Notre Dame. For three years he studied Latin and other subjects under the guidance of Father Emmerich. The priest and his student often went on walks together to visit some of the religious shrines in the area. On one of these pilgrimages, John was unusually quiet and thoughtful.

"Father," he began, "I've been thinking...more and more, I feel that God is calling me to be a priest. What do you think? Is this a dream that could come true? Could I really become a priest someday?"

Father Emmerich's heart soared. This was exactly what he'd been hoping for. If only John's father would agree!

"I think it's a fine idea," Father Emmerich said. "But you have years of study ahead of you. Keep working hard, pray to God for guidance, and we'll see how your family feels about the idea."

But that Sunday, when John approached his father, the reply wasn't encouraging.

"John, I know this will disappoint you," Mr. Berchmans slowly replied. "But you're going to have to stop studying and begin learning a trade. What about making shoes, as I do, or maybe tailoring? I'll need your help in supporting the family, especially since your mother has been so sick."

What a blow this was to poor John! "But, Father," he protested, "If I have to stop studying, I'll never become a priest. Isn't there any other way?"

Kindhearted Mr. Berchmans felt the boy's disappointment. "Let me speak to Father Emmerich, and we'll see if we can come up with something," he said.

At last a solution was found. Canon Froymont, a priest at the Cathedral of Mechlin, was looking for a servant. He agreed that John could live with him as a servant while studying at the archdiocesan junior seminary.

It was a great day for John! "Thank you, Lord," he prayed that night. "And please bless my family, who are making such sacrifices so that I can prepare to become a priest."

At the age of thirteen, John went off to Mechlin to become a servant to Canon Froymont. He performed all his duties with a quiet efficiency and cheerfulness that made him well-liked by all. When the canon went duck hunting, John went with him. Patient as always, the boy set about training the priest's dog to retrieve the ducks. He also spent long, happy hours at his studies. More and more, he felt sure that God was leading him down the path to the priesthood.

~~~~~~~~~~~~~~

Three years later, in 1615, the Jesuit Fathers opened a college in Mechlin, and John enrolled there at once. A year later, he was pleading with his father to let him enter the Society of Jesus. Neither his father nor Canon Froymont was very enthusiastic about the idea. "We need parish priests," argued the canon. "With the Jesuits, you'll study for years, and then probably go off to the missions. Why not stay here in Belgium?"

John didn't want to displease his father or the canon, but in his heart, he knew that this was God's will for him. Finally his father gave his consent. John was overjoyed! At the age of seventeen, he was accepted as a Jesuit postulant, and within a few months he began his novitiate. His happiness was broken only by the death of his beloved mother a few weeks afterward. Later, his father entered a diocesan seminary. He, too, had decided to become a priest!

As a novice, John lived much the same way as he had before, with Mass and meditation every morning, long hours of study, and assigned chores. One phrase he wrote often in his personal notebook was, "Give great importance to little things." John had quickly realized the importance of doing each task, even the smallest, well. He was especially careful to make every conversation with his brother Jesuits holy—by being cheerful, honest, and thoughtful. He was one of the most popular young men in the novitiate.

Two years passed quickly. In April, 1618, John's father was ordained as a priest. Later that year, on September 25, it was time for John to make his first profession as a Jesuit. He took his vows, and was sent to Antwerp to study philosophy. After only three weeks, the Jesuits decided that it would be best for him to move to Rome to continue studying. Before John could return to Mechlin to say good-bye, his father unexpectedly died.

Soon after John arrived in Rome, his teachers realized what a brilliant student he was. He was able to carry several difficult subjects at the same time.

More importantly, John always tried to grow in holiness. Father Massucci, the spiritual director for the senior students, wrote: "After Blessed Aloysius Gonzaga, with whom I lived in the Roman College during the last year of his life, I have never known a young man of more exemplary life, of purer conscience, or of greater perfection than John."

In May, 1621, John was in his third year of study in philosophy and ready to take his final exams.

Although the exams were very difficult, John passed easily. His teachers were so impressed that, that summer, they chose him to take part in a public debate on the Catholic faith. Only the most learned and skilled debaters were allowed to participate. Many people would come to watch and listen, and the debaters had to be prepared to speak on many different topics. John didn't have time for even a short vacation before he began studying for the debate. Even though that summer was unusually hot, he stayed in Rome and worked hard to get ready.

August 6, the date of the debate, was very hot and humid. John hadn't been feeling well for several days, but he hadn't mentioned it. *I'm sure I'll be able to participate in the debate and then take a few weeks to rest in one of the Jesuits' country houses,* he thought. The debate went well, and everyone agreed that John Berchmans was one of the most brilliant young men they had heard in many years. But the next

Soon after John arrived in Rome, his teachers realized how brilliant he was.

afternoon, before he could even leave for the country, John became gravely ill.

Somewhat embarrassed by his sickness, the young man tried to joke with the priests who were attending him. But the doctors weren't laughing; John's illness was serious. They didn't know what was causing the fever and pain. Within a week he had become very weak, and even though he remained cheerful, John knew that he was dying. The doctors had no more ideas, and the best they could do was to try to keep the fever down and make him as comfortable as possible.

On August 11, Father Cornelius Lapide (a famous Jesuit biblical scholar) asked John if he had anything to confess. They both knew that the end was very near. In Latin, John answered peacefully, *"Nihil omnio."* (Nothing at all.) The Jesuit community came to his room in procession, bringing the Holy Eucharist to their dying brother. John spent his final night in prayer, and on the morning of August 13, he quietly went to God. John Berchmans had indeed died young, and he would be named a saint, as he had hoped. He is the patron saint of altar servers.

One of the beautiful things about John Berchmans was his cheerfulness. Whether he was at home taking care of his mother, or in the novitiate doing chores or studying, he was always kind and pleasant. His strongest desire was to be a saint—to be like Jesus—and his one goal was to be a priest. With John Berchmans, we can pray, "Jesus, help me to be holy. Help me to be a saint."

St. Martín de Porres

(1579–1639)

November 3

Young Martin de Porres skipped up the stone steps of the Cathedral of Lima and slipped into the cool, dark sanctuary. There, where no one could see him, he gazed up at Jesus on the crucifix. "O Jesus," he whispered, "the beggar looked so happy when I gave him the bread and fruit. He was so thin. Please help Mother not to be angry with me. I know you won't let us go hungry."

Martin had felt dizzy with joy when he gave the food to the beggar. He still felt happy as he knelt in the church. But as he walked out of the church into the hot, busy street of Lima, his stomach felt slightly knotted. Understandably, his mother was never pleased when he came home from the market with empty hands.

Martin darted through the crowded streets until he reached the small dwelling on the outskirts of Lima where he lived with his mother and his little sister,

Juana. He quietly slipped through the narrow door. His mother was cooking dinner. He paused for a moment to listen to her sweet, low voice as she sang to herself. How he loved her!

But now, his mother saw him and her voice became angry. "Martin, where is the bread? You know how hard I work to feed you and your sister. Have you given away our food again?"

"But, Mama, didn't you explain to me last night that Jesus said, 'Whatever you do to the least brother you do to me'? How could I walk by and not give the beggar what I had?"

Ana Velasquez sighed, then smiled. Looking into her son's sensitive young face, she thought of his father, the Spanish nobleman Don Juan de Porres. She, a poor woman of color, had given birth to his two children, Martin and Juana. Don Juan had left Ana to raise the children on her own. He had felt that she would never be accepted by his Spanish family and friends. The pain of rejection was softened only by Ana's deep conviction that in the eyes of God all people are brothers and sisters. If Martin was overly generous, it was because she had so often taught him about Jesus, who was so kind to the poor.

No, Ana couldn't remain angry. Besides, she had good news for her young son.

"Sit down, Martin. I have something to tell you— something more important than the bread and fruit you've given away."

Martin sat on a short wooden stool. "What is it, Mama?"

"It's your father, Martin. He's come back to Lima, and he'll be coming to visit us tomorrow. He has something important to tell us."

The next day, Ana, Martin, and Juana were waiting for Don Juan. It had been so long since the children had seen their father! What was in store for them?

"Martin, Juana, I've decided that it's time for the two of you to join me in Ecuador. Both of you will live with me, meet your cousins, and get some schooling. Your mother will be a housekeeper for a woman here in Lima."

~~~~~~~~~~~~

Several years passed. Martin and Juana were happy living with their father in Ecuador. Then something unexpected happened: Don Juan was appointed governor of Panama, and he couldn't take the children with him. He decided that Juana would remain in Ecuador with his family and Martin would return to Lima to live with Ana. "You'll soon be a man, Martin," Don Juan said, "and it's time to begin thinking about the kind of work you'd like to do."

Later that year, Martin was happily settled back in Lima. Life was much easier now, because they had financial help from his father. One day, his mother had some news for him. "Señor Rivero, the barber on Calle de Fuentes, stopped by this afternoon. He heard how well you did in school last year and he wants you as his apprentice. Imagine, Martin, he's going to pay for your help while you learn from him!"

In the sixteenth century, barbers did much more than cut hair and trim beards. The local barber was expected to know the remedies for fevers and other sicknesses. His shop was full of the herbs and powders that were used as medicines. He was able to drain infected wounds and even to pull teeth. His gentle hands were expected to set broken bones and ease pain. A barber's work was important indeed!

Twelve-year-old Martin's first duty was to learn the names and uses of the medicines. Carefully, he dusted the shelves of bottles that lined the walls of the shop.

Señor Rivero taught him to recognize the valuable herbs and leaves of the Peruvian countryside. As the boy gathered them and spread them out to dry, he dreamed of the day when he would be able to treat the sick and injured himself. As his mother had taught him, Martin tried to see the wounded and suffering Christ in everyone: "'Truly I tell you, just as you did it to one of the least of these who are members of my family, you did it to me'" (Mt 25:40).

Dr. Rivero was pleased with his young apprentice. Martin learned quickly. His long fingers were steady and firm. After a year or so, the doctor started leaving Martin to tend the shop while he went to visit the sick in the hospital or in their homes.

One afternoon Martin was preparing a batch of herbs when screams and shouting broke his quiet thoughts. A fight! This happened often between the Peruvian Indians, the black slaves, and the proud Spanish.

Suddenly the shop door burst open and angry Spaniards dragged in a wounded and bleeding Indian. "Where's the doctor! Boy, quick, call the doctor! This Indian can't die or I'll be charged with murder!"

The panicky Spaniard roughly shoved Martin aside and ran through the shop looking for Señor Rivero. The other men yelled at Martin to get out of the way. After all, what could this black youth do for a dying man? But Martin was already heating water to clean the wounds as he ripped up strips of clean cloth for bandages and pulled bottles of medicine from the shelf.

The wounded man relaxed under Martin's care. The other men began to calm down. In a few moments they were watching in awe. The relieved attacker, a rough Spanish soldier with a fiery temper, was grateful that his victim wouldn't die. He tried to slip some gold pieces into Martin's hand, but Martin wouldn't accept them.

"No," he said, "I've done nothing for you and I don't need your gold. You should give it to this Indian, whose children will go hungry while his wounds are healing and he can't work."

Ashamed, the soldier tossed the coins into the Indian's lap and fled the shop.

Word of Martin's skill and generosity spread throughout Lima. Señor Rivero was pleased when people came and asked Martin to care for them. After all, he was growing old, and another doctor was badly needed in this rough section of the city...why not Martin?

~~~~~~~~~~~

Martin's reputation as a holy and skillful doctor was spreading throughout the city. It was very difficult for a black man to earn a living in Lima; most blacks were slaves. But Martin had been born free. He could easily earn a good living by practicing medicine. Everyone came to him: the poor and abused Peruvian Indians; the despised and often mistreated African slaves; the Spaniards who had conquered this vast land of the Incas. To Martin, the color of a person's skin made no difference. He was firmly convinced that all people were created in God's image and that Jesus Christ had suffered and died for all.

By the time Martin was seventeen, however, he knew that he would not be taking Señor Rivero's place. Instead, Martin felt certain that God was inviting him to become a Dominican lay helper. After saying good-bye to his friends and making sure that his patients would be cared for, Martin packed his few clothes and set out for the Dominican Priory of the Holy Rosary.

Father Juan de Laranzana sighed. He had heard of the young man in front of him: Martin de Porres, son of a poor black woman and of a Spanish nobleman; Martin, the apprentice surgeon of Lima; Martin, who would give away his own meal if a hungry person walked by. Father de Laranzana knew that Martin refused to accept payment from the poor. Most of all, the priest recalled the young man's reputation as a devout and holy person. Yet Martin was not educated beyond basic reading and writing.

Father Juan smoothed the front of his long white habit while he thought about what to say. "Martin," he finally began, "do you know what you are asking? We Dominicans are an order of preachers. We are teachers, Martin. Scholars. What do you hope to accomplish by joining us?"

Martin was not disturbed by the priest's question. Before this meeting, Martin had spent long hours praying and thinking. He wanted to live as much as possible like Jesus, and for this he felt he must choose the most humble work. "Father, you're right," Martin responded. "The Dominicans are great scholars, and I'm barely able to read. You are great preachers, and who would listen to me? But I'm not asking to become a preacher or a scholar. I want only to be a lay helper in this holy priory. A *doñado,* who would work hard, serve the brothers and fathers here, and share in their life of prayer."

Martin's sincerity couldn't be denied. *To accept him seems reasonable enough,* thought Father Juan. "Very well, Martin," the priest said, "you may come to live as a lay helper in our priory."

After weeks of "trying out" this new life, Martin was allowed to wear the long white tunic and black cloak of a Dominican. Father Juan appointed him assistant in the infirmary. Martin was also appointed the community tailor and barber. Brother Martin felt right at home in the priory. It was like a dream come true!

In those days, when a young man entered the priory to become a priest, he received a special haircut called a tonsure. His hair would be cut short all around, and the middle of the head would be shaved. Everyone who saw such a young man would know that he was on his way to becoming a priest.

Brother Martin had great respect for the priesthood. He especially liked to cut hair for the tonsure because it was so symbolic. He was careful to cut the hair very evenly and to make the shaved spot perfectly round. Most of the young men were pleased to have their hair cut so well. They were proud to have everyone know that they were on their way to ordination. But one day a different sort of man came for his tonsure. He was from a very rich, noble family. He wasn't happy about having his carefully groomed head shaved. He had a plan all figured out.

"Listen, Brother," he said boldly. "You don't need to cut my hair quite so short, nor shave it to the skin."

"Oh?" replied Brother Martin kindly. "Aren't you coming for the tonsure?"

"Yes, I am," answered the proud young man. "But I'm a Spanish nobleman studying for the priesthood, and you're nothing but a black boy dressed up in Dominican robes. Therefore, you must cut my hair as I say."

The other young men expected Brother Martin to become angry at the unjust remark. Instead, Brother Martin said nothing. He simply motioned for the man to be seated, and then preceded to cut his hair in the usual manner.

When the haircut was over, the young nobleman put his hand on his head. How upset he was! "You stupid boy!" he screamed. "Didn't I tell you how to cut my hair? Why didn't you do as I said?"

Brother Martin waited a minute, then calmly said, "My friend, look at the robe we wear. It is made of white and black cloth. Both colors contribute to the Dominican habit. And if you are pleased to wear the Dominican robes, should you not be pleased to have your hair cut in the Dominican style?"

The other young men in the room clapped and cheered. Brother Martin's humility and common sense had won their respect.

Soon Brother Martin became a wise friend to many of the seminarians and novices who came to confide their hopes and fears to him. Brother Martin helped many (including the proud young nobleman) to improve their attitudes and to follow God's call with joy.

Brother Martin's wisdom and holiness were not lost on his superiors. Nine years after Brother Martin had become a lay helper, he was invited to become a full member of the Dominican community, a lay brother. Through prayer, Brother Martin came to understand that this was now God's will for him. What a joyous day it was when he made his solemn vows! Brother Martin was well known in Lima, and his many friends were very pleased.

~~~~~~~~~~~

"Brother Martin, we won't have enough food," whispered Brother Sebastian.

"Have we ever run out?" Brother Martin asked.

"Well, no. But we have to feed all the brothers here in the dining hall, plus all the townspeople who are here for food. The pot wasn't even full when we started. Don't you think we should serve each person a little less, so we don't send some away with nothing?"

Brother Martin looked up. There were people lined up outside the door, waiting for their portions of bread and soup. There were old men bent over their walking sticks, young mothers with babies and toddlers, and teenagers. Poverty in Lima seemed to spare no one. Brother Martin thought about Jesus, who had miraculously multiplied loaves and fish to feed a hungry crowd. Quietly, Brother Martin said to his companion, "Tell me, Brother, is anyone here less hungry because we have less food? No. The Lord knows how many people depend on us. Let's serve them generously."

Brother Sebastian talked about that afternoon for years to come. In spite of his fears, there was plenty of food for everyone! There was even some left over for Brother Martin's animal friends, the dogs and cats of the neighborhood.

The next day was Brother Martin's day off. He was grateful for the chance to spend some time with his best friend, Brother Juan Masias. And so Brother Martin set out walking across the city to the Dominican Priory of St. Mary Magdalene.

"Brother Martin!" exclaimed Juan as he saw his friend coming up the priory walk. "I was hoping you would come today. I have the whole day free."

"Yes, Brother Juan. So do I. In fact, I came to propose an idea to you."

Brother Martin looked up. There were people lined up outside the door, waiting for their portions of bread and soup.

"I'd be excited to hear it," Brother Juan said sincerely. "Why don't we go into the orchard to discuss it?"

Once they had found a shady spot, Brother Martin began. His deep brown eyes were gazing across the orchard, but it was obvious that his mind was far away from the pleasant priory yard. "Yesterday we had more people than ever in the food line. And so many children! It seems they have no place to go, no one to care for them."

Brother Juan twisted a blade of grass between his fingers, studying Brother Martin's face as if to find an answer there. Like all big cities, Lima had a large number of abandoned children. The luckier ones became apprentices to craftsmen, or servants in large households. But many faced a hard life of stealing, jail, and hopeless poverty.

"If we don't help these children," Brother Martin said, "I'm afraid for their futures. How will they ever learn that they have a loving Father in heaven?"

"Brother Martin, what can we do? There are so few of us and so many needs. We have too much to do already!"

"I know, Juan," Brother Martin said. "But I've got an idea, and I'm sure it will succeed. We'll need a building and teachers, and maybe some dedicated women who will be able to care for these young ones." As Brother Martin spoke, his face and eyes lit up.

"Martin, you're incredible!" Brother Juan shook his head. "You'll probably have the building ready by the time we go for evening prayers!"

Brother Martin only laughed.

A month later, Brother Juan visited him. "So, Brother, how are the plans coming along?"

Brother Martin smiled as he motioned his friend to a chair. He had good news. "Last Wednesday, I spoke with the archbishop." Brother Martin's eyes glowed with the memory. "Oh, Juan, truly the Lord does hear the cry of the poor."

"Brother Martin, what did you tell the archbishop? What did he say?"

"I told him about the children and about our hopes." Brother Martin stood and put his hands firmly on Juan's shoulders. "And the archbishop said that he knew a good family who would surely contribute enough money to build a house and a school!"

Juan clutched his friend's arms. It was almost too good to be true, but there was still more. Brother Martin continued, "The archbishop will ask some good women to come to care for the children. The school even has a name already: the Orphanage and School of the Holy Cross. It will welcome any homeless or orphaned child who comes to its door."

Together, the two brothers sang a hymn of praise to God. Their dream was on its way to becoming a reality. And, even today, Holy Cross continues to provide a home for the orphaned youngsters of Lima!

~~~~~~~~~~~~

One day, a stranger arrived at the gates of the priory. While visiting with several of the friars there, he happened to see Brother Martin hurrying by on his way to the infirmary. "Why, that was Brother Martin!" cried the stranger. "I haven't seen him for years, not since I was in a Turkish prison in Algeria. He used to come among us slaves to feed us, cure our sicknesses, and give us hope. I owe my life to him. When did he come to Peru?"

"Oh, you must be mistaken," replied one friar. "Brother Martin has never been out of Peru in his life!"

"But that's not true!" exclaimed the stranger. "Whenever we needed him, he was there. He even provided me with money to buy my freedom! I know it was Brother Martin!"

The other friars exchanged glances. One of them smiled. "Brother Martin has received many gifts from God. One of them is called *bilocation,* the ability to be in two places at the same time. This isn't the first time we've heard stories of this remarkable ability. Some even call him 'the Flying Brother' or 'the Miraculous Missionary'! We've heard stories from people who live in China, Japan, Africa—all over the world. There's no doubt that Brother Martin is truly a very holy person!"

In the summer of 1639, the archbishop of Mexico City became seriously ill while visiting Lima. Even though he had the best doctors in Lima available to him, the archbishop asked for Brother Martin to come to him. He was afraid he would die, and he had heard of Brother Martin's fame as a healer. Sure enough, the archbishop was well soon after Brother Martin's visit. The archbishop was so pleased that he invited Brother

Martin to return with him to Mexico to be his personal physician.

Sadly, Brother Martin's superior gave his consent, grateful that the archbishop would not leave with Brother Martin until after the end of the summer. Brother Martin seemed unaffected by this sudden change of plans for his life.

One day while Brother Martin was cleaning the priory, a young priest asked him, "Brother Martin, won't you be glad when you get to the archbishop's palace in Mexico? There you will be well treated and will probably even have servants waiting on you!"

"No, Father. Servants will not wait on me. And as for this work I am doing now, there is nothing I'd rather be doing at this moment than cleaning our beautiful priory."

A few days later the whole community took notice when Brother Martin showed up wearing a crisp new habit. Brother Martin had not worn a new habit since he had entered!

"Surely you must be planning to wear that habit to Mexico soon, Brother Martin," commented the superior.

"No, Father. This is the habit I shall soon be buried in," Brother Martin said simply.

Father Superior was greatly upset by this. He counted on Brother Martin for the work that he did, but even more for his friendship and sound advice.

Later, Brother Martin met a friend who was often sick. "Please pray for me when I die, Brother Martin," the friend said. Brother Martin put his hand on his friend's shoulder and said quietly, "I shall die first. Please pray for me."

Sure enough, within a week Brother Martin was in bed with a fever. He knew that soon he would go to meet the God whom he loved so much. One by one, his friends came to visit the brother who had been their physician and friend for so many years. Each day Brother Martin grew weaker, until one evening the community was called to begin the prayers for the dying. Gathered around his bed in the small room, the entire community sang the Hail, Holy Queen and chanted the Creed. As they neared the end of the Creed, Brother Martin sighed, smiled, and peacefully died.

It seemed that the whole city of Lima came for Brother Martin's funeral. Thousands and thousands of people passed silently by the coffin. From that day forth, in the years that followed, miracle after miracle was reported in Brother Martin's name. Among his own Dominican brothers, and from all over Peru, people recovered from incurable diseases and wounds. From 1639 until today, St. Martin de Porres remains a friend to all who suffer. He is the special patron saint of African Americans. His feast day is November 3.

Martin de Porres is famous for his great charity to all people and also for his gentle love for animals. But Martin is especially known for his love for prayer and his ability to be a good friend. We can be like Martin when we try to accept every person as a son or daughter of God, without distinction or prejudice.

St. Jane Frances de Chantal

(1572–1641)

Holding her infant son in her arms and surrounded by her three young daughters, Jane waved good-bye to her husband and his friends as they rode off. Baron Christopher de Chantal, an officer in the French army, was going out hunting with his good friend, Monsieur d'Aulezy, and some of their neighbors. Jane was smiling as she and her children went back into their large house. How she loved this *château* in Bourbilly, France, with its lovely gardens, stables, and farmlands!

Jane's mother had died when Jane was a small child, and often, as the young woman cared for her own children, she prayed to the Blessed Mother to watch over and guide her from heaven. Little did she realize how much she would need those prayers in a very short while!

Later that day, Jane was joined by her friend Madame d'Aulezy. "What game do you suppose the men will bring back from the hunt, Jane? I hope they'll shoot a deer. Perhaps we should have a dinner party next week, before Christopher has to leave again."

"I think that's a wonderful idea! Let's do it," Jane replied. But as the two friends sat planning the guest list, they heard the sudden clatter of hooves and men's loud voices. Jane hurried to the front door. She cried out as she saw Christopher's body slumped over his horse, which Monsieur d'Aulezy was leading up to the house.

"My God, forgive me! Forgive me!" Monseur d'Aulezy was almost hysterical. The other hunters pushed him aside and carried the bleeding man into the house. By sheer accident, Christopher's best friend had shot him in the leg, badly wounding him. Jane fainted when she saw her husband's ashen face.

"We've sent for the doctor, Jane," one of the men was saying as she revived. "I'm afraid it doesn't look good...."

The year was 1601, and there was little knowledge of how to prevent infection. The doctor did his best to remove the bullet, but within a week, it was clear that Christopher wouldn't survive. A devout Catholic, he gathered his small family around and called for the priest to come and celebrate Mass. He received the sacrament of the Anointing of the Sick, accepting his coming death without bitterness. He forgave his friend over and over, and begged Jane to do the same. But poor Jane was already so overwhelmed with grief that she could barely get up each morning to care for the children. At the funeral, she broke down completely and fainted again.

Four months passed, and Jane remained deeply depressed. She lay in bed and cried day and night. Her young daughters and infant son were left in the housekeeper's care. At last, her father, a wealthy politician from Burgundy, wrote Jane a strong letter. "Consider your love for your children, Jane, and take care of them," he urged, "at least for Christopher's sake." The letter stirred something within her, and little by little the young widow regained her strength.

Although Christopher had left her a large amount of money, the estate belonged to her father-in-law, and the old baron asked Jane and the children to move to Monthelon and live with him. Sadly, Jane packed their belongings and said good-bye to the home she had loved so much.

The baron was almost eighty, and often difficult to live with. The children had to keep very quiet and not disturb him. He had a housekeeper whom he trusted to run the house, so Jane had to obey the woman's unreasonable rules and had little control over her own life. More and more, Jane turned to prayer and to reading the Scriptures to find strength and encouragement. She fasted often, and begged God to send her a spiritual director who would lead her to do God's will.

Then, one Lent, she went to stay with her own father in Dijon, where a famous bishop, Francis de Sales, was preaching. The first time that she saw him and heard him preach, Jane was certain that he was to be her spiritual director. Since Bishop Francis was an old friend of her father's, it was easy enough to arrange a meeting. The bishop was immediately impressed with Jane. Although he could see she was sad, he could also see that she was a brave and generous person who sincerely wanted to do the very best she could for God and for her family. He spoke with her often, and they wrote many letters to each other. Little by little, he encouraged her to spend more time with her friends and family. "It's all right for you to pray and fast," Bishop Francis advised Jane, "but your first duty is to be a good mother, a good daughter, and a good friend."

Under Bishop Francis's direction, Jane felt alive and happy again. But while she had many friends and lots to do, she still loved her times of prayer and meditation. In fact, as she watched her children grow up, she found herself thinking more and more about becoming a nun. Finally she presented the idea to Bishop Francis. As usual, he showed no surprise at what she said, but neither did he encourage her. Instead, he told her, "Jane, this is no small matter you are considering. Let me think about it and pray about it for a while. I'll let you know what I think when I return this spring."

Jane sighed. Bishop Francis would be away for at least four months. But trusting his wisdom and concern for her, she agreed to say nothing to anyone else, but to pray daily for the Lord to guide them. Eagerly she waited for his return, and when spring finally came, so did the bishop. She asked him to come for dinner. After they had eaten, he suggested that they take a walk. "Jane," he began quietly, "I have something to ask you."

Trusting Bishop Francis's wisdom and concern for her, she decided to pray daily for the Lord's guidance.

Jane could only think that he was going to tell her that she should not join the cloister—but she wanted it so much! "What is it, Bishop Francis? I'm prepared to follow your advice."

"I have plans to begin a new community of women in the diocese of Annecy," the bishop went on. "They won't be cloistered, but will be able to go around the city and countryside to help everyone in need. The sisters' model will be Mary, our Blessed Mother, who traveled to visit and assist her cousin Elizabeth, and they will be called the Congregation of the Visitation of Holy Mary." They walked a few steps more in silence. Then the bishop continued, "And I'd like you to be the first member and the guide for those who will join you."

With her head spinning and her heart pounding, Jane could only exclaim, "Yes! Yes!" She had always helped her neighbors in times of need, and often she had thought with sadness that joining the cloister would end that work. But now she could live a life of prayer and community while still helping her neighbors!

At first, Jane's family wasn't happy with her plans. But they began to soften when her oldest daughter announced her engagement to Bishop Francis's younger brother. After all, the holy bishop would be part of the family now! Jane's heart ached as she thought of leaving her other children. She finally decided that her two younger daughters should come with her to Annecy. One would soon be married anyway, and the other had always suffered poor health.

(In fact, she died soon after the move.) Jane was most concerned for her fifteen-year-old son, Celse-Bénigne. Finally she arranged for him to live with her father, whom he loved deeply, and finish his schooling with a tutor. Even so, the day she left home was a very emotional one.

With tears in her eyes, she knelt in front of her elderly father and asked for his blessing. Gently he put his hands on her head and said, "Go with my consent, Jane. I offer you to God, a daughter as dear to me as Isaac was to Abraham. Go where God calls you. I shall be happy, knowing you are in his house. Pray for me."

"Go where God calls you." As the years passed, those words of her father became the strength and guiding force of Jane's life. Other women joined her, and Bishop Francis opened one convent of the Visitation Sisters after another. There were many difficulties. Francis's dream of sisters visiting people in need wasn't understood by other bishops. In the end, the Visitation Sisters didn't have the freedom Bishop Francis had hoped for, but their initial spirit and desire to serve everyone in need continued.

Jane traveled constantly from one house to another, encouraging the sisters here, helping them out of troubles there, praying for them and guiding them. Jane's once rigid ideas had gradually softened. Bishop Francis's advice, "Be humble. Be meek," had had an effect. Mother Jane Frances was known everywhere for her kindness, serenity, and wisdom.

Mother Jane Frances's life was never without its trials and sorrows. Just a year after she received her religious habit, her father died, and she had to return home to settle his affairs. A few years later, in 1622, her beloved friend and spiritual guide, Bishop Francis, also died. In 1627, her son, now a soldier, was killed in battle. Soon afterward, the plague struck France. This deadly disease killed many members of her family and of her religious community. Jane courageously led her sisters in caring for the sick and for the children who were left orphaned.

By 1636, there were over sixty-five communities of Visitation Sisters. In 1641, the Queen of France invited Jane to Paris to open yet another community, which she gladly did. But on her way back to Annecy, Mother Jane Frances de Chantal died. All of France mourned the woman whom so many had come to know through the good works and prayers of the Visitation Sisters. In 1767, Jane Frances was canonized a saint.

From the time that her mother died when Jane was a small child, Jane had to face many problems and sorrows. Even though she must have often felt like giving up, she kept trying to do her best in the situations in which she found herself. As a wife, as a widow, as a mother, and as a foundress of a religious community, St. Jane Frances de Chantal never stopped loving God, believing in his love for her, and sharing that love with others. We can imitate her by praying for God's help whenever we feel like giving up in a difficult situation.

St. Isaac Jogues   St. René Goupil

(1607–1646)   (1606–1642)

OCTOBER 19   OCTOBER 19

In the mid-seventeenth century, several Jesuit missionaries from France settled among the people of the Huron nation in what was called New France, now southeastern Canada. They lived with the Hurons, learning their language, eating their food, and sharing their lives of hunting and fishing. Why did the missionaries do this? They wanted to carry out the command of Jesus to his disciples: "Go into all the world and proclaim the good news to the whole creation" (Mk 16:15-16).

One of these missionaries was Father Isaac Jogues. He arrived in the New France settlement of Ihonatiria in 1636, and was readily accepted by the Hurons. The Hurons gave him the name Ondessonk, which means "bird of prey" (like an eagle or hawk). He became one of their favorite blackrobes. (The Hurons called all priests "blackrobes" because of the long black cassocks they usually wore.) In 1639, after an outbreak of smallpox, Ihonatiria was abandoned, and the Jesuits built a new mission settlement called Sainte Marie.

In the summer of 1642, Father Jogues was chosen to lead a trading expedition back downriver to Three Rivers and Quebec to obtain supplies for the long winter ahead. A group of Huron Christians under the command of their fiercest chief, Ahatsistari, went with him. Ahatsistari was a famous warrior who had taken the baptismal name Eustace when he became a Christian. The expedition also included a French layman named William Coûture. William was a *donné*, or volunteer, who had dedicated his life to helping the Jesuits in their North American missions. The trip was a dangerous one, because of the possibility of an attack by the Mohawks, a "nation" of the Iroquois group of Indians. The Mohawks were sworn enemies of the Hurons.

After a month of traveling, the small fleet of canoes reached Three Rivers safely. There they were joined by another *donné,* René Goupil, a French doctor. Together the group continued safely on down the St. Lawrence River to Quebec to pick up the rest of their supplies and medicines.

On August 1, they set off to return to Sainte Marie. More Hurons had asked to join them, and the traveling party now included forty members in twelve canoes. "If we're attacked, brothers," said Father Jogues, "remember always to be faithful to Jesus, the Son of God, who has given his life for you!"

The Hurons nodded in agreement. One by one, they pledged loyalty to their baptismal promises.

With strong, sure strokes, the Hurons guided their canoes through the choppy water. Hour after hour,

Father Isaac Jogues was accepted by the Hurons. They gave him the name Ondessonk, which means "bird of prey," and considered him one of their favorite blackrobes.

they paddled steadily upstream. By nightfall they had covered almost thirty miles.

"Brothers," said Eustace, "we must decide what route to follow tomorrow. We could travel in the open waters, safe from ambush, but that way is long, as you know. Or we could pass through the northern channel—a shorter route that holds many dangers."

"We've heard of no bands of Iroquois nearby," said an older brave. "Let us take the channel." Everyone agreed to take the northern route.

In the stillness of dawn, the men gathered about Father Jogues as he led them in prayer. Then they boarded their canoes and slipped cautiously through the reeds until they reached open water. The entrance to the northern channel lay a short distance beyond.

The twelve canoes stroked on into the channel. The waterway was so narrow that they were forced to travel single file. Anxiously the men watched the tree-covered island to their left and the densely forested area to their right. When a stretch of weedy swampland opened up between the channel and the shore, everyone sighed in relief.

Suddenly, war whoops split the air! The swamp came alive with painted bodies. Musket shots rang out. Eustace and his men shrieked, pulled out their bows, and shot arrows at the enemy Iroquois while continuing to paddle fiercely toward them.

Chief Eustace thundered, "Great God, to you alone we look for help!" Father Jogues raised his hand and pronounced words of absolution over his people. Then he turned to a young brave beside him who had been hit by a bullet. He was a catechumen, almost ready for Baptism.

"Do you wish to be baptized now, Atieronhonk?"

"Yes, Ondessonk, before we are captured or killed!"

The priest cupped some water in his hand and poured it over Atieronhonk's head, baptizing him Bernard. Then the canoe rammed into the weedy shore.

Only half of the Huron canoes had come within range of the Iroquois muskets. The others had turned around swiftly and escaped downriver to safety. Eustace was left with about fifteen braves, plus René and William, to face thirty Iroquois. The Iroquois had retreated to the forest's edge, while the Hurons crept toward them through the swamp grass.

Another blood-curdling shriek split the air—this time from the river! Eustace turned. Eight canoes of screaming Iroquois were bearing down on them! The Hurons were now completely surrounded.

Soon the men were engaged in hand-to-hand combat—about five Iroquois to each Huron. One by one the Hurons were captured. The Iroquois roared in triumph at each new victory.

Crouched in the tall river grass on the shore, Father Jogues watched helplessly. As a priest, he was forbidden to join in the battle. Jesus had given his life for the Iroquois just as much as for the Hurons. All the missionary could do was to wait and pray.

If I crept through the grass to that thicket on the right, he thought, *I could run through the forest and escape.*

But how could he abandon the Hurons? The Christians among them were only recently baptized. And among the captives were some who were almost ready to receive the sacrament. Father Jogues rose to his feet and picked his way through the brush back to the Iroquois who were guarding René. The braves stared at him in amazement, waiting for some kind of attack.

"Don't be afraid!" the priest shouted. He stretched out his arms as a sign of surrender. Several Iroquois cautiously approached him—then sprang upon him, kicking him and beating him, tearing off his long cassock. They dragged him over to the other prisoners.

"Don't tie me," Father Jogues told his captors. "I won't try to escape as long as these Hurons remain your prisoners. They are my bonds. I will never abandon them!"

The Iroquois were shocked at his words, but they didn't bind him. Father Jogues approached René. "My brother," he said, "God is our Lord and Master. What he has permitted can only be for our good. So be it."

"Yes, Father," the doctor replied. "God has permitted this. May his holy will be done. I love and cherish God's will with all my heart."

Father Jogues next turned to his Huron friends. "Take courage, brothers. The torments we will suffer now are as nothing compared with the glory to come. God will not let us suffer anything beyond our strength."

He faced the unbaptized catechumens among the Huron captives.

"We are near death, brothers. Do you wish to be baptized in the name of the good God of whom we have spoken so often?"

"Yes, Ondessonk!" they answered, and Father Jogues used drops of water squeezed from his own torn, wet garments to baptize them in the name of the Father, and of the Son, and of the Holy Spirit.

As he finished, shrieks and whoops rang through the forest. A large band of Iroquois appeared, leading Eustace. It was he, the famous Huron chief, whom they had especially wanted to capture in this raid!

The priest hurried to the great chief's side, only to be pushed away by angry Iroquois, who threw Eustace to the ground and tied him up. Without expression, Eustace declared, "Ondessonk, I will remain faithful to God our Father, whether I live or die."

Meanwhile, William Coûture had managed to escape. He ran steadily down a forest trail toward the French settlement. Surely he could make it within a day.

Yes, he could make it. But what about his companions? Could William return to security while they faced torture and death? No, it was better to die with them, he decided. William turned and headed back up the trail. Thus, William, too, was captured. In fact, before William rejoined his companions the Iroquois beat and tortured him. When Father Jogues ran to embrace and bless William, their captors, suspicious of his actions, beat him and René also.

The next day, with twenty Hurons and the three Frenchmen as captives, the seventy Iroquois boarded their canoes and threaded their way through a maze of channels until they reached the main river. Once they were sure that they hadn't been followed, they beached their canoes, held a council, and celebrated their victory.

That night, on a hilltop south of the St. Lawrence River, Father Jogues grieved, not because of the sufferings that he knew were coming, but because almost no leaders remained among the Huron Christians. These men who had been captured would soon have become the first catechists among their people. Now they would suffer and die as Christians—but they would never teach their people about Jesus.

The next day the warriors and their prisoners made their way southward to the land of the Mohawk Iroquois. René Goupil, wounded himself, treated the injuries of his fellow prisoners and even those of the Iroquois. Father Jogues marveled at the doctor's gentle cheerfulness, his submission to God's will, and his eagerness to give up his life for the Lord Jesus.

Years before, when he had been a Jesuit novice, René's poor health had prevented him from making his religious vows. Later he had felt unworthy. Now, however, he asked Father Jogues's permission to make the vows of a Jesuit brother.

Father Jogues gladly gave permission. While traveling in an Iroquois war canoe, René pronounced the vows of consecration he had memorized years before. He and Father Jogues were now spiritual brothers. In the hard days ahead they would strengthen and encourage one another.

On the eighth day after the attack, the travelers met a band of two hundred Iroquois warriors. They greeted the raiding party with shrieks of triumph, then sprang upon the captives, beating and pounding them mercilessly.

"The gauntlet!" urged one brave.

"The gauntlet!" went up the cry.

Each warrior rushed off and returned with a club or thorny rod. They formed two facing rows stretching from the beach to the top of a hill. All the prisoners were lined up. The older Huron men came first, followed by William, more Hurons, René, more braves, and finally Father Jogues.

The first Huron was pushed between the two rows of Iroquois, and began to run up the hill, while stinging blows from the clubs rained down on his head, his back, and his legs. The shrieks grew more savage as one man after another was forced to run between the rows of Iroquois warriors.

Father Jogues watched it all. He knew that the Iroquois were suspicious of the blackrobes. He knew he would suffer the worst torture.

The last Huron was halfway up the hill. Now it was Father Jogues's turn. He stepped forward and began to run between the lines of savage, swinging clubs. He felt pain—stabbing pain, dull pain, pain that sent his head reeling and spinning. Someone tripped him. He tottered to his feet and ran on blindly, only to find his path blocked by another Iroquois, and another, and another. He broke away again and again and stumbled on. Blows and kicks rained upon him. He fell again and knew no more.

When Father Jogues woke up, he found himself near a wooden platform on the hilltop. William and

René were there, too. The Iroquois tried to make him stand, but he sank to the ground. They took blazing sticks and held them against his arms and legs. One seized his hand and cut off his thumb with a sharp knife. Another held a burning coal against his fingers. Father Jogues lost consciousness again.

When he regained his senses, the braves lunged for him. A wiry young figure stepped before them—it was Chief Eustace's young nephew, Paul. "Torture me!" he urged them. "Torture me as cruelly as you like! I will take this man's place."

The Iroquois threw the Frenchmen down from the platform, but instead of attacking Paul, they fell upon Eustace, the Huron chief, slashing him from head to foot, holding blazing torches against the wounds to seal them so that he wouldn't lose too much blood and die right away. True to his people's sense of honor, Eustace never showed how much pain he felt.

"Keep remembering," Father Jogues called out to his friend, "keep remembering that there is a God who sees everything and who will reward everything that we suffer for his sake."

"Ondessonk, I will remain faithful even until death!" the chief shouted back.

At long last, the Iroquois were done for the night. They stumbled sleepily down the hill to their campground, leaving the Frenchmen and Hurons lying bruised and bleeding in the moonlight.

The next day the Iroquois and their prisoners resumed the journey southward. Most of this trip would be overland on foot. The prisoners were forced to trot and carry heavy packs on their backs. Father Jogues and René, worn out from torture and lack of food, couldn't keep up with the group, no matter how hard they tried. They dragged along behind—and talked of escape.

"I must stay with the Huron Christians," the priest told René. "But you could easily escape now that they've relaxed their guard. Perhaps we can persuade William to go with you."

"I won't leave you, Father," replied René. "I'll die with you, if that's God's will!" And so the two remained with their Huron comrades.

They finally arrived at Ossernenon, located where Auriesville, New York, is today. The date, Father Jogues calculated, was August 14—the vigil of the feast of Mary's Assumption into heaven.

"Lord Jesus Christ," he prayed, "I thank you that on the day that the whole world rejoices in the glory of your Mother's Assumption, I may share some part of your sufferings and cross."

Another journey came soon. Another Iroquois village and more torture. Another journey, and still more torture. How long could this go on before they died? It seemed impossible that they would live another day.

Then the Iroquois took Father Jogues and hung him by his arms from the crosspiece of a longhouse. As the weight of this body pulled on his arms more and more, he begged his tormenters to loosen the ropes a little. They tightened them instead. *They acted justly,* he thought. *I thank you, Lord Jesus, for letting me experience how much you suffered for me on the cross, since the whole weight of your most sacred body hung, not from ropes, but from your hands and feet pierced by nails.* Then, as he was about to lose consciousness, a young brave cut him down.

The next day a council was held—and at first it seemed that the Frenchmen would be killed. But many of the braves wished to end the war with the French and urged that the blackrobe and his companions be left alive. At last that group won. It was decided that the Frenchmen would live as slaves among the Iroquois.

And their Huron companions? Three would die, one in each village; the others would become slaves.

That night, Father Jogues and René witnessed the bloody death of Eustace's nephew Paul, who had offered himself to the Iroquois as a victim in place of the priest. Shouting out his hope in a better life to come, Paul died with great courage and faith.

Over the next village some miles distant, the sky glared red. There, another Huron brave was being burned.

And in the farthest village, William watched Eustace die, bearing his tortures with calm courage, telling his Huron friends not to let his death stand in the way of a future peace between them and the Iroquois.

Father Jogues and René were taken as slaves by the Iroquois chief who had captured them. The two Frenchmen were so weak that they couldn't work and could barely drag themselves from place to place. To add to their misery, they were half-starved, and since food was scarce that fall, they were given only a little ground corn and some raw squash each day.

At last the Iroquois realized how sick their prisoners were and started to give them some fish and a few pieces of meat. As soon as the Frenchmen could hobble about again, they were sent into the fields with the women of the village to help harvest corn and vegetables.

Father Jogues knew how to get along well with the Indians, for he had lived among the Hurons for six years. He understood how superstitious they could be, and avoided doing anything that would arouse their rage. He warned René to do likewise. But the doctor, accustomed to openness and sincerity, didn't understand how some of his actions could anger the Iroquois.

But he did anger them. His gestures when he prayed made them think that he was a sorcerer weaving spells against them. His Christian virtues of gentleness and kindness seemed cowardly. The Indians wanted to kill him.

It seems that the Iroquois reasoned this way: If they killed Father Jogues, the French would never agree to peace, for he was a blackrobe. But this other man seemed less important. If he died, so what? A story could be made up to explain his disappearance. To make their deed easier, the Iroquois separated the two Frenchmen, giving Father Jogues to another master.

René didn't guess that the Iroquois were planning to kill him. He would often go out to play with the young Iroquois children. One day he picked up a child of three or four and placed his own cap on the child's head. The little boy laughed. René made the Sign of the Cross over the child's head.

A wild scream came from the boy's grandfather, who had been sitting in the shadows watching. "You have put an evil spell on the child!" he cried. The old man flew at René in a rage, tore the boy away from him, and began to beat and kick the prisoner.

Later the same day, Father Jogues came to the longhouse. He called René out. "Come and pray with me," he invited. They walked through the village and up a lonely hill toward their favorite prayer spot.

"I heard about what happened this morning," the priest began. "Our lives are in danger, especially yours."

"I'm not afraid of death, Father," the doctor replied, "so long as I am in God's grace."

The priest heard René's confession, as he had done every day, and absolved him of his sins. They knelt together and offered the Lord Jesus their lives and their blood, asking him to unite their sacrifice to his own for the salvation of the Iroquois.

On their way back down the hill, they began to pray the Rosary, as was their custom, with Father Jogues leading and René answering. Two braves met them on the trail. One of them was the uncle of the child over whom René had made the Sign of the Cross. "Go back to the village," he growled.

They walked down the slope together, the missionaries saying their Hail Marys softly, the braves stalking behind them.

"You walk ahead," one of Iroquois abruptly commanded Father Jogues. "You stay here," he ordered René. The priest gazed intently at the glaring man, then walked on a few steps. A rustle made him whirl —just in time to see a tomahawk crash down on René's head. "Jesus, Jesus, Jesus!" called the Jesuit brother, as he crumbled to the earth.

The priest rushed to his side. René was still alive. Father Jogues again prayed the words of absolution over his dying friend. Seeing that René was still breathing, the Iroquois struck him a final blow.

Now it's my turn, Father Jogues thought, falling to his knees. He prayed an Act of Contrition as he waited for the braves to tomahawk him.

"Get up," commanded the grim-faced uncle. "I have no power over you. You belong to another family."

A mob from the village soon swarmed to the spot, babbling excitedly. Father Jogues was led away to his longhouse for fear that someone would kill him, too.

René had been so cheerful, so kind, so obedient, and he had just recently made the vows of religious life. Father Jogues was comforted by the thought that René's beautiful soul must have winged its way straight to heaven on that September 29, 1642—the feast of St. Michael the Archangel.

The possibility of death haunted Father Jogues continually, because only a few of the Iroquois wanted to keep him alive in case of a peace treaty with the French. Most suspected him of being in league with evil spirits, and would have killed him the first chance they had. Yet day after day passed, and Father Jogues survived.

If I'm going to live after all, he thought, *I must try to find a way to teach these people about God.* He learned more of their language, and found ways to slip in a word here and there about the Creator of all peoples. After all, hadn't these Iroquois, too, been redeemed by the blood of Jesus?

That fall Father Jogues accompanied a hunting party into the Adirondack Mountains. He helped the women carry the food and gear. During the weeks in the mountains he went into the forest daily to pray in the vast solitude, where no one had ever before spoken the name of Jesus. Peeling the bark from a tree in the form of a cross, the priest interceded for the native people.

But the Iroquois, spying on him continually, blamed the scarcity of elk and deer on his prayers and on the cross. They mocked him and beat him often. This, along with hunger, lack of clothing, the cold November snow, the memory of his past sins, and the fear of torture and death, plunged Father Jogues into the depths of discouragement. Then it seemed that a voice spoke to him, saying, "Serve God from love, not from fear. Don't worry about yourself." Renewed in spirit, the missionary returned to the village with the hunting party.

The Iroquois put him to work taking care of a sick brave—one who had tortured him severely a few months before. The man was dying of a horrible disease that covered him with sores. Father Jogues nursed the sick man for two weeks.

Little by little, his master and his family began to like the priest. They asked him many questions, and eagerly listened to his answers. But as soon as he began to speak about the Christian God, they lost interest.

Father Jogues was more successful among the sick. He visited them daily, as he had once done among the Hurons, and he taught them about eternal life. A few adults agreed to be baptized. He also baptized many infants who were near death.

Father Jogues went among the Huron and Algonquin prisoners in the three Iroquois villages, comforting them and hearing the confessions of the Christians. He warned them against praying openly, because it would make their captors angry. Joseph, one of the prisoners, became accustomed to carrying on an almost continual conversation with God. He was delighted when Father Jogues taught him to pray the Rosary, which from then on he secretly recited.

In his travels, the priest often saw William Coûture, who had been taken by a family in the third village. He was still fervent in his prayers and was doing well, considering the tortures he had gone through.

In March, some children told Father Jogues that they had found René's bones in the ravine. Tenderly, the priest gathered up those precious relics and buried them beneath a pine tree. He prayed over the remains of North America's first martyr.

The sister of Father Jogues's master had grown very fond of the priest. She was a kind old woman who called the Jesuit missionary her "nephew." In May of 1643, she took him with her when she and a band of braves went down to the Dutch settlement to trade skins and furs.

At Rensselaerswyck, also called Fort Orange, Father Jogues met and spoke with the Dutch governor, but he didn't try to escape. He had his new Christians to look after.

On Pentecost, back in his "own" village, he secretly baptized an Algonquin woman prisoner who was about to be burned alive. He managed to do it while pretending to give her a drink of water.

A few days later new prisoners arrived—Huron Christians and a Frenchman. Fortunately, they had not been tortured, but the priest's heart sank to see so many of "his" people captive and in exile. A few days later, in the neighboring villages, the Iroquois killed a hundred Huron prisoners. Father Jogues's grief knew no bounds.

That summer the Iroquois continuously attacked the French, Hurons, and Algonquins along the St. Lawrence River. One of the war parties took two captive Hurons with them to carry baggage. These managed to slip away and hurried to tell the French about René, William, and Father Jogues.

Meanwhile, Father Jogues was paddling his master's canoe down the rivers south of the Catskill mountains. One day he met a very sick young man who called him by name. "Ondessonk, do you remember the man who cut your bonds when you were at the end of your strength?"

The priest thought back to that terrible night he had been suspended from the wooden beams. "Yes, I remember very well," he replied. "I owe a lot to that man. I've never been able to thank him. Do you know him?"

"It was I who did it. I took pity on you and loosened the bonds."

The priest embraced him. "I have often prayed for you," he said. "And now I have a gift for you." He told the dying man about the reward of eternal life and what he must believe to attain it. After he had spoken, the man asked for Baptism. He died just a few hours later.

Then began the 200-mile journey back to the Iroquois villages. Father Jogues could hardly wait to get there. In his year among the Iroquois he had baptized seventy children and adults belonging to five different tribes, and he was content to remain among them as long as God should be pleased to keep him there.

"Nephew," the old chief's sister said to Father Jogues almost as soon as he had come home, "prepare to go fishing with the braves and me in the great river below the Dutch settlement."

So Father Jogues was off again. He and his companions stopped at Rensselaerswyck for about a week. During this time he wrote a letter telling about René's martyrdom and his own sufferings and labors among the Iroquois. He addressed it to his superior in France. The Dutch promised to send the letter with the first ship sailing to Europe.

A few weeks later, Father Jogues came to Rensselaerswyck again on his return trip from the fishing area. An angry band of Iroquois braves met him there.

What had happened? Before leaving on the fishing trip, Father Jogues had sent a note to the French fort on the St. Lawrence warning the settlers of a future Iroquois attack. An Iroquois chief had delivered the message, not knowing what it was about. When the men at the fort read the warning, they immediately began firing at the Iroquois.

"You have betrayed us!" the Iroquois screamed upon seeing Father Jogues. "You shall die!"

The Dutch governor urged Father Jogues to escape on a ship bound for France. The priest hesitated, then said he would pray about it. Lying awake that night, he thought the matter through. Now that he knew the Iroquois so well, it seemed he would be more valuable to the missions alive than dead. He could escape to Europe, return later to New France, and eventually go back to the Iroquois people when the heat of their anger had cooled.

After a hair-raising escape, Father Jogues spent over a month lying on hard planks in a hot Rensselaerswyck attic while his leg swelled with infection from a dog bite. At last he was smuggled on board a ship going down the Hudson River. He was on his way to France!

~~~~~~~~~~~~~~~

It was Christmas morning, 1643, when Father Jogues set foot on French soil. His heart pounded with joy as he headed for the nearest church. For the first time in seventeen months he made his confession and received Holy Communion. A few days later, tattered and worn, he presented himself at the Jesuit house in Rennes. What joy flooded the members of the community as they gathered around their brother, who had suffered so much for Jesus! They gasped at the sight of his scarred and twisted hands and the thinness of his once powerful body. They shuddered when he related the tortures, and rejoiced when he told them of René's courageous martyrdom and the seventy baptisms.

But Father Jogues had only three things on his mind. First he visited his mother. Then he wrote to Pope Urban VIII and requested permission to celebrate Mass, even though his injured hands could no longer hold the host exactly the way priests were supposed to hold it in those days. The Holy Father quickly granted this permission. He wrote to Father Jogues, "It would be a shame if a martyr of Christ were not allowed to drink the Blood of Christ." Then Father Jogues requested permission from his superiors to leave once again for the missions of New France.

In the spring of 1644, a small ship left France and made its way across the Atlantic, battling storms and bad weather all the way. Before it reached the St. Lawrence River, every passenger on board had made his confession to Father Jogues.

How happy the missionary was to see the wooded shores of his beloved New France! Through the trees, here and there, he glimpsed the dwellings of the Algonquins. He was home among "his people" again!

At Quebec, his fellow Jesuits greeted him with open arms. They were overjoyed to find him alive and well. Their own news was not so happy, though. The Iroquois were still raiding the Hurons and Algonquins, destroying both Indian nations little by little.

Father Jogues's superior assigned him to Montreal, where a fervent Christian community lived. He spent the winter there.

The following spring, a peace council was held between the French and the Iroquois, and some prisoners of the Iroquois were released. A temporary peace treaty was made. It was renewed the following fall. But the French were uneasy. They felt they couldn't trust the Iroquois.

"Eat a little meat," his companions often urged Father Jogues during the long winter months at Montreal.

"No, thank you," was the reply. "When I go back among the Iroquois I don't want my thoughts to keep turning to the pleasures and comforts of this place."

His one desire was to return to the Iroquois—to the same people who had captured, tortured, and enslaved him.

His chance came in midwinter, when Iroquois ambassadors returned to renew the peace treaty. They told Father Jogues that they would be happy to have him live among them; his "aunt's" longhouse was waiting. Father Jogues asked his superior to allow him to go.

And so that May he returned to the Iroquois country as an ambassador of the French governor, accompanied by a surveyor named John Bourdon. He went joyfully, because this was what he had hoped to do. Yet to his superior he admitted, "My poor body trembles when I remember everything that has gone before. But our Lord, in his goodness, calmed me, and will calm me still more. Father, I desire what our Lord desires. How I would regret it if I lost such a wonderful opportunity. I wouldn't want to be responsible if some souls didn't hear the Gospel preached!"

Most of the Iroquois were happy to see Father Jogues again, especially because he was as kind and friendly as ever. The Turtle Clan and the Wolf Clan (to which Father Jogues's "aunt" belonged) welcomed him eagerly. But the warlike Bear Clan listened grimfaced to the peace pledges between the Frenchmen and their tribesmen.

After the peace councils, Father Jogues found time to instruct several sick people and to baptize them and a few dying infants. He also reassured the Iroquois about a locked black box he had left in his "aunt's" longhouse three years before. The box contained his vestments and other items used at Mass, but the Iroquois suspected that it held a demon. Father Jogues smiled, showing the native people how to open the chest with the key. He even let the braves examine all its contents. At last they seemed convinced that the box was harmless. "We will keep the black box here, Ondessonk, until your return," they promised.

The peace mission having been completed, Father Jogues and John Bourdon traveled the long route back to Montreal, where they made their report to the French governor.

The following fall, Father Jogues and a young *donné* named John de la Lande set out for the Iroquois country to spend the winter. With one Huron as their companion, they paddled the long, lonely river route through the still forests. Eventually, they left the lakes and rivers behind, and set out through the mountains on foot. It was a route that Father Jogues knew well by this time. After several days they drew near to Ossernenon.

Suddenly, they saw a band of Iroquois coming up the trail toward them. The priest called to them, only to see them disappear into the brush. A moment later, furious shrieks pierced the air, and painted warriors leaped out of the forest and seized the missionaries, dragging them down the trail to the village.

A great mob bore down on them. Father Jogues could see that the Bear and Wolf Clans were fighting among themselves. Some of the Wolves grabbed the missionaries and rushed them to the safety of his "aunt's" longhouse.

Why had the Iroquois had this sudden change of heart?

"Two tragedies came to us this summer," explained his "aunt." "A terrible sickness swept through the villages, killing many, and the corn crop was destroyed by worms. These evils were blamed on your black box, Ondessonk." The Bear Clan had aroused the people to take the warpath against the Algonquins,

Hurons, and French. It was one of the war parties that had met Father Jogues and John on the trail.

All night long the Wolves and Bears argued over what to do with the blackrobe and his young companion. The next day, the warriors left to hold council in another village, leaving the Frenchmen free until an agreement concerning their fate was reached.

At sundown Father Jogues went with a young Wolf brave to have supper in a Bear longhouse. He had received an invitation, and he dared not refuse.

As the priest stooped to enter the low doorway, his young Wolf friend sensed danger, but it was too late. A tomahawk suddenly swung out from behind the doorpost, and Father Jogues fell to the ground. The Bear braves began to celebrate. They had finally killed Ondessonk, the great sorcerer! Now they would be free of evil spirits.

The sad news quickly reached his "aunt's" longhouse, where Wolf braves continued to guard young John de la Lande. They warned John not to go outside because it was too dangerous. As the hours ticked by and all fell silent, the braves fell asleep around the fire. John felt a burning desire to find and bury Father Jogues's body. He crept silently out of the longhouse, never noticing the warriors waiting in the darkness. A tomahawk felled him before he could cry out.

The next day, a messenger arrived with the decision of the Iroquois council: the French prisoners were to be set free. Sadly, the news had come too late to prevent the tragic deaths of Father Jogues and John de la Lande.

Within a year after Father Jogues's death, the Iroquois had again taken the warpath, slaughtering many Hurons and Algonquins. In 1648 and 1649 they killed five more Jesuit priests—John de Brebeuf, Anthony Daniel, Charles Garnier, Noel Chabanel, and Gabriel Lalement. God, nonetheless, poured an abundance of graces upon the Iroquois people. Many of them were soon converted, and a few years later, the Mohawks had a young maiden of their own on the path to sainthood—Kateri Tekakwitha.

Father Jogues grew to love the Iroquois. He worked to spread faith in Jesus Christ among them, as he had done among the Hurons. A good way to show love for God and to do his will is to try our best in whatever circumstances we find ourselves, and to want to love others just as Jesus loves us.

Bl. Kateri Tekakwitha

(1656–1680)

July 14

Bright Star leaned back against a birch tree and looked up at the blue sky. It was so peaceful here at the edge of the forest. *Can the talk of war with the Iroquois really be true?* she wondered.

Suddenly she heard the distant sound of drums. But not just any drums—war drums!

I must hide and pray for my people, the young woman thought. *May the great God save us from the warriors of the Mohawk Nation!* Swiftly and silently, Bright Star disappeared into the dense forest.

Night fell. The young Algonquin woman was alone on her knees in the cool darkness. "O God, don't let my people be destroyed," she begged. "We have only you to help us. Only you."

The last star was fading when Bright Star heard a wild, triumphant cry behind her. It was an Iroquois warrior!

She began to run—but it was too late. Another Iroquois jumped from the bushes and grabbed her by the wrists. "We'll bring you to our village as a slave!" he cried.

"Wait!" ordered the first warrior. "I am chief of the Turtle Clan. I will decide!"

The brave relaxed his grip and waited.

The chief looked at Bright Star. Never had he seen a more beautiful young woman. "This woman has found favor in Great Turtle's eyes. She will be my wife. I have spoken."

Bright Star followed Great Turtle. Her journey would be long and hard. "Jesus," she whispered, "be with me and protect me."

Great Turtle took Bright Star to live with him in the Valley of the Mohawks. Although she was an Algonquin, her captors didn't treat her harshly. She was a kind person and a hard worker, and everyone came to love her. Great Turtle took her as his wife, and soon they were blessed with a beautiful baby girl.

For a moment, Great Turtle forgot all about his many worries, his war councils, and his tribal meetings. He proudly held the infant in his arms and asked, "My wife, what shall we name our little one?"

Bright Star wanted to give her child a Christian name, but she didn't dare ask Great Turtle. He wasn't a Christian, and he didn't understand her religion.

"Let's call her Tekakwitha," she said.

"Good!" agreed Great Turtle. "Tekakwitha means 'she who moves everything that is before her.' Yes, that is a good name." He gently placed the sleeping child in her mother's arms. "I will return soon," he promised as he headed out the door of the lodge.

Bright Star's eyes filled with tears. "Someday," she said softly, "someday I will have the blackrobes pour the water of life on you, my little one. Then you, too, will be a child of God."

"Hush! You must be careful what you say," warned Anastasia, an old Christian woman who was Bright Star's friend. "If you are not careful, you will anger the tribal council. Then all of us Christians could be punished."

"You're right, Anastasia," said Bright Star. "But I will still try to make Great Turtle understand the Christian religion and love Jesus. My husband must become a Christian, too!" The young woman kissed her child and laid her on a mat. "The blackrobes are far from here," she said to Anastasia, "but I'll do my best to teach Tekakwitha about Jesus and his Mother Mary."

"You do well, but be careful, for her uncle and her aunt are not Christians either. In fact, they hate the blackrobes."

"I know. Will you promise to take care of Tekakwitha if anything should happen to me?"

"Yes," Anastasia replied. "I promise."

~~~~~~~~~~~~

Almost every night, when the stars were twinkling in the sky, Bright Star crept out of her lodge and knelt in prayer. She had never given up hope that Great Turtle and Tekakwitha would be baptized. The following year, she was praying also for the baptism of her new baby son!

With two children to care for, Bright Star's life was busy and happy. Soon little Tekakwitha was following her everywhere, full of curiosity and always asking questions. She loved to hear stories, especially about Jesus, his Mother, and the saints.

One morning, while Tekakwitha was playing in the forest, she heard a heavy rolling of drums.

"What does that mean?" she asked out loud.

Soon the sound came through the trees again. It was a strange new way of beating the drums. Tekakwitha was frightened.

"Mama!" she cried as she ran toward the lodge.

Bright Star came out and the child threw herself into her mother's protecting arms.

"Why are they beating the drums like that?" asked Tekakwitha.

Bright Star shook her head sadly. "My little one, a terrible sickness has come to our tribe. Many of our people have already died from it. The white man calls it smallpox. When it comes, it usually kills."

"But Father is a great chief and warrior," Tekakwitha answered proudly. "He will fight and conquer this sickness."

"My little one, it is not in his power to do so. Only God can help us. We must pray."

As she was speaking, Bright Star closed her eyes. She hadn't felt well all morning. If only she could rest, perhaps this sick feeling would go away...her head was swimming.

"Mama!" cried Tekakwitha. "What's wrong?"

But Bright Star could no longer hear. She slumped to the ground, hot and feverish.

Anastasia came running as soon as she heard Tekakwitha scream. She tried to help Bright Star, but she could do nothing for her. The good woman ran to check on Tekakwitha's little brother. He lay so still on his mat—too still.

~~~~~~~~~~~~

"Don't cry, Tekakwitha," Anastasia soothed. "You're the daughter of a great chief. You must rest so you can fully recover from this terrible illness that has taken your family and left you weak and scarred."

"Yes," Tekakwitha quietly answered. "But I miss my mother, my father, and my little brother!"

"I miss them, too, Tekakwitha. But they're in heaven with Jesus. And someday we'll join them there!"

"Anastasia," begged Tekakwitha, "why can't I live with you?"

"My little one, your uncle, Thunder Cloud, is now the chief of the Turtle Clan," answered the older woman. "He has the right to take you as his daughter. He loves you. You'll be treated well."

"But my aunt doesn't smile. She certainly doesn't like me," said Tekakwitha sadly. "I wish I didn't have to go. I'll never become a Christian now."

Anastasia wrapped her arms around the girl. "Don't worry," she replied. "Someday you'll become a Christian, and you'll help others become Christians, too."

Her uncle, Thunder Cloud, was fond of Tekakwitha and treated her well, but her aunt, Light Feet, disliked her and was jealous of the attention that her husband gave the girl. Yet Light Feet never dared hurt Tekakwitha, knowing how angry that would make her husband.

~~~~~~~~~~~~~~~

Time passed. Tekakwitha was now eleven years old. All the girls in the Mohawk village worked hard, hoeing and harvesting the crops of corn, squash, and beans, doing weaving and beadwork, and collecting firewood and water. Light Feet made her frail niece work harder than all the rest. Tekakwitha never complained, but she was often exhausted. Because of the smallpox she had survived as a child, she was small for her age, and her face was scarred with pockmarks. The disease had also left her with poor eyesight. The sunlight hurt her eyes, and she tried to stay inside the lodge or in the dark forest as much as possible.

One day, as Tekakwitha sat weaving a new mat, Anastasia arrived at the lodge to visit her. The older woman seemed excited. *What good news can she have?* Tekakwitha wondered.

"Tekakwitha!" Anastasia exclaimed, "the blackrobes are here! I heard them speaking with your uncle. They'll be staying here at the lodge for three days. Your good mother's prayers have been answered. Perhaps you can be baptized now."

"That would be wonderful!" the girl responded. "I want so much to become a child of God."

One day, Anastasia came to visit Kateri. The older woman brought exciting news!

"Tekakwitha!" called Light Feet sharply. "Come and help me prepare the meal. But remember—you are not to speak to the blackrobes."

Once the food was ready, Tekakwitha went out to draw some water. On her return she saw the three blackrobes—Jesuit missionaries who had come to speak to the Mohawk chiefs about a peace treaty with the French.

After the meal, as Tekakwitha was clearing away the dishes, one of the missionaries came up to her. "Are you Tekakwitha?" he kindly asked.

"Yes," she answered in surprise.

"I am Father Pirron. Tell me, do you love God as much as Anastasia said you do?"

Tekakwitha's face reddened. "Yes. I do love him and his Mother, Mary. I would be so happy to learn more about them."

"Well, pray to Jesus and Mary, and try to always be good and patient with everyone," the priest advised her. "You'll be happy soon."

But Tekakwitha would have to wait many years until she could be baptized.

~~~~~~~~~~~~~~

"Tekakwitha, come quickly!" Light Feet called. "We must dress well. We will have guests share our table tonight." Soon all was ready, and a group of Mohawks arrived. The men sat together and talked and smoked. The women, too, were busy talking.

Once the men stopped smoking, Thunder Cloud motioned to Light Feet. She got up and handed a bowl of cornmeal porridge to Tekakwitha. A brave sitting next to Tekakwitha extended his hands to accept the bowl from her. Tekakwitha understood. By this action they would be married!

Tekakwitha felt trapped. She wanted to belong only to God. Throwing down the bowl, she ran from the lodge. Her uncle and the brave ran after her, but she managed to escape them.

"I will punish her for this!" screamed Light Feet. "She has brought dishonor upon our family."

From then on, Tekakwitha was treated harshly and given the hardest work. But she never complained. She was happy to be able to offer her sufferings to God. Whenever someone hurt her, she repaid them with kindness. Tekakwitha's only desire was to imitate Jesus in her daily life. She knew that Jesus and Mary were watching over her.

One day, while she was home alone, she was surprised by a visitor. It was a blackrobe!

"Father de Lamberville is my name," he said, smiling. "Anastasia told me you'd like to talk to a blackrobe."

"Yes! Please, Father, may I be baptized? I want to belong to God."

"But first you must know something about the Catholic faith."

"My mother was a Christian. She taught me many things, and so did Anastasia," the young woman responded.

Father de Lamberville asked Tekakwitha many questions. He was very surprised when she answered all of them quickly and correctly.

"You know a great deal about the Catholic faith, Tekakwitha, but before I can baptize you, you must have your uncle's consent. Then I will prepare you for the sacrament of Baptism."

Tekakwitha asked Thunder Cloud that very night. "Uncle, you know how much I want to learn about the God of the blackrobes and be baptized a Christian. Please, I ask your permission."

Thunder Cloud looked at her for a long time. He disliked the blackrobes and the Christian religion, but he loved his niece. After speaking to Father de Lamberville, he reluctantly gave his consent. Of course Light Feet was angry. She didn't want Tekakwitha to be baptized. But Thunder Cloud had spoken.

On Easter Sunday, April 18, 1676—Tekakwitha's twentieth birthday—she finally heard the beautiful words: "I baptize you in the name of the Father, and of the Son, and of the Holy Spirit." Tekakwitha chose the baptismal name Kateri, after a favorite saint of hers, Catherine of Siena. That day, Kateri was the happiest young woman in the whole Turtle Clan!

But her joy was soon turned to sorrow.

"I have come to say good-bye," said Anastasia. "I am going north to the Christian mission of St. Francis Xavier in New France. There I will be able to worship God in peace."

"Take me with you," pleaded Kateri. "I'll ask my uncle to let me go."

But Thunder Cloud refused. "Never will I let you leave our clan!" he exclaimed. Sadly, Kateri remained with her uncle and aunt.

After the young woman's baptism, Kateri's aunt made her suffer more, scolding her and refusing to give her food when she wouldn't work in the fields on Sundays. Other villagers ridiculed her when she prayed. Even the children taunted her and threw stones at her. Because Kateri continued to refuse to marry, the elders of the tribe also became very angry with her. Once, a young brave went so far as to threaten her with a tomahawk! Life as a Christian was becoming more and more dangerous.

There was great excitement one day when an Oneida chief, who had become a Christian, arrived in the village with Father de Lamberville. The chief's Christian name was Louis. He and a companion were now preaching about Jesus among the tribes of the Mohawk Valley.

Kateri was filled with joy. She eagerly drank in the words of those Native American missionaries.

That evening, Kateri spoke to Father de Lamberville. "Please, Father," she begged, "help me to leave here and travel to the mission of St. Francis Xavier, as Anastasia did. I want to be free to live as a true Christian."

"I'm worried about your safety here, Kateri," the Jesuit answered. "The villagers seem so upset with you. I'll ask Louis if you can travel north with him. But since you don't have your uncle's permission, it will have to be in secret, under cover of darkness. Can you be ready to leave in three days?"

"Yes, Father!" Kateri exclaimed. "I'll be ready!"

Three days later, Kateri slipped out of the lodge as her uncle and aunt slept. She joined the missionaries, and the little group fled northward. It was a journey of more than 200 miles through forests, swamps, and rivers.

When at last they reached the Christian settlement, Kateri was overjoyed to see Anastasia.

"Kateri! How happy I am to see you!" cried the older woman. "Did your uncle give his consent?"

"No, Anastasia. I know that he's very angry. He tried to track us. But God was good to me and didn't let him find us."

"You'll live with me," said Anastasia. "Come, I'll show you our lodge."

Kateri immediately began living as she had always desired. Even when it was bitterly cold, she went to church every morning at four o'clock to begin her prayers. Then she participated in the Mass that was celebrated in the settlement each day.

Anastasia enjoyed Kateri's company and spoke to her enthusiastically about God and the saints. Kateri listened attentively. She wore her rosary beads around her neck and prayed the Rosary often. She helped the people in the village who were sick and poor, and took great joy in caring for the children. Kateri was also very devoted to the Blessed Sacrament and to the cross of Christ, spending hours on her knees in the village chapel. When she was in the forest gathering firewood, she often fashioned crosses out of sticks and spent time in prayer there, too.

Because of her devotion and her deep understanding of her new religion, she was soon granted permission to receive Holy Communion. This was a great honor, because in those days newly-baptized Christians usually had to wait several years for this privilege. Kateri received her First Communion on Christmas morning, 1677. From that day on, she went to receive the Lord Jesus frequently.

One day Kateri couldn't get up. She was too ill even to go to Mass.

"What's wrong?" asked Anastasia.

"I—I can't move. I feel pain all over," murmured Kateri.

Anastasia ran to call a priest. "I'll come at once," said Father Cholonec.

Kateri smiled when she saw him. "Don't worry, Father," she said, "I won't die until tomorrow. You may rest tonight."

The following day she received Holy Communion and the sacrament of the Anointing of the Sick. Then she died peacefully. She was only twenty-four years old.

A few minutes after Kateri's death something strange and wonderful happened. Her face, scarred from the smallpox she had suffered as a child, became smooth, bright, and glowing! She was beautiful! Everyone who witnessed this miracle knew that Kateri was very special. She became known as the "Lily of the Mohawks."

In 1980, Pope John Paul II beatified Kateri Tekakwitha. She is the first native North American to be declared "blessed" by the Catholic Church.

Sometimes we have to wait many years for something we want very much, just as Kateri Tekakwitha waited years for her baptism. The important thing is never to stop praying and trusting that God will give us what we want, if it's for our good.

St. Margaret Mary Alacoque

(1647–1690)

OCTOBER 16

Margaret was the fifth of seven children born to the Alacoque family in Janots, a small town in Burgundy, France. Margaret's father was a public official, and her family lived in a large house surrounded by farms. Her mother taught the children prayers and Bible stories.

When Margaret was only eight, her father died unexpectedly of pneumonia. Madame Alacoque became so sick from grief that she could no longer take care of her children. Margaret was sent away to a boarding school run by Franciscan Sisters.

Margaret loved the peace of the convent. She liked to get up early and go into the chapel to hear the sisters chanting the psalms. The sisters often found her in the chapel at night praying the Rosary. In fact, Margaret became so well known for her prayers and love for Jesus that she was able to make her First Holy Communion when she was only nine years old. At that time, most children were not allowed to receive Communion until they were at least thirteen.

Margaret treasured her time with the sisters. She often spoke to Jesus in her heart. *O Lord,* she prayed, *when I am old enough, please let me enter the convent and consecrate my whole life to you.* But when she was eleven, Margaret became very ill with rheumatic fever and had to leave the school. A relative came to take her back to Janots.

The girl was shocked to find that one of her uncles had moved into her house and taken control of all her father's money and property. Her mother and brothers and sisters (who were still too young to protest) were being treated as servants in their own home! But for almost four years, Margaret was too sick to think much about it. During that time, she was barely able even to get out of bed.

As she began to recover, Margaret missed the long hours she had spent praying in the chapel at her school. "Uncle," she said timidly one day, "now that I'm better, I'd like your permission to go into the village and pray at the church each day."

"Don't be ridiculous!" he sharply answered. "If you want to pray, do it here in the house. It's a waste of time, anyway!"

But Margaret wasn't discouraged. Every day she went to ask his permission. Occasionally he would say yes; most of the time he said no.

For the sake of her mother, Margaret tried to make the best of the situation. She even began to make friends with some of the young men and women who frequently came to the parties her uncle held. Soon both Margaret's mother and her uncle were encouraging her to decide which of the young men she would like to marry. Margaret was so well liked that she could have her pick! Yet something made her hesitate. She remembered the promise she had so often made to Jesus: to enter the convent and consecrate her whole self to God.

"It's your duty to marry," her mother told her. "Choose one young man or another, but choose someone."

Margaret was praying after Holy Communion one day, asking God to help her know what to do, when Jesus appeared right in front of her. He was so powerful and handsome! But he looked sad, too. "I have chosen you to be my own," said Jesus. "We were happily promised to each other when you were still very young...before the world looked so attractive to you."

Margaret realized that she was crying. She had been thinking of abandoning God's call for an earthly husband! She saw how foolish she had been. "My Lord," she promised, "even if it should cost me a million lives, I'll never be anything but a religious."

Her mind was made up now, and she was firm when she told her family that she wanted to become a religious sister. "Please send away all the young men who want to marry me," she said. At the age of twenty, she entered the community of Visitation nuns at Paray-le-Monial and took the name Sister Margaret Mary.

Sister Margaret Mary's love for God grew deeper all the time. She spent hours adoring him in the Blessed

Sacrament. "Oh, my God," she would say, "I love you so much that I want to be consumed by love, just as a candle is consumed by the flame!"

After Margaret had spent many peaceful, happy years in the convent, Jesus appeared to her on the feast of St. John the Evangelist and invited her to rest her head on his heart, just as St. John had done at the Last Supper. This was the first of many times that Jesus came and spoke to her during her life as a religious. Jesus told Margaret that she had been chosen to tell all people about his love for them and to explain the devotion to his Sacred Heart. He told her about the pain he suffered because people hardly seemed to know that he was waiting for them in every tabernacle all over the world, longing to be their closest friend. They hardly talked to him at all; they hardly ever told him they loved him; they hardly ever gave their whole hearts to him who had given his whole heart to them!

Jesus told Sister Margaret Mary, "My Divine Heart is so on fire with love for people that it cannot hold the flames of love inside any longer. My love must spread to others through you!"

Jesus told her, too, that many people were in danger of losing heaven because of their sins. He asked her to have a special feast day established to honor his Sacred Heart, so that people who loved him could pray for those who did not. He asked that, on the first Thursday evening of each month, people make a holy hour, meditating on what he suffered in the Garden of Gethsemane just before his passion. Then they were to receive Holy Communion at Mass on the first Friday of the month.

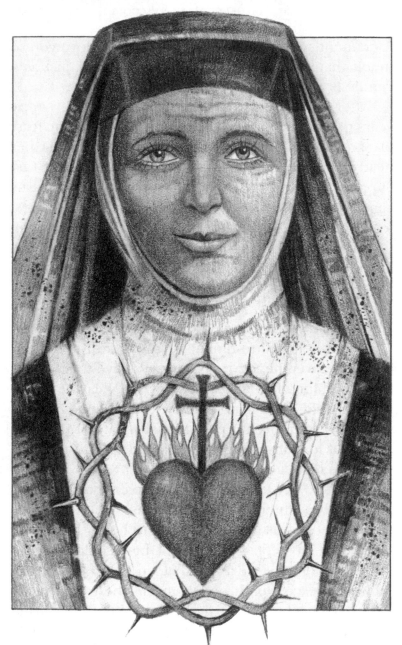

Jesus told Margaret to tell all people about his love for them and explain the love they must have for his Sacred Heart.

This message of Jesus was a reminder that he had become man to show us how to live as children of God, and that he had suffered and died for the love of all people. This message was important, because in the days of Margaret Mary many people had forgotten how much Jesus loved them. They thought of God as a harsh judge and were afraid to receive Holy Communion. They thought that God loved only a few special people.

Sister Margaret Mary found it very hard to tell the sisters in her community about her visions of Jesus. Many of the sisters thought that she was making them up. It was only after many years, and with the help of a good priest named Father Claude de la Columbiere, that the sisters began to believe her.

In June of 1686, the sisters at Paray-le-Monial celebrated the feast of the Sacred Heart for the first time. By then, Sister Margaret Mary had been appointed directress of novices, and she was able to explain to the young sisters how Jesus wanted all people to pray on the first Friday of the month.

Eventually, news of the visions and of Jesus' request to make known the love of his Heart for all people spread throughout France. Sister Margaret Mary would later become known all over the world as the apostle of the Sacred Heart. But she wouldn't live to see the devotion spread far. In 1690, she became ill and died suddenly but peacefully. Before she died, she said, "My only need is God, and to lose myself in the Heart of Jesus."

Whenever we see a picture or statue of the Sacred Heart of Jesus, we can remember that the message Jesus gave to St. Margaret Mary was that he loves each and every one of us. We should always trust in the love and mercy of Jesus.

St. Benedict Joseph Labre

(1748–1783)

Twelve-year-old Benedict Joseph Labre looked hopefully at his uncle. "Do you really think I can come and live with you, Abbé Francis?"

"It's entirely up to you," the priest answered. "You might have a vocation to the priesthood. If you come to be my helper, I'll teach you some theology and Latin. You'll need to know those subjects if you want to be a priest someday."

In the mid-1700s, a twelve-year-old was practically an adult. Benedict thought and prayed about what his uncle had said. Before long, he had made up his mind. He said good-bye to his family and went to join his uncle, the *curé,* or parish priest, of Erin.

Years passed. Benedict was a diligent and intelligent student, but he learned more than theology and Latin. He learned how to pray and how to serve others. Then one day a traveler came through Erin. Benedict listened as the visitor spoke about a group of monks called Trappists. "These men give their lives to God as no others do!" the visitor said with conviction.

The story impressed Benedict. More than anything, he wanted to live with and for Jesus alone. After some time, Benedict confided to Abbé Francis, "Uncle, I feel God is calling me to be a Trappist monk."

But Benedict's family didn't want him to rush into anything. "Besides, your other uncle, Abbé Vincent, thinks that you might be more suited for life in the Carthusian Order," his father told him. The Carthusians, however, suggested that Benedict needed more time to be sure of his vocation.

Over the next two years, Benedict tried twice to join the Trappists, but the monks wouldn't accept him. Then he tried the Carthusian monastery. He was accepted there but only stayed for six weeks. Benedict next decided to try applying to a different Trappist community. In 1769 he was finally accepted into the Abbey of Seven Fountains. For a while, everything went fine. Benedict was very happy working and praying with the others. But, no matter how hard he tried, he worried that he wasn't keeping the monks' rule well enough. (He really was, but he couldn't stop worrying about it.) Then he came down with a terrible fever. Sadly, the abbot told Benedict, "My son, you are a very good and holy young man. But it seems that God wants you somewhere else. Go back to your family. The Lord will guide you."

Benedict returned home, saddened and confused. "What do you want me to do, Lord?" he prayed. "I'm ready to give you everything. So why can't I become a monk?"

Benedict decided to make a pilgrimage to Rome. Along the way he stopped at every shrine, always praying to know how he could best love and serve God. This was the first of the many pilgrimages that Benedict would make.

Like all eighteenth-century pilgrims, Benedict traveled on foot and begged for food. At convents or monasteries he slept in shelters set up for travelers. Whenever he wasn't near a shelter, he slept outdoors.

Benedict soon discovered that thieves and criminals often pretended to be pilgrims. This made things difficult. Sometimes children made fun of the pilgrims, throwing rocks at them. At first Benedict didn't know how to react. He wasn't a criminal! He had never hurt anyone, and he was certainly not lazy! Then Benedict realized that Jesus had been treated in the same way.

Other travelers, as well as homeless beggars, became suspicious of Benedict. They thought he had a hidden agenda because he was good to everyone, never gambled or got drunk, and never used bad language. Benedict would say, "These things offend God—and they're not good for you, either. Try to work if you can. If you can't work, be good to the people who take care of you."

Benedict gradually came to understand that God was calling him to live among the street people of

Rome, accepting insults, hunger, dirt, and bad smells. Benedict spent whole days praying for the other homeless people. Once he wrote to his mother: "I'd like to hear news about you and my brothers and sisters, but it isn't possible to receive a letter, because I don't have any address."

One day a priest saw Benedict sitting by the road. His legs were swollen and cut. "Benedict, what's wrong?" the priest exclaimed. The young man couldn't even walk. Father helped him to the church shelter and had him registered as a permanent guest. (Usually men could stay only three nights in a row.) When he felt better, Benedict helped at the shelter. He knew, though, that soon he would reach the day he had been waiting for: the day he would join Jesus in heaven.

Holy Week was Benedict's favorite time of year. He looked forward to the beautiful Mass of the Lord's Supper on Holy Thursday and to the special Good Friday services. But his friends at church noticed that Benedict was paler than usual during the Holy Week of 1783. At the end of one of the services, Benedict fell to the floor.

Gently, people carried the holy beggar to a nearby home. A priest hurried to give him the sacrament of the Anointing of the Sick. When Benedict died, the whole city of Rome mourned. At his funeral, so many people came to pray that the army had to direct traffic! Many people who hadn't known Benedict were surprised. They had heard of holy priests, holy nuns, and holy kings or queens. But a holy beggar?

Benedict wrote to his mother: "I'd like to hear news about you and my brothers and sisters, but it isn't possible to receive a letter, because I don't have any address."

After Benedict's death, hundreds of miraculous cures were attributed to his intercession. Benedict Joseph Labre was canonized by Pope Leo XIII in 1881. He is the patron saint of beggars, the homeless, and of people who suffer from mental illness.

St. Benedict Joseph Labre, the holy beggar, is a model for everyone who is searching to know God's will, and for everyone who, for whatever reason, is traveling the streets with no place to call home.

St. Elizabeth Ann Seton

(1774–1821)

JANUARY 4

Four-year-old Elizabeth sat on the porch steps, watching big, puffy clouds floating in the sky above. Her uncle William came to the door. "Elizabeth, dear," he said, "let me sit with you. Are you crying because your little sister has died?"

The small girl turned. "I'm not crying for Kitty, Uncle, because I know that she has gone to heaven. And I wish I could go to heaven to be with her, and with my mother, too!"

William held out his arms to hug the child. "Yes, Elizabeth, God loves us tenderly, and someday we'll all be together in heaven! But that time is a long way off."

Within a few years, Elizabeth was helping her new stepmother around the house and caring for new baby sisters. She enjoyed teaching the little ones their prayers and playing "school" with them.

Elizabeth's father, Dr. Richard Bayley, was a wealthy and generous man. He helped as many of New York's poor as he could, treating them just as well as he treated patients who could afford to pay for his services.

One day another doctor asked him, "Could you assist me with a difficult and dangerous operation?"

"I have a very full schedule," Dr. Bayley replied, "and I'm tired, besides. Surely you can find another assistant."

"I doubt if another would be willing," his friend quietly answered. "I'll be sorry to tell the family of your refusal. They are poor people—penniless."

Dr. Bayley jumped to his feet. "Poor?" he asked. "Why didn't you say so before? Let's go at once! They shouldn't be left without care simply because they can't afford it."

At nineteen, Elizabeth had grown into an intelligent and prayerful young woman. She had delicate features and beautiful dark eyes. William Seton, a young businessman, fell in love with her and asked her to marry him. In 1794, since they were Episcopalians, they were married in an Episcopal Church in New York City.

William and Elizabeth were very happy, but a heavy burden soon fell on them. After the death of his father, William had to take over the family business and support his twelve brothers and sisters. Elizabeth was sad to see him becoming worried and tense. She helped with the bookkeeping and tried to find ways to keep his courage up. She knew the Bible well and often consoled her husband with thoughts and prayers from Scripture.

Soon Elizabeth and William had five young children: Anna Maria, William, Richard, Catherine, and Rebecca. Elizabeth saw each of her children as a gift from God, and was careful to help them to grow up obedient and kind.

In 1803, William became very sick with tuberculosis. The doctors suggested that a change of climate might help him.

"Leave the younger children with us, Elizabeth," urged kind relatives. "You'll be able to take better care of William that way." Sad as she was to be separated from her little ones, Elizabeth agreed. She, her husband, and their oldest child, Anna Maria, set sail for Italy, where William had spent some time as a young man. They were to stay with some old friends of his, the Filicchi family.

But when the ship reached port after seven long weeks, William was placed under quarantine by the Italian officials. They could see that he was very ill, and they knew that he had just come from New York, where there had been an outbreak of yellow fever. Elizabeth couldn't convince the officials to allow her family to continue on to the Filicchis' home.

The building in which the Seton family was isolated was dirty, cold, and damp. William's condition grew worse and worse, despite the good food and medicines that the Filicchis sent him. Elizabeth watched helplessly as her husband suffered violent coughing spells. Soon he was coughing up blood.

After a month of quarantine, the little family was released on December 19 and moved to an elegant lodging house provided by the Filicchis. But it was too late. Elizabeth watched as William became weaker and weaker. He died in her arms two days after Christmas. He was only thirty-five years old. Elizabeth was heartbroken, but she knew she had done everything she could. William was buried the next morning.

The Filicchis were very kind, and asked Elizabeth and her daughter Anna Maria to stay with them for a few weeks. One day Elizabeth went to church with them. The services amazed her, because she had never before attended the liturgy of the Roman Catholic Church. She went to church with her new friends again and again.

One morning, at the elevation of the Sacred Host, Elizabeth thought of the words of St. Paul—"discerning the Body of the Lord"—and tears began to flow down her cheeks. Was Jesus truly present here, as St. Paul said he was? Oh, if only he were!

At that time in Italy, the Blessed Sacrament was often carried through the streets in procession. Whenever she saw a procession pass by her window, Elizabeth had a deep sense of loneliness. If only she could believe that God was truly present in the Eucharist! One time she fell to her knees and prayed, "My God, bless me if you are truly present. My soul desires you!"

Another time, Elizabeth saw one of Mrs. Filicchi's prayer books on a table. She opened it and found a prayer to the Blessed Mother. Elizabeth said the prayer slowly. She was sure that Jesus wouldn't refuse his Mother anything, and that Mary would have only love and mercy for the souls for whom her Son had suffered. Elizabeth prayed, and she felt that the Blessed Mother was *her* Mother, a tender, compassionate Mother. Feeling a sense of relief and hope, she cried herself to sleep that night.

~~~~~~~~~~~~~~~

The return ocean voyage to New York had been long, but Elizabeth forgot the hardships and all her worries when she was reunited with her younger children again. She felt sure that even though William was gone, God would take care of them all!

"I have good reason to place my trust in you, my God," Elizabeth wrote in her diary. "Whom do I have in heaven except you? And whom on earth besides you?"

She had been thinking long and carefully, and had decided to become a Roman Catholic. By now she was convinced that Jesus was truly present in the Blessed Sacrament, and she longed to participate in the Mass and to receive Holy Communion.

The family of Elizabeth's husband objected strongly. They didn't like the Roman Catholic Church and threatened to have nothing to do with Elizabeth if she should take this step. But she continued to pray, and finally knew what she must do. On March 14, 1805, the thirty-year-old widow was received into the Catholic faith at St. Peter's, the only Catholic church in New York City at that time.

After receiving the sacrament of Reconciliation for the first time, Elizabeth began to prepare for her First Holy Communion, which she received on the feast of the Annunciation. "At last," she wrote, "God is mine, and I am his!"

Elizabeth's relatives did abandon her, as they had threatened to do, leaving her and her children without income. But she was at peace. She took a job as a schoolteacher. At night she played the piano while her five children sang and danced. After the children had gone to bed, she washed and mended their clothes. At midnight she would go to bed, only to rise early the next morning and walk several blocks to go to Mass. It was a hard schedule, but Elizabeth didn't mind. When William had been alive, he had scolded her for working too hard, and she had replied, "Love makes all effort easy." Now it was love—for her children and for her faith—that made such a difficult time "easy."

Elizabeth was eventually introduced to Father Dubourg, a young priest from Baltimore, Maryland, who told her that there was a great need for a school for girls in his city. Could Elizabeth open such a school? Elizabeth loved to teach, and there were many Catholics in Baltimore. She and her children would be welcomed there. Elizabeth said yes.

But Father Dubourg had even more ambitious plans for Elizabeth. "Would you consider forming a new congregation of religious sisters?" he asked. "If you become the foundress of this congregation, you will be the mother of many daughters."

Elizabeth didn't feel capable of what Father Dubourg was asking her to do. But after praying about it, and asking the advice of a priest who was guiding her, she agreed to try—as long as she could keep her three daughters with her. (Her two boys were already attending a Catholic boarding school.) Elizabeth trusted in God and began the new community. Eventually, Archbishop John Carroll approved a rule for the sisters which would allow Elizabeth's daughters to live with her.

As the superior of the new religious congregation, Elizabeth was now called Mother Seton. Soon several young women joined her. By 1812, twenty sisters were sharing a common life of prayer and teaching. They became known as the Sisters of Charity of St. Joseph.

Elizabeth and her community experienced many difficulties. Several of the sisters died because of hardships suffered during the War of 1812. Then Elizabeth's oldest daughter, Anna Maria, died of tuberculosis at the age of sixteen, after having pronounced her vows as a Sister of Charity. At about the same time the foundress's youngest daughter, Rebecca, injured her leg. A tumor began to grow and Rebecca, who was only ten, suffered for months. Elizabeth stayed at her bedside day and night, telling her about the beauties of heaven that would soon be hers. Little Rebecca was in great pain, and Elizabeth marveled at her patience. After Rebecca's death, Elizabeth wrote to her son William, "If you had been given the opportunity of seeing our Rebecca fly to heaven as a little angel, you could not be more certain that she is with God."

Just as she had always been a good wife and mother, Elizabeth was also a wonderful religious superior.

Soon, several young women who wished to become teaching sisters joined Elizabeth. By 1812, twenty women were sharing a common life of prayer and work.

She gave her sisters a marvelous example of prayerfulness, calm, generosity, and self-sacrifice. She looked after each sister and each young pupil as diligently as she had looked after her own children.

But Elizabeth herself became ill with tuberculosis. Her thoughts were fixed on heaven, as they had been when she was a child. As she grew weaker day by day, she knew that her own death was coming. "Eternity seems so near," she would exclaim. "Think of it when you feel oppressed or annoyed. It will be a beautiful endless day!"

After receiving the sacrament of the Anointing of the Sick, Elizabeth said, "Thank you! Oh, how grateful I am!" Then she said to her sisters, "Pray for me!" The next day, praying, "Jesus, Mary, Joseph," she peacefully went to join her loved ones in heaven.

Mother Elizabeth Ann Seton was canonized by Pope Paul VI in 1975. She is the first person born in the United States to be honored as a saint of the Catholic Church.

St. Elizabeth Seton faced many problems and sorrows in her life, but she never lost her trust in God. We can try to imitate her by remembering that God is with us in everything that happens to us—in happy times and in sad times.

St. Bartholomea

(1807–1833)

July 26

"Let's see which of us will become a saint first!"

Sister Frances, who had spoken, smiled as the young students crowded about her shouting, "I will!"

"No, I'll be the one!"

"How do you know?"

Eleven-year-old Bartholomea Capitanio, who was new at the school, stared in amazement at her teacher. A saint? Could *she* really become a saint?

"Well, let's draw straws," Sister Frances was saying as she walked over to the closet where they were kept.

Meanwhile, Bartholomea ran across the courtyard to the chapel, rushed inside, and fell to her knees before the Blessed Virgin's altar. "Heavenly Mother," she begged, "let me draw the longest straw! I promise you I'll become a saint, no matter what it costs!"

She quickly said three Hail Marys and hurried back to the classroom, sure that her desire would be granted.

The drawing began. Soon it was Bartholomea's turn. With a trembling hand, she pulled out a straw and stared at it.

"Look!" another girl cried. "Bartholomea got the longest straw!"

In a moment, Bartholomea was running back to the chapel to offer a prayer of gratitude. She knew that drawing the straw wasn't the *reason* she would become a saint, because to become holy means to cooperate with all the graces God gives us. But now that the thought had come to her, she couldn't get it out of her mind.

~~~~~~~~~

Bartholomea had only recently come to live at the school of the Sisters of St. Clare after a rather unhappy childhood. Her father was addicted to alcohol and had a violent temper. Many times he would come home angry and suspicious, ready to quarrel at the slightest excuse. Sometimes he would hurt Bartholomea's mother and even drive her out of the house.

Because Bartholomea's mother feared for her daughter's safety, she had sent the girl to live at the sisters' school. That was where Bartholomea made her resolution to become a saint.

No sooner had the girl made her decision than she set about finding a way to accomplish it. She wrote: "I have decided to become a saint. That is the goal to which you, my God, invite me. It's an ambitious saying, which would be full of pride if I didn't place all my confidence in you, my God. I propose to become a saint by the practice of three virtues: humility, self-denial, and prayer. Mary, my dear Mother, please help me become a saint."

Bartholomea's love for prayer and her strong desire to become a saint didn't prevent her from being a popular person at school. In games and skits, she usually played the part of the mother or the teacher. She loved to make up stories to entertain her companions. Often she would take smaller neighborhood children to church and teach them their prayers in front of the Blessed Virgin's altar.

After hearing a sermon about how much Jesus suffered because of our sins, Bartholomea promised, "Oh, Jesus, I don't want to offend you again—ever!"

~~~~~~~~~~

When Bartholomea was fourteen, her nine-year-old sister, Camilla, also came to stay at the boarding school. Like the girls' father, Camilla had a quick temper and was used to having her own way. She was always getting into trouble with her teachers. This made Bartholomea feel terrible, even though she wanted the sisters to correct Camilla for her own good. She knew how difficult Camilla's life had been at home with their father. She tried her best to persuade Camilla to be good and to take her classes seriously. But Camilla was jealous of her older sister and treated her rudely.

In her final two years of school Bartholomea helped the sisters teach the younger children. She was a good teacher and the children loved and trusted her. They knew she was their friend.

When Bartholomea completed her studies, her parents called her home. They wanted her with them. As much as she wanted to stay at the school and become a sister herself, Bartholomea obeyed and returned home. Her father's drinking problem was worse than ever, but he was fond of Bartholomea and sometimes listened to her when she tried to calm him. Meanwhile, her mother needed help caring for the family.

Now that Bartholomea was an adult, she would often go out to find her father when he was drinking and bring him home before he got into an argument.

Once she stopped at the house of one of his friends.

"Yes, your father was here, but he's gone to the tavern. If you want, I'll go call him."

"No, I'll go," Bartholomea replied.

"Into a tavern?" the man asked. "Aren't you afraid?"

"No. I'll go," the girl calmly answered.

She found her father playing cards. Seating herself nearby, she said, "Papa, as soon as you finish this hand, I need to speak with you."

She led him out—and home! No one in the tavern had dared to say a rude word to her, because of her courage, modesty, and devotedness.

Another time, a neighbor insulted Bartholomea's father. Her father tried to control his anger at first, but as insult followed insult, rage welled up in his heart and he lunged at the other man.

Bartholomea ran up to him and urged, "It's not worth it, Papa. It's not worth it. Come on, let's go home!" Father and daughter turned and left quietly.

Her father's drinking problem was worse than ever, but he was fond of Bartholomea and sometimes listened to her when she tried to calm him.

The young woman had acquired such strength and courage because of the daily schedule she had made for herself. This schedule included daily Mass and a visit to the Blessed Sacrament, an hour of meditation each morning, and another half hour of prayer at night.

Never forgetting that her whole life belonged to Jesus, Bartholomea knew that he was with her at all hours of the day. Jesus called her to her household duties, urged her to be kind, assured her that he would never abandon her, and asked her to perform every action only for him.

Bartholomea loved God so much that she wanted to convince as many people as she could to love him, too. Not long after she returned home to live with her parents, she opened a private school right in the house, where the young village children could come to be taught. Soon she ran out of space and moved the school to a larger house.

The young woman was a wonderful teacher, and her students learned quickly. They learned other things along with reading, writing, and arithmetic. They learned humility, kindness, and patience! At the end of the year, parents were amazed to see how better behaved even their most rebellious children had become.

Bartholomea's teaching method was to love her students and to sacrifice herself for them. Seeing that she really cared for them, the children responded with all their best efforts. Every day she proposed a virtue for them to practice and told them *how* they could practice it. Often she rewarded those who tried the hardest.

Bartholomea knew that some students learn faster than others, and she helped each one without showing any partiality. She never hesitated to point out their mistakes, but did it so kindly that they immediately tried to improve.

Pastors of parishes in the nearby towns began to send teenage girls to Bartholomea so she could train them to be teachers. Within a few years, Bartholomea's influence had spread throughout the whole region—about eighty-four villages!

Bartholomea wasn't just a teacher. When two older women, Catherine and Rose Gerosa, opened a hospital for the poor, they begged Bartholomea to take charge of the hospital's finances, and she accepted the duty. She often visited the sick in the wards, stopping to say a comforting word and encourage each patient to prepare for confession and Communion. Upon her arrival, word would pass joyously from person to person: "Bartholomea's here!"

Once two soldiers were admitted to the hospital, sicker in soul than they were in body. They had no interest at all in God or religion. But Bartholomea's holiness, together with her prayers for their conversion, brought God into their lives.

Another man, who had led a very sinful life, refused at first to listen to Bartholomea's gentle urgings. After a time, however, her prayers won out. He made a good confession and firm resolutions and, upon leaving the hospital, became a religious brother.

Whenever he heard anyone speak of Lovere, where Bartholomea lived, he would say, "There's a saint in that town!"

~~~~~~~~~~

Bartholomea never gave up her concern for her father. One summer he became very sick. As his health grew worse and worse, she prayed with him, urging him to say with her prayers of love, contrition, and resignation to God's will. Like a lamb, he did everything she told him to do.

When her father made his last confession, he confided to the priest that it was his daughter who had helped him prepare it. He knew that Bartholomea was the means of his conversion, and he kept her near him till the end. When he died, toward the end of October, 1831, Bartholomea wept, but she had the consolation of knowing that he had died a changed man. She assisted at many Masses for the repose of his soul.

~~~~~~~~~~

After her father's death, Bartholomea continued to teach children and to care for the poor and the sick. But more and more clearly she saw the need for a new religious congregation to carry on these works. There was so much good to be done, and so few people to do it!

Bartholomea's friend, Catherine Gerosa, joined her in the project. At first they encountered many obstacles that seemed to block their plans. But one by one these were overcome, thanks to the firm faith and unfailing prayers of the two holy women.

The Sisters of Charity of Lovere were founded on the feast of the Presentation of Mary, 1832. As the new congregation began, Bartholomea's own work on earth was drawing to a close. In April, 1833, she came down with a fever that rose higher and higher. Her mother and sister (and, in fact, the whole village) were very sad, because she was only twenty-six years old.

"Mama, listen," Bartholomea soothed. "You know that everyone has to die. If I were to live forty more years, I'd still have to die. This is the moment when God in his mercy has chosen to receive me into paradise. Don't be saddened by my death, but instead thank God!"

To die meant to abandon her new religious Institute at its very birth and to leave it in other hands. It was a great sacrifice, but to Catherine Gerosa, Bartholomea said, "In heaven I'll be more useful to the Institute than I would have been on earth."

On July 26, Bartholomea grew weaker. From time to time she kissed the crucifix and a small statue of the Blessed Virgin. Then, murmuring prayers and smiling as if dropping into a deep sleep, she passed into eternal life.

~~~~~~~~~~~~~~~~

"What shall I do now?" Catherine Gerosa kept repeating to herself. "I'm good for nothing. It's better for me to return home! Without Bartholomea I can do nothing; she was an eagle; I'm an ox."

But Bartholomea's confessor told Catherine to have courage. The Institute was necessary, he declared. She must pray and have faith.

"Le's go ahead then," Catherine agreed. "God wants to show us that he's the one doing everything—not us!"

Soon more young women, former pupils of Bartholomea, came to join Catherine. Bartholomea's sister, Camilla, also came. In 1835, on the feast of Our Lady's Presentation, they received the religious habit.

The Institute grew quickly and spread throughout northern Italy, even sending missionaries to India and Brazil. A hundred years after its founding, the congregation numbered over 8,000 sisters in more than 600 places around the world. The sisters cared for abandoned children, elderly people, people with leprosy, the mentally ill, the plague-stricken, and the homeless. They worked in hospitals, orphanages, and public and private schools.

Bartholomea Capitanio was declared a saint in 1950 by Pope Pius XII. Catherine Gerosa, co-foundress of the Sisters of Charity of Lovere, was canonized as St. Vincentia Gerosa that same year. All this happened because an eleven-year-old girl once made a decision to become a saint—and did something about it!

Bartholomea was able to overcome the difficulties of living with an alcoholic parent because she prayed for God's help every day. Now that she's in heaven, we can ask St. Bartholomea for strength and courage to face our own problems with faith and confidence in God's loving care. We can ask her to help us want to become saints, too!

St. Joseph Cottolengo

(1786–1842)

APRIL 30

One day in the year 1827, a young family from France was traveling near the city of Turin, Italy. Unexpectedly, the mother of the family, who was ready to give birth, became very sick. The father hurried to take her to the city's hospital, but the hospital refused to admit her because the family had no money to pay for her care. Someone who had seen their desperate situation had called a priest, hoping that he could help them. But when he arrived, it was too late. He gave the woman the sacrament of the Anointing of the Sick, and baptized her newborn baby daughter. Sadly, both the mother and the baby died.

Father Joseph Cottolengo was the priest. As he stood by, helpless to do any more, the woman's husband and her three little children sobbed desperately.

Father Cottolengo thought of how that woman and her baby might have been saved if the city hospital had only taken her in and cared for her. As he thought about it, he made a resolution: that sort of thing would never happen again in Turin!

It didn't take the determined priest very long to put his plan into action. He found a small building near the city center that could be turned into a hospital. He opened it up and brought in the most desperately sick people he could find. The Vincentian Sisters and the Brothers of St. Vincent came to help him. But in 1831 there was an outbreak of cholera (a very dangerous fever) in Turin, and the city authorities ruled that Father Cottolengo had to close the little hospital. They feared it might be a source of the illness.

Father Cottolengo didn't give up his idea. He asked various families to take in the sick people, and the sisters helped care for them. He waited, looked around, and soon found a small, run-down house on the outskirts of Turin in a neighborhood called Valdocco. This would be his next hospital! Volunteers helped to renovate the building, which Father named the Little House of Divine Providence.

On April 27, 1832, a little cart pulled by a donkey came bumping along the road to the house. In the cart was their first patient—a man with a diseased leg. Father Cottolengo's dream was coming true!

More and more patients came. Soon another house had to be built, then another and another. Streets were built between the houses, and before long there was a whole complex of buildings filled with people who had all kinds of sicknesses. Father Cottolengo founded a group of religious sisters to live at the hospital and help care for the patients.

Father Cottolengo was busy all the time, making sure that all the needs of the sick, of the sisters, and of the other nurses were provided for. He worked hard, but he prayed even harder, because only help from God could keep his great project going. They needed food, medicine, supplies, and more. Doctors came to help. Father Cottolengo founded more religious communities to serve the residents. The Little House became famous throughout Europe.

People began to wonder what would happen when Father Cottolengo was no longer with them. Would God still provide without the faith and prayers of the holy priest?

That question bothered the king of Italy, too. One day he sent for Father Cottolengo and asked him if he had made any plans for the future. For a minute the priest didn't say anything. He walked over to the window and looked down into the big square below. "If you please, Your Majesty, come look at this," he said. There below them the palace guard was changing. One group of soldiers was dismounting from their horses; other soldiers took their place. It all happened very calmly and without excitement.

"That's just the way someone will take my place when God calls me. Don't you think so, Your Majesty?"

The king was impressed. From that time on, he had great respect and admiration for Father Cottolengo. He always spoke of him as "my friend Cottolengo."

To Father Cottolengo, patients in his Little House were the most important people in the world. When he was with them, nothing could take him away. One day an archbishop came to visit. He found Father Cottolengo playing ball with a mentally ill man named Doro.

"I would like to speak with you, Father," said the archbishop.

"I'm delighted to see you, Your Excellency," replied the priest. "I'm playing with this man right now, and he might feel offended if I stop. I hope you don't mind waiting."

So the archbishop waited—and even kept score for the players! He didn't mind, because he realized that every person is very special in the eyes of God.

~~~~~~~~~~

Saints can be described in many ways, depending on what virtues they practice the most. "Love" and "hope" both describe St. Joseph Cottolengo very well, but another virtue stood out even more clearly in him, and that was "faith": his faith in Divine Providence (the care God has for us). "Every time someone new enters the Little House," he said, "more bread comes down from heaven—and the best thing about it is that *I'm* not the one who makes it come; it's Divine Providence that takes joy in raining down the blessings one by one."

Father Cottolengo was never worried and never discouraged. When things seemed the worst, he was happiest. Then he felt that the Providence of God was very close. Sometimes he could predict the arrival of something they needed almost to the exact minute. One day, for instance, the hospital ran out of flour, rice,

The patients in the Little House were the most important people in the world to Father Cottolengo.

and noodles. It was almost mealtime, and there were thousands of sick people to feed!

The cook was worried. She hurried to Father Cottolengo. "Oh, Father, there's nothing to prepare!"

"Really? Well, put the kettles on and start the water boiling. Let's not waste any time."

As soon as the water was boiling in the big kettles, the doorbell rang. There was a large wagon full of bread and rice that someone had donated!

"The Little House will grow as long as it doesn't have a steady source of income," Father Cottolengo often said. "It will grow as long as it has nothing."

One day Father Cottolengo had to leave on a trip. His brother, Father Louis Cottolengo, came to take his place. "Here's the money bag, Louis," said Father. "Spend whatever you need to, but never look inside the bag to see what's left. If you do as I say, the money will last."

Many, many expenses came up in the days that followed. Father Louis had to pay out a great deal of money. He was amazed that the little bag always provided whatever he needed—and more! It didn't seem possible that it could have held so much!

Another time the sisters' superior came to Father Joseph Cottolengo looking quite upset. "What's the trouble, Sister?" he asked kindly.

"I have so many things to buy, Father, and this is all the money I have!"

"That's all? Let me see it."

She handed it to him. It was a very small amount. "Quite right," said Father Cottolengo. He walked over to the window and tossed the money outside!

"That's all right," said Father Cottolengo. "It's been planted now. Wait a few hours, and it will bear fruit."

That evening a woman came to see Father Cottolengo. She donated a large sum of money. "To help you in your good work, Father!"

Another time a sister came and asked, "Father, what are we going to do? There isn't any bread. There's no flour, no potatoes—there's nothing! And it's almost dinnertime!" She held up a very small coin. "This is all we have!"

"Give it to me," replied the priest. He flung the coin out the window. "There! Now we really have nothing, and Providence has to provide! Go to the church and pray," he told the sister. "I'll go and pray, too. When noon comes, send everyone to the dining hall as usual."

Noon came and everyone went to the dining hall as usual. There was a knock at the gate. Someone hurried to open it. And what came rolling in through the gate but wagon after wagon, loaded with meals that were already cooked! The meals had been prepared for a regiment of soldiers who were in the field on battle maneuvers. But the soldiers had been delayed, and their officers had decided to send the food to the Little House so that it wouldn't be wasted.

One day the sister who did all the shopping told Father Cottolengo that she didn't want to do it any longer.

"And why not?" asked the priest.

"The storekeepers want us to pay our bills before they sell us anything else!"

"You have no faith," replied Father. "As a penance, say Psalm 51, the *Miserere,* and then go out as usual."

The sister didn't say a word. She prayed and left.

At her first stop, the storekeeper came up and handed her a receipt for what had been owed: "A lady came and paid me for you, Sister!"

This happened again and again, all along the street. One woman even handed the sister some extra money. "The lady left it for you," she said.

Father Cottolengo listened to the story without surprise. *He* knew who the mysterious Lady was—the Blessed Mother!

Once a very angry man came to the Little House and demanded payment of his bill. "I won't leave until you pay every single cent!" he roared.

"I don't have even one cent," replied Father Cottolengo.

The man said something nasty.

"Please don't swear," said Father Cottolengo. "Come back tomorrow, and we'll pay it all."

"Nothing doing! I'm not moving from here until you pay up!"

"All right," agreed the saint. "Wait just a moment, please."

It was very quiet for a minute. Then Father Cottolengo reached into his pocket very slowly. When he pulled his hand out, it held two large rolls of money.

There are many stories like these about the faith of St. Joseph Cottolengo. His life was full of miracles. In fact, the miracles have continued since his death. Even to this day, the Little House of Divine Providence runs smoothly, operating on the gifts of God!

Even when things seem to go wrong, let's be like St. Joseph Cottolengo and trust in God, who always watches over and cares for us. God can bring good out of every situation!

St. Dominic Savio

(1842–1857)

MARCH 9

Dominic Savio was the son of a blacksmith who lived in the small town of Riva, in northern Italy. Even when he was very small, he liked to pray. Each morning, Dominic would get up at five o'clock with his father and go to his parish church to serve Mass. When he was seven years old, Dominic was allowed to receive his First Communion. This was a big exception at that time, because most children weren't permitted to receive Communion until they were older. On that wonderful day, Dominic told Jesus all the secret hopes of his heart. He made a promise to Jesus, whom he called "my special friend." Dominic even adopted a motto, which he afterward told to his pastor: "Death, but not sin!" This was the sort of motto that a hero would have, and Dominic would prove to be a hero in living up to it.

Dominic wanted to imitate Jesus as closely as he could. And this wasn't always easy. Once, he had just changed schools. His new teacher, a priest, didn't know him well yet. Some of the other boys decided to take advantage of the situation to get Dominic into trouble. It was winter, and the classroom was heated by a wood-burning stove. One of the boys came up with an idea. "Let's put some snow in the stove so that the fire will go out and the wood won't burn. Then it'll be so cold that Father will have to let us out early!"

When the fire died out, the priest opened the stove and found the snow. "Who did this?" he sternly demanded. The frightened culprits pointed to Dominic. Although surprised, the priest believed the other boys. As a punishment, he made Dominic kneel on the floor for a long time. Dominic obeyed without trying to defend himself. He knew that if he explained what had really happened, the other boys would receive a much worse punishment because they were always in trouble. *Jesus suffered so much for things he was falsely accused of,* Dominic thought. *This is a small thing I can do to try to be like him.*

By the time Dominic was twelve, he knew that he wanted to be a priest more than anything else. And he was eager to begin the studies that would prepare him for ordination. The priest Don Bosco (whom you'll read about later in this book as St. John Bosco) encouraged Dominic and admitted him to the Oratory of St. Francis de Sales in Turin. This was a special school Don Bosco had founded for boys. There, Dominic happily began his studies.

When he wasn't studying, Dominic often visited the Blessed Sacrament by himself or with friends whom he

By the time Dominic was twelve, he knew that he wanted to be a priest more than anything else.

invited. At other times, he'd be found telling stories about the saints to a group of eager boys gathered around him. On Fridays, Dominic gave up the usual games and went to chapel to honor the sorrows of the Blessed Virgin in a special way. "Let's stop in for a prayer to the Blessed Mother," he'd encourage his friends. Every Sunday he taught catechism to younger children.

Dominic was well-liked and was a peacemaker. Once, two of his companions were having a pretty serious fight. Each had even picked up a large rock to throw at the other. Right at that point, Dominic stepped between them. "Get out of the way!" one of the angry boys yelled.

But Dominic wouldn't budge. "You'll have to hit me first," he quietly responded. And for a minute, it looked as if the bully was going to do just that!

Then Dominic pulled a small crucifix out of his pocket and held it up. "You won't hit me? Then hit *him!*"

This was too much for the boys. They realized that they were wrong. They dropped their rocks. In a few minutes they were shaking hands and apologizing.

Each week, Dominic went to confession. He received Jesus in Holy Communion every day. He urged his friends to go to confession regularly, and even founded a club to encourage the other boys to receive Holy Communion often. The members of the club tried to be good Catholic students in every way and had a great devotion to Mary.

Dominic once exclaimed to Don Bosco, "I have to become a saint, Father!" And he never lost sight of that goal. Dominic was always encouraging his friends to do good deeds and to avoid everything that might lead them to sin. But he never pretended to be wearing a halo himself! He was a lively, normal teenager, always at the center of the action, whether at a ball game or taking part in a school play.

When Dominic was fourteen, he became very ill. He was sent home to his parents in the hope that the change of climate would help him recuperate. How hard it was for Dominic to leave his teacher and friend, Don Bosco! He had a feeling that they wouldn't meet again—except in heaven.

Back at home, Dominic grew worse instead of better. The parish priest was called to administer the sacrament of the Anointing of the Sick and bring him Holy Communion. The boy felt all the strength draining out of his body, but he was peaceful. Suddenly a change came over him. Dominic sat up in his bed and held out his arms as if reaching for someone. His eyes shone. "Oh, what a beautiful sight!" he exclaimed. Then, with a smile on his lips, Dominic went to meet Jesus.

Dominic Savio's life was very short and very ordinary! He was a good friend and a good student, but he wasn't "the best" at anything. He didn't live long enough to become a priest. But Dominic is a saint—one of the youngest, too— because he let his love for Jesus guide him in everything he did. We can do the same thing, with St. Dominic's help.

St. Bernadette Soubirous

(1844–1879)

April 16

The town of Lourdes in southern France was enveloped in a blanket of fog on that February 11, 1858. In the damp, one-room home of the Soubirous family there wasn't even a bit of wood left to light a fire.

"We'll go get some, Mama," volunteered the girls, Bernadette and Toinette. Their friend Jeanne was eager to go, too.

Thinking of her older daughter's asthma, Mrs. Soubirous protested, "Bernadette, don't go out. Your cough might come back again."

"Don't worry, Mama," Bernadette reassured. "I'll put on my hooded cape. I won't get cold." Her mother wearily nodded and the three girls rushed out.

Bernadette, the oldest of the four living Soubirous children, wasn't as strong as her sister Toinette. Her asthma often made her miss school and religious instruction classes. Because of this, she hadn't yet been allowed to make her First Communion, even though she was already fourteen years old. But Bernadette loved God with all her heart.

Bernadette, Toinette, and Jeanne ran off toward the wooded area of Massabielle to look for firewood. To get there they had to wade across a shallow stream that flowed into the Gave River. Toinette and Jeanne kicked off their wooden shoes and, squealing loudly, splashed through the icy water. Bernadette, who wasn't supposed to get wet, threw some rocks into the stream, trying to make a path to walk on. But the water was too high and covered them.

When her sister and Jeanne had run ahead, Bernadette suddenly heard a sound like a gust of wind. She looked around in surprise. The air was still and the tree branches weren't even moving. Suddenly, a hollow in the rocky cliff by the stream filled with light and a beautiful young Lady appeared!

The Lady smiled and motioned for Bernadette to come closer. Not knowing what to do, Bernadette drew nearer to the Lady, dropped to her knees, and reached for her well-worn rosary beads. The Lady seemed to be about sixteen or seventeen years old. She wore a long white dress and veil. A blue sash encircled her waist, and she held a large, white rosary. When the Lady made the Sign of the Cross and began to finger the beads of her rosary, Bernadette also began to pray the Rosary. As she prayed, Bernadette noticed that the young Lady silently moved her lips only during the "Glory be to the Father, and to the Son, and to the Holy Spirit," at the end of each decade.

Once Bernadette finished praying the Rosary, the Lady disappeared. Bernadette was still kneeling on the damp ground when Toinette and Jeanne returned carrying their bundles of branches. "You could at least help us!" Jeanne complained. Impulsively taking off her shoes and stockings, Bernadette waded across the frigid stream and quickly gathered up a pile of branches. "Why did you tell me that the water was cold?" she said as she put her stockings and shoes back on. "It wasn't cold at all!" Toinette and Jeanne looked at one another in amazement.

On the way home, impatient Jeanne ran ahead, and Bernadette ended up telling Toinette what she had seen at the grotto in the cliff. "Promise me you'll keep it a secret," she begged. "I promise," Toinette answered. But once in the house, Toinette told her mother what Bernadette had seen. Mrs. Soubirous went upstairs and repeated the fantastic story to Aunt Romaine. Everyone agreed that Bernadette must have been imagining things!

The following Sunday, February 14, Bernadette and some friends—armed with a bottle of holy water in case the Lady didn't come from God—returned to the grotto. Bernadette knelt and began to pray the Rosary. The girls followed her example, waiting expectantly. "She's there!" Bernadette suddenly exclaimed." The others couldn't see anything. "Quick! Throw the holy water!" urged one of the girls. Bernadette sprinkled some of the holy water toward the young Lady. "If you come from God, stay!" she cried, "but if not, vanish!"

When the Lady made the Sign of the Cross and began to finger the beads of her rosary, Bernadette also began to pray the Rosary.

The Lady moved up to the very edge of the cliff's hollow, bowed her head, and smiled. Bernadette's face lit up with joy.

After this apparition, the news reached the city officials. They didn't believe the story, but were eager to find out more about it, thinking it might be some sort of trick of Bernadette's to obtain money for her parents. Bernadette's father had lost his job, and her family was very poor.

On Thursday, February 18, the beautiful young Lady appeared for the third time. Holding out paper, pen, and an ink bottle, the girl begged her, "My Lady, please write your name and tell me what you desire of me."

As soon as Bernadette had made the request, she grew worried. Had she been too bold? She held her breath. The Lady smiled and began to speak. "It is not necessary," she said softly. "Would you do me the favor of coming here for fifteen days?"

"Yes!" Bernadette exclaimed.

The Lady continued, "I do not promise to make you happy in this world, but in the next."

Bernadette visited the grotto each day for the next three days. Each day, more and more townspeople followed her there. By the third day, there were over a hundred spectators crowded into the space around the grotto, but only Bernadette could see and hear the Lady.

Soon after this, Bernadette was taken to the office of Police Commissioner Jacomet, who asked her many confusing questions and then accused her of lying.

Bernadette calmly answered everything. She even corrected all the false information that the commissioner wrote down and then read back to her in an attempt to trick her.

"Now, listen," stormed Jacomet, "if you don't promise not to return to the grotto, you'll be sent to jail!" Just then, François Soubirous arrived on the scene. Immediately Jacomet turned his anger upon him. "You're her father," he shouted. "If you don't stop this deception, you'll both go to jail!"

"Believe me, sir, I'm tired of the whole thing myself," François declared. "Bernadette will not go to the grotto at Massabielle again."

"See to it!" snapped Jacomet. "Now take her home!"

But Bernadette had made a promise to the Lady. Touched by his daughter's sadness, François gave in and allowed her to return again and again to the grotto. And, since no one was breaking any laws, the police really couldn't do a thing about it!

The eighth time that the Lady appeared to Bernadette, she asked the girl, "Would you mind kneeling and kissing the ground as a penance for the conversion of sinners?" The Lady's face was sad. This made Bernadette feel sad, too.

"Of course, my Lady," Bernadette replied. "I will do it with all my heart." She kissed the ground several times, and then the visit was over.

On February 25, the morning of the ninth apparition, Bernadette made her way to the grotto through an especially large crowd and knelt in prayer as usual.

As she began to pray the Rosary, the Lady said, "Go to drink and wash yourself in the spring. Then eat some of the grass you find there."

Bernadette was puzzled. There was no spring of water! *Maybe it doesn't matter where I take the water from,* Bernadette thought, as she stood up and began to walk toward the river.

But the Lady motioned with her finger for Bernadette to come back and look for the spring in an area beside the grotto. Returning to the spot shown her by the Lady, Bernadette got down on her hands and knees and began to dig in the reddish soil. When she had made a small hole, a few drops of muddy water appeared at the bottom. Three times she tried to drink the water and three times she had to spit it out because it was more mud than water. Finally, on the fourth try, she managed to swallow a few drops. Next, she "washed" her face with the muddy water. Finally, she ate some of the leaves of one of the wild plants growing nearby.

The onlookers gasped. They didn't understand what Bernadette was doing.

But later that afternoon, a small trickle of water began to flow from the hole Bernadette had dug. People enlarged the hole and the water continued to increase. Soon it was clear and clean. Some of the townspeople filled bottles with the water and even gave it to those who were sick. People who drank the water felt peaceful and happy. (Today the water of the spring flows into great tanks. Persons who visit Mary's shrine at Lourdes may drink the water and bathe in it.

Tests have shown that it is ordinary water, but over the years, many persons have experienced spiritual or even physical healings by using it as a sign of their trust in God.)

On March 2, after visiting the grotto for the thirteenth apparition of the Lady, Bernadette, accompanied by two of her aunts, went to see her pastor, Father Peyramale. He had heard of the events at Massabielle and had followed the bishop's advice not to go to the grotto. But now Father Peyramale would have to take some sort of stand on the apparitions, because the Lady had given Bernadette a message for him.

"The Lady asked me to tell the priests that she wants the people to come to the grotto in a procession," Bernadette nervously declared.

"A procession!" the priest roared. "Doesn't she know that only bishops can order processions? She should have sent you to the bishop, not to me." Turning to Bernadette's aunts, the priest ordered, "Take this girl home and keep her there!"

As soon as they were out the door, Bernadette's Aunt Bernarde ran home. Walking with her Aunt Basile, Bernadette suddenly remembered another thing the Lady had asked her to tell Father Peyramale. "We have to go back!" Bernadette exclaimed. "I forgot to tell him something important!" But Basile refused to face the angry priest again.

When she got home, Bernadette tried to get her parents to go back to the rectory with her. But they also refused. That evening she finally convinced a neighbor to go with her.

This time there were three other priests with Father Peyramale. "The Lady also told me to tell you to have a chapel built at Massabielle," Bernadette blurted out.

"The Lady!" the pastor boomed. "What's her name?"

"I don't know."

"Well, you'll have to ask her. Tell her that the pastor doesn't deal with people he doesn't know. Tell her I need to know her name."

On March 25, Bernadette hurried to Massabielle with the first rays of dawn. The beautiful Lady was already there in the hollow of the rock when Bernadette arrived. It was the sixteenth time that she had appeared to Bernadette. Bernadette gathered her courage and pleaded, "My Lady, won't you be kind enough to tell me who you are?"

Three times the young girl dared to question her. Finally, the Lady opened her arms and extended them toward the earth. Lifting her gaze to heaven and joining her hands over her heart, she said, "I am the Immaculate Conception." And then she was gone.

Eagerly the crowd questioned Bernadette:

"Did she tell you her name?"

"Is it really the Blessed Virgin?"

"I don't know," she murmured as she ran to find Father Peyramale. The name the Lady had told her was one that she had never heard before. All the way to the rectory she kept repeating the strange words to herself so she wouldn't forget them. What in the world could they mean?

Pushing open the rectory door, Bernadette practically shouted, "'I am the Immaculate Conception!' The Lady told me, 'I am the Immaculate Conception.'"

The pastor gasped. "It must be a mistake. Do you know what that means?"

"No, Father," Bernadette admitted, shaking her head. "But that's what the Lady said. I repeated it all the way here."

"Go home now. I'll see you another day," Father Peyramale managed to say.

After Bernadette left, the priest thought long and hard about what she had said. Only four years before, Pope Pius IX had solemnly declared it a dogma, or truth of faith, that Mary, the Mother of Jesus, was conceived without original sin. This was not something a young, uneducated girl from the country would ever have heard of. So if the Lady had said, "I am the Immaculate Conception," it could only mean that she was the Blessed Virgin Mary!

~~~~~~~~~~~~

On June 3, Bernadette received her First Holy Communion. In the silence of her heart she spoke to her God: *O Jesus, I love you. Forgive all sinners and save them. For them I offer you my life.*

The joy of her First Communion prepared her to say good-bye to her beautiful Lady. It was the evening of July 16, 1858, when Bernadette asked her aunt, "Aunt Lucille, will you come with me? The Blessed Virgin is waiting for me."

Willingly, her aunt accompanied her to the grotto. A tall fence had been placed around it to keep the crowds away. Bernadette and her aunt stopped on the opposite side of the Gave River. They knelt, gazing up at the grotto.

Soon Bernadette's face lit up with a smile, and her aunt knew the Blessed Mother had appeared. Bernadette prayed the Rosary with the Lady for the last time. This was her farewell visit, and Bernadette knew it. She fixed her gaze on the splendor of her Lady, who appeared more beautiful than ever before. As the figure of the Virgin slowly disappeared, Bernadette was left with a peaceful heart.

"I shall not see her again on this earth...but I *will* see her again!" she declared.

~~~~~~~~~~~~~~~~

Thousands of people had heard of Bernadette's visions and many traveled to Lourdes, wanting to talk to her. She decided to find shelter from the crowds. At first, Bernadette went to stay as a boarder at the local convent of the Sisters of Charity of Nevers, the same sisters who had taught her in school. She did housework for them. One day the bishop came to visit. "What do you intend to do, Bernadette, in return for what the Blessed Virgin has done for you?" he asked her.

"I would like to live with the sisters, to pray and work as their maid, Your Excellency," Bernadette replied.

"But to stay in the convent for good, you must make vows, like the sisters," the bishop answered. "Have you ever thought of entering their congregation?"

"Your Excellency," Bernadette protested, "I'm poor and ignorant."

But poverty and ignorance matter little when a person wants to serve God. Within a year, Bernadette had made up her mind to join the Sisters of Charity.

She left Lourdes for the city of Nevers, where the Mother General of the Sisters of Charity accepted her into the community.

"Bernadette," said the Mother General, "I hope you will be happy among us. What do you know how to do?"

"Very little, Reverend Mother. I know how to peel potatoes and scrub pots."

"In the house of the Lord," replied the Mother General, "one duty is just as important as another. Tomorrow you'll begin to work in the kitchen."

On July 29, 1866, the bishop came to give Bernadette the habit of the congregation. "From now on," he said, "you will be called Sister Marie Bernarde."

People were always coming to the convent trying to get a glimpse of Bernadette because she had seen the Blessed Virgin. But the little sister found many ways to hide from them. For example, once she was passing through the hallway when a gentleman came to the front door. "Sister," he said to her, "please be so kind as to call Bernadette here for a moment."

"Yes, of course," Bernadette answered with a smile, hurrying off as if she were going to look for someone. Several minutes passed. The gentleman approached the sister who took care of answering the door. "Isn't it possible to see Bernadette?" he asked.

"But you were speaking with her," the sister answered in surprise, "and the way she escaped from you, you shouldn't even hope to see her again!"

One day another sister asked Bernadette, "Have you ever felt that you were better than the rest of us because you were so favored by the Blessed Virgin?"

Bernadette was amazed. "Don't you know that the Blessed Virgin chose me because I'm the most ignorant?" she replied. "If she had found anyone more ignorant, she would have chosen that person."

Another time she said, "I served as a broom for the Blessed Virgin. And when she no longer had any use for me, she put me in my place, behind the door. That's where I am and where I will stay."

~~~~~~~~~~~

The Blessed Virgin had told Bernadette, "I shall not make you happy on this earth," and Bernadette knew that suffering was her mission. Before long, she became very sick with tuberculosis.

As Bernadette lay dying, she murmured, "Holy Mary, Mother of God, pray for me, a poor sinner...." She closed her eyes and leaned gently on the arm of the sister who was sitting beside her. Now, at last, she would see her Lady again—but this time, it would be in heaven.

~~~~~~~~~~~

Today the spring that Bernadette dug at the request of the Blessed Mother continues to bubble up and call people to Mary's shrine. Trains bring the sick to Lourdes from all over the world. At the shrine of Our Lady of Lourdes, people find Jesus. In the Most Blessed Sacrament, he passes among the rows of sick, who wait in the square in front of the beautiful basilica (a large church built in a special design). While the priest blesses the people with the monstrance containing the Blessed Sacrament, they pray:

"Jesus, have pity on us!"

"Lord, let me see!"

"Lord, I want to walk again!"

While not everyone receives a physical cure at Lourdes, many people experience spiritual healings there and return home with more faith and trust in God and peace in their souls.

Long processions make their way from the grotto to the square in front of the basilica. Just as Bernadette used to do, the people recite the Rosary together and ask God's forgiveness and blessings through Mary's intercession.

St. Bernadette never became proud of the special favor God gave her. She knew that the Blessed Mother's visits to her were God's gift, and not something she deserved. Let's always be grateful, because everything we have is God's gift to us. Let's also love the Blessed Mother as Bernadette did. Mary always brings us closer to her Son, Jesus.

St. John Bosco

(1815-1888)

JANUARY 31

John Bosco was born in the Piedmont region of
northern Italy to a poor peasant family. His father died
when John was only two years old. His mother,
Margaret, was a good and religious woman, a hard-
working widow who taught her son to be kind and
faithful. John spent his early years as a shepherd, but
his mother wanted him to be educated, too. He was
fortunate to be able to study with their parish priest,
who taught him reading, writing, and religion. John
loved his schoolwork, and could often be seen out in
the fields with a book in his hands.

One night when he was nine years old, John had a
dream. He was standing in the middle of a group of
children who were fighting and swearing. He tried to
tell them to stop, but they wouldn't listen. Then he
tried to *make* them stop by using his own fists. But
that didn't work either. Suddenly, he saw a man in
white coming toward him. The man was smiling. "You

will make them your friends with love," the man said. "With meekness and charity, you will conquer them."

"Who are you?" asked the surprised boy.

"I am the Son of the Lady your mother has taught you to pray to so often. Ask my Mother for help!"

Then the Blessed Mother appeared in the dream. "Look!" she exclaimed, and John saw that the violent children all around him had changed into wild beasts. "As I do with these wild beasts, so will you do with the children," Mary told John. And the beasts became meek lambs as she spoke. "Make yourself humble, strong, and robust," she added. "At the right time, you will understand everything!"

From then on, John knew that his special purpose in life would be to help children.

One day his mother took him to a country fair where he watched the stunts of the acrobats. An idea came into his mind. Back home again, he stretched a rope between two trees and tried to walk it.

Of course, he fell many times. His brother Anthony laughed. But John wasn't discouraged; he just tried again and again. Soon he could easily walk the tightrope. But he didn't stop there. He learned other acrobatic stunts. Now he was ready for his "show"! One Sunday night, he invited some adults and children to watch as he performed. They clapped enthusiastically as he began. Then John, who had another motive, started a hymn to Mary. Everyone joined in. "Now unless you say the Rosary while I perform, I might fall and break my head!" John exclaimed. So the crowd began to pray. At the close of his performance, John sat down and repeated the sermon the priest had given that morning at Mass. He did that because he realized that many of the people in his audience hadn't gone to church that day.

John knew he wanted to be a priest. To pay for his education, he took part-time jobs and learned many skills, including carpentry, tailoring, and shoemaking. He asked his mother if she would be able to support herself if he entered the seminary. He knew she'd have to make many sacrifices.

"Don't worry about me," his mother told him. "Do what God wants you to do. I'm poor, I was born poor, and I want to die poor." So, at the age of sixteen, John Bosco entered the seminary and began his studies for the priesthood.

John hadn't forgotten the dream. Whenever he could spare a moment from his studies, he would gather together all the ragged and lonely boys he could find. He took them on outings and taught them about God.

When John was ordained to the priesthood in 1841, the whole village turned out for his first Mass. Tears of joy streamed down his mother's cheeks. From then on her boy would be known as Don Bosco. ("Don" is an Italian title of respect for a priest.)

After his ordination, Don Bosco went to Turin to complete his studies. This large Italian city was experiencing many problems. At that time there was a great deal of political unrest in Italy. Small independent states were moving toward unity as a republic. Many people who had lived on farms in the rural areas headed for the cities, looking for work. Cities like Turin weren't able to cope with this sudden influx of people. The results were overcrowding, slums, high unemployment, homelessness, poverty, and crime. There weren't nearly enough schools for all the children moving into the cities.

Many teenagers and younger children were living on the streets, unable to find work. They became thieves, and were often picked up by the police and thrown into prison. There hardened criminals taught them how to commit even worse crimes.

Don Bosco visited the jails and hospitals, the streets and the alleys, talking to young people. He was shocked at the conditions in which so many of them lived. "O Lord," he prayed, "help me to serve these young people in such desperate need. Show me the way to begin."

One day Don Bosco was in the church sacristy, preparing to celebrate Mass, when he heard a commotion. Turning around, he saw the sacristan scolding a ragged young boy. "What's wrong with you? You don't even know the first thing about serving Mass. Get out of here and don't come back!"

The young priest hurried over. He sent the sacristan away. "Would you like me to teach you how to serve?" he asked the boy. Gratefully the youngster nodded his head. After Don Bosco had finished the lesson, he asked the boy to bring his friends with him the next day.

Soon Don Bosco had many pupils. Every Sunday morning they came to participate at Mass and go to confession; in the evening they came to study catechism and sing hymns. Many of these boys were homeless. The priest found a place for them to live. His mother came to Turin to help him take care of them. The boys lovingly called her "Mama Margaret." The little school grew and grew, moving several times to larger quarters.

One evening as Don Bosco was walking through a deserted area, a strange thing happened. Two men came up behind him. The priest knew they wanted to beat and rob him. Suddenly a huge gray dog roared out of the shadows and leaped at one of the robbers. The other turned and fled. Don Bosco called the snarling dog away from the man he was about to attack, and that man ran away too. The dog then walked quietly home with the priest before disappearing into the night.

Don Bosco named the dog "Grigio," which means "gray" in Italian. Don Bosco had many enemies who thought he was going too far in his work to help homeless boys. Some of these men went so far as to organize plots to kill him! Many times, when the priest was in danger, Grigio would appear out of nowhere and lead him to safety.

Was this really an ordinary dog? Who was his owner? "What does it matter?" Don Bosco said. "I only know that throughout many dangers, this animal protected me providentially."

Soon Don Bosco realized that a religious congregation was needed to take care of and teach the boys—and not only boys in his own city, but all over

After a few years, Don Bosco realized that a community of religious was needed to take care of homeless boys, both in his own city and in other parts of the world.

the world. And so, in 1859, he founded the Salesian Society, which he named after St. Francis de Sales. Don Bosco's little school eventually grew into the famous Salesian Oratory. Many of the pupils who graduated from the Oratory went on to become teachers in other Salesian schools. Don Bosco watched his congregation grow and spread all over the world.

Don Bosco died in 1888. By that time, the Salesians were helping over 130,000 children in 250 locations worldwide. In 1934, Don Bosco was canonized by one of his greatest admirers, Pope Pius XI.

From his early childhood, St. John Bosco wanted to help others get closer to God. One way we can do this is by trying to act as Jesus would act. Our good example will help our friends.

St. Thérèse of Lisieux

(1873–1897)

Thérèse Martin, born in Alençon, France, on January 2, 1873, was the youngest in a family of five girls. Zelie Martin, her mother, died of cancer when Thérèse was only four years old. To be closer to their mother's family, the Martins moved to the town of Lisieux soon after Zelie's death. Little Thérèse was raised by her older sisters, Pauline and Marie.

One day, Pauline showed Thérèse how all the people in heaven are completely happy even though some have more glory than others. She did this by taking a cup and a thimble and filling each with water. "Now," she asked, "which is the fullest?" Thérèse was puzzled, for neither of them could have held another drop. "That's how it will be in heaven," Pauline said. "Every soul will be completely filled with happiness, but some will have more room for it, because they had a greater love of God when they lived on earth." Then and there, little Thérèse decided to let herself be filled with a great love of God.

Pauline also taught her younger sister all about the religious feasts. Thérèse's favorite was Corpus Christi, when the Blessed Sacrament was carried in procession through the streets of the town. The children would spread flowers along the road in front of it. Thérèse thought that each flower was like a kiss to Jesus in the Eucharist.

When Thérèse was ten years old, her beloved sister Pauline left the family to become a Carmelite nun in the monastery at Lisieux. Carmelite nuns are cloistered, which means they spend all of their days, and part of their nights, too, in prayer and meditation, and they don't leave their monastery. Thérèse was terribly upset that Pauline wouldn't be at home with her any more, acting as her "second mother." But Pauline explained, "Thérèse, the sisters at Carmel live for God alone. This is what I want to do with my whole heart. It will make me very happy."

At that moment, Thérèse knew that she, too, wanted to live for God alone, and that someday she would enter religious life as a Carmelite.

The following year, on the day of her First Holy Communion, Thérèse told Jesus that she was entirely his. She was crying for joy. That day she listed her resolutions for progress: "I will never let myself become discouraged. I will say the *Memorare* daily. I will try to be humble."

When the Holy Spirit came to her in Confirmation, Thérèse felt great joy. She understood that she was receiving strength for the spiritual battles that would come in her life.

~~~~~~~~~~~~

Thérèse couldn't bear the thought of anyone going to hell. She knew that Jesus wanted everyone to be happy with him forever in heaven. She prayed often for the conversion of those people who refused to love God and obey the commandments.

When Thérèse was fourteen, the newspapers were filled with reports about a murderer named Pranzini who was going to be executed but wouldn't repent of his crime. This was her chance to pray for a *particular* sinner! "Dear God," she prayed, "send Pranzini the grace of repentance, because of the merits of the passion of Jesus!" She prayed long and hard for that man, and offered sacrifices for his conversion. At the same time, she confided to Jesus: "He's my first sinner, so please give me a sign that he's been converted—any little sign."

The day of the execution came. And what did the newspapers say about the criminal's death? Just before he died, the murderer had asked for a priest, whom he had ignored until then. The priest held up a crucifix, and Pranzini kissed it three times. He was sorry for what he had done! Thérèse had her sign. She knew that her "first sinner" had been converted.

By this time, Marie had joined Pauline at the Carmelite monastery, and Thérèse's sister Leonie had become a Poor Clare nun. Only Celine and Thérèse were left at home. Thérèse still wanted to enter Carmel. She wasn't sure how she should tell her father, because he loved her very much. Now that he was growing old, he would feel so lonely without her! But Jesus was calling her, and she had to answer. Thérèse chose a beautiful spring evening, the feast of Pentecost 1887, to break the news to her father. "Papa," she began as they walked together in the garden, "I want to enter Carmel."

Mr. Martin had suspected that Thérèse wanted to give her life to God. Although it was a great sacrifice to let his daughters go, Mr. Martin felt privileged to have them serve God as sisters. But Thérèse was so young...only fourteen. With tears in his eyes, Mr. Martin hugged Thérèse after she told him how strong her desire was. "You have my permission," he quietly told her.

But there was a problem. Thérèse's uncle Isidore was her legal guardian, and he insisted that she was too young to enter such a strict Order. Thérèse cried, but then she prayed for a miracle—and waited.

Three painful days passed, and Thérèse went back to her uncle's house. "Thérèse," began Uncle Isidore, "I've been praying about your request—and God has let me know that it's right for you to enter Carmel." Thérèse had her miracle!

Thérèse applied for admission to the convent. The nuns were willing to accept her, but Father Delatroette, the priest who supervised the monastery, wasn't. "She's too young for this demanding way of life," he insisted. "She can't be accepted until she's twenty-one!" Not ready to give up, Thérèse appealed to the bishop. But he didn't want to make a decision

On a spring night when she and her father were walking together in the garden, Thérèse forced herself to speak.

until he had discussed the matter with Father Delatroette. Thérèse left the bishop's house in tears.

Three days after the visit to the bishop, Mr. Martin, Celine, and Thérèse set out for Rome with a pilgrimage group from their diocese. Thérèse planned to bring her case to the Holy Father. After all, if he said that she could enter the monastery, everyone else would have to agree! On the way, the pilgrims visited many beautiful and holy places, including the House of Loreto, where, according to legend, the Holy Family had lived when at Nazareth, and which had been carried to Loretto, Italy, by angels hundreds of years before.

The pilgrims finally reached Rome, and the day for their audience with the Pope arrived. Everyone was told not to speak to the Holy Father. But Thérèse had to! So when her turn came to kneel and kiss his ring, she bravely asked, "Holy Father, in honor of your jubilee, allow me to enter Carmel at fifteen." Pope Leo XIII bent toward her and kindly replied, "You will enter if it is God's will." Then two papal guards lifted Thérèse to her feet and led her away.

Poor Thérèse! It seemed that the journey had been in vain! She, Celine, and their father were very sad as they began their return trip to France. But Thérèse kept on praying. About a month after she returned home, the bishop unexpectedly agreed to let her enter the Carmelite monastery after Lent the following year!

Thérèse entered Carmel on April 9, 1888, which was the feast of the Annunciation that year. She began her religious life by offering her prayers, works, and sacrifices especially for priests. When the time came to receive her religious name, she received the name Sister Thérèse of the Child Jesus of the Holy Face.

Thérèse had a strong desire to become a saint, and she asked God's help to do each duty in the best way possible out of love for him. Her famous "little way" to God was made up of prayer, humility, and love. Thérèse was convinced that anyone could become holy by simply loving God and doing even the smallest action well for the love of God. Whether it was time to sweep the hall, pray, or help care for a sick sister, Thérèse did it as if it were the most important thing in the world.

Thinking of this "little way" of holiness helped Thérèse to give an extra bright smile to the sister who annoyed her the most. When someone didn't approve of the way Thérèse did something, she would do it all over again in the way the other person suggested. She accepted the cold in the winter and the heat in the summer without complaining. Sometimes it was difficult, because her cell was terribly cold in wintertime, and often she hardly slept at all. But she never let the other sisters know about it, and she tried to be as cheerful and full of energy in the daytime as she would have been after a full night's rest.

One Christmas, Thérèse's sister Pauline, who was now the prioress of the monastery, asked Thérèse if she would write down the story of her life. Thérèse was surprised. She couldn't imagine why anyone would be interested! But she did as she was asked. She called her autobiography *The Story of a Soul*. Thérèse also wrote poetry and prayers.

Sister Thérèse was developing a troublesome cough. Eventually she became very sick, and started to cough up blood. She became weaker and weaker. When the doctor was called in, there was nothing he could do to save her. She had a very painful, fatal form of tuberculosis.

Thérèse's final days were filled with almost unbearable pain. Thérèse knew she wasn't suffering by herself. She felt herself united to Jesus on the cross. Like Jesus, she offered all her pain to God in reparation for sin, and so that sinners would repent and return to God's love. She also prayed in a special way for priests and missionaries, that they would always know how much love God has for them. She was only twenty-four years old when she died in 1897.

A year after her death, the bishop gave permission to publish Thérèse's autobiography, *The Story of a Soul*. Soon the book had been translated into thirty-five languages! People all over the world have learned about her "little way." In 1925, Thérèse was declared a saint. In 1997, a hundred years after her death, Pope John Paul II named her a "Doctor of the Church," which means that her writings have helped people everywhere to learn about what we believe and how we live as Catholics.

To St. Thérèse, "little things" were what mattered. She never did anything special or outstanding, but she did everything with great love. Thérèse shows us that love is what brings us very close to God.

St. Gemma Galgani

(1878–1903)

APRIL 11

"But, Father," protested the young mother, "I don't think we should name the child 'Gemma' as my brother-in-law wishes. I've never heard of a saint in heaven by that name—and I certainly want my little one in heaven one day!"

"Certainly gems are to be found in heaven," consoled the priest. "Let's hope this child will be a heavenly gem."

And so the day-old infant was baptized Gemma Umberta Pia Galgani on March 13, 1878.

Mrs. Galgani was a very good mother. She went to Mass and received Communion every day. When her children were still small, she taught them about the importance of avoiding sin and trying to please God in every way. Often she showed Gemma the crucifix and said, "See, Gemma, this is Jesus, who loves us and died on the cross for us." The little girl would take the crucifix from her mother's hands and kiss the figure of Jesus.

Every Saturday, Mrs. Galgani prepared Gemma's three older brothers for confession. She took them to church herself whenever she could. When Gemma turned seven and was preparing for her first confession, her mother was very happy to see how serious the child was.

One day Gemma's mother said something that must have puzzled the little girl: "Oh, I wish I could take you with me! Would you come?"

"Where are you going?" Gemma asked in surprise.

"To heaven, where Jesus lives with his angels."

"Yes! Yes!" exclaimed Gemma, her eyes shining at the thought.

Young as she was, Gemma soon came to understand that her mother was very ill. Every day she became weaker, and soon she couldn't get out of bed.

"This disease is highly contagious," the doctor declared. "The children must be sent away."

But Gemma cried and refused to go. Finally, her father sent the boys away and kept Gemma home.

The little girl became her mother's nurse and took care of her every need. Often she knelt beside her mother's bed and prayed the Rosary with her.

When Gemma received the sacrament of Confirmation, her first thought after thanking God was to pray for her mother. It seemed to her she heard a voice asking, "Will you give me your mother?"

"Yes," she answered silently, "but only if you will take me, too."

"No," was the reply. "You must stay with your father. I will take your mother to heaven, but will you give her up willingly?"

Gemma bravely said yes to God.

When she reached home and saw her poor mother suffering so patiently, Gemma began to cry, but she didn't say why.

Mrs. Galgani seemed to get better for a little while, then her severe pains returned. Gemma stayed by her side, praying. The young girl felt as if her whole world had fallen to pieces. Gemma wanted so much to stay with her mother until her mother went to heaven, where she would have no more suffering and pain. But her father couldn't bear to see Gemma watch her mother suffer, so he sent her to stay with her aunt in another village.

~~~~~~~~~~~~~~

Months later, Gemma came back to an empty house—even though it was full of children, and her father was there as always. Gemma hid her own sorrow and became the comfort of the whole family. Whenever she saw one her brothers crying over their mother, she gently said, "There's no need to cry. Mama is in heaven. She's not suffering any longer—and she suffered so much!"

Every day the little girl went to a school taught by the Sisters of St. Zita. She paid careful attention in class, and joined in the games during recess. The sisters noticed that she always had a smile for everyone.

First Communion day was one of the most wonderful days of Gemma's life. She prepared herself carefully, with sincere sorrow for all her sins. As soon as she had received the Sacred Host, she felt Jesus' presence in her soul.

But one day all her joy was gone. Until now Gemma had felt a strong love of God, an attraction for prayer, a longing for heaven. Suddenly, she felt nothing at all. Life seemed empty, without purpose or meaning.

She knew in her mind that God loved her and that heaven awaited her—but she *felt* nothing. It became difficult to pray, difficult to work, to play, to laugh.

In spite of how she felt, Gemma kept on praying every day. She continued to smile, although she felt sad inside. She worked as energetically as ever, although she felt like doing nothing at all. She gave generously to the poor, as she had always done.

In that time of darkness, Gemma's faith and love grew strong, because she had to *force* herself to have faith; she had to *force* herself to love. When at last a feeling of happiness returned to her, she had become much more convinced of God's special love for her.

Not long after the darkness lifted from Gemma's soul, another sorrow came into her life. Her brother Gino, who had entered the seminary, contracted a dangerous disease. He returned home, and Gemma nursed him for many long, anxious months, but in the end he died.

Within three years, Gemma's father also died, and she and her brothers were left orphans and utterly poor.

Gemma was nineteen at the time. An aunt took her in and urged her to marry a nice young man, a doctor's son, who had fallen in love with the quiet, attractive young woman. But Gemma wanted her heart to belong only to Jesus. She wanted to become a nun.

The young man persisted. So did her aunt.

"My Jesus," Gemma prayed, "deliver me from this distressing situation."

The deliverance was immediate and painful. Gemma developed a terrible disease in her spine, followed by deafness and almost complete paralysis.

Gemma suffered intensely, with the crucifix as her only consolation. Almost continuously she meditated on Jesus in his passion. She began reading the life of St. Gabriel Possenti and prayed to him for help.

Gemma felt drawn to St. Gabriel, because he had had a great devotion to the passion of Jesus and to Mary, as she did. One night, Gabriel appeared to Gemma and invited her to make a vow never to get married and to give her life totally to God. Overjoyed, Gemma made her vow the very next morning, after the priest had brought her Holy Communion.

She was growing weaker and weaker. The doctor could see no hope. Quite willing to die if it were God's will, Gemma waited patiently.

One night she heard St. Gabriel praying the Our Father. He paused in the middle, and Gemma tried to finish the prayer, although she was in such great pain she could hardly speak.

Together she and her guest said the Hail Mary and Glory Be—and repeated the prayers eight more times. It was a novena!

"Do you wish to be cured?" asked the saint.

"It doesn't matter to me," replied the suffering young woman. She only wanted to do God's will.

"Yes, you will be cured. I'll come each night at this time, and we'll pray together to the Sacred Heart of Jesus."

Several nights passed in that way. The novena was almost over when the priest came to hear Gemma's confession and bring her First Friday Communion. After Communion, Gemma could feel Jesus asking her, "Gemma, do you wish to be cured?"

Overwhelmed by his tenderness, Gemma couldn't answer.

"My daughter," said Jesus, "I give myself completely to you, and you must belong entirely to me. I am your Father, and my Mother will be your mother. My fatherly help can never fail those who abandon themselves into my hands. You will be all right, even though I have taken away those who loved and helped you the most."

Gemma was cured! Everyone in the house cried for joy.

What a consolation it was to the orphan Gemma to have the Blessed Mother as her own Mother! She had always loved our Lady, but now she turned to Mary with all the trust of a small child. In every need she sought her heavenly Mother's help. "Keep my heart with you in heaven," she prayed.

Often she pictured to herself that tender Mother standing at the foot of the cross, suffering silently with her Son. Seeing those two most gentle people in such agony, Gemma felt an intense desire to suffer with them.

"How deeply I feel your sorrow, my Mother, seeing you at the foot of the cross, but do you know my greatest sorrow? It is that I cannot comfort you; on the contrary, I feel worse, because I myself have been a cause of so much of your suffering."

"My Jesus," Gemma prayed one day, after having been refused entrance into a convent because of her

Gemma would imagine Mary, the Mother of Jesus, standing at the foot of the cross, suffering silently with her Son. Seeing those two most gentle people in such agony, Gemma felt an intense desire to suffer with them.

poor health, "I want to love you—oh, so much—but I don't know how."

"Do you wish to love Jesus now and forever?" a voice asked. "Then never stop suffering for him. The cross is the heritage of the people God has chosen."

Every Thursday night and Friday morning, Gemma began to feel the sufferings of Jesus' passion. During those hours, she bore the stigmata—the wounds of Jesus—in her hands, feet, and heart. The pain was intense—and in addition to this, she felt weighed down by the burden of the world's sins. Each Friday afternoon, the wounds would close up and fade to small white scars.

"I shrink every time I look at the cross," she wrote, "because I feel I could die thinking of the pain of it, yet in spite of this, my heart welcomes the sufferings." Why? Because Jesus had suffered, and Gemma loved Jesus very much.

Gemma's last months on earth were filled with intense pain. The darkness of spirit she had felt years before returned to her. The devil tempted her to despair. Life was empty of all joy.

Gemma turned to her heavenly Mother and asked Mary to intercede for her. She continued to talk to Jesus, even though she could not feel his presence.

One day a nurse asked her, "What would you do if our Lord let you choose between going to heaven at once and staying on earth to suffer more and add to his glory?"

"It would be better to stay and suffer," Gemma replied. "Jesus' glory always comes first."

On Wednesday and again on Thursday of Holy Week, 1903, Gemma received Holy Communion. Then, on Good Friday at about ten o'clock, she exclaimed, "I have to be crucified with Jesus."

Lying on her sickbed, she extended her arms as if she were on the cross. She said nothing, and on her face was an expression of suffering, but also of love and calm. She remained that way for three and a half hours.

Gemma continued to suffer the rest of that day and most of the next. Holy Saturday evening she received the sacraments of Anointing and Eucharist for the last time. Then, bowing her head as Jesus had on the cross, Gemma Galgani commended her soul to God.

She was twenty-five years old.

Gemma was buried in the Passionist convent of her city, Lucca, where she had longed to live during her lifetime. This is the inscription on her tomb:

"Gemma Galgani from Lucca, most pure virgin, being in her twenty-fifth year, died of tuberculosis but was more consumed by the fires of divine love than by her wasting disease. On the eleventh of April, 1903, the vigil of Easter, her soul took its flight to the bosom of her heavenly Spouse. Beautiful soul—in peace with the angels."

In every sorrow, including her parents' deaths, St. Gemma turned for help to Jesus in the Eucharist and to the Blessed Mother. Whenever something makes us sad or causes us suffering, we should "talk it over" with Jesus and Mary. They love us and know what we need, and they will always help us.

St. Frances Xavier Cabrini

(1850–1917)

Maria Francesca Cabrini was born to a farming family in Sant'Angelo, in the Lombardy region of Italy, in 1850. Little Francesca, whom her family nicknamed Cecchina, liked to listen to the stories of missionaries that her father read aloud to the family every evening.

"I'm going to be a missionary, too!" she told her older sister, Rosa, one day.

"You? You're too small. Missionaries must be strong!"

"I'll grow," Cecchina promised.

Cecchina loved to think about her favorite missionary, St. Francis Xavier, and his great love for Jesus, and how he had traveled all over Asia and was headed for China when he died.

"Do Chinese children know about Jesus?" she asked.

"Some do, but many have never heard of him," answered Rosa patiently.

"How much I'd like to tell them about him!" the little girl exclaimed.

As Cecchina grew to be a young woman, her desire to be a missionary grew with her. In spite of her poor health, she trained to be a teacher. Cecchina was sure that God was calling her to enter the convent, but because she had been sick so much, the superior of the Daughters of the Sacred Heart told her each time she applied, "This isn't for you. You're not strong enough for our way of life!"

Each time, Cecchina said to herself, "God's will be done." But she still wanted to serve him as completely as possible. She put her faith in the Lord, trusting that, through hard work and prayer, she would eventually understand his plan for her.

When she was twenty-two, Francesca received a request from Father Serrati, a priest in the nearby town of Vidardo. He wanted her to come to teach in the school there, since the regular teacher was ill. Francesca was already very busy helping Rosa teach in their local school. She didn't think she'd have time to take on this new job. "Think of it this way, Francesca," the priest encouraged, "it will be a kind of missionary adventure." Francesca prayed over the idea and agreed to help. She went to work with an energetic will and fervent prayers—and succeeded.

Francesca was such a success, in fact, that even though she was supposed to act as a substitute teacher for only two weeks, she ended up teaching in

Vidardo for two years! Meanwhile, Father Serrati, now Monsignor Serrati, had been transferred to Codogno, a larger town. There was an orphanage there called the House of Providence. It was in financial difficulties and was badly in need of new administration. Monsignor Serrati knew just the person to straighten things out—Francesca!

Things weren't easy for Francesca at the House of Providence. She had to deal with some people who always wanted their own way and argued a lot among themselves. Francesca worked hard to keep the peace and still get things done. She succeeded. And her dream of becoming a religious sister came true!

Bishop Gelmini eventually allowed Francesca and seven other young women who worked with her at the orphanage to make their first religious vows. "I'd like you to serve as the superior of the community," the bishop told Francesca.

"May I have your permission to take a new name, Your Excellency?" Francesca asked. "I'd like to add the name Xavier to my baptismal name, in honor of my favorite missionary saint, St. Francis Xavier."

"Of course," the bishop replied with a smile. "From now on you will be known as Mother Frances Xavier Cabrini."

Not long after, Bishop Gelmini closed the orphanage and sent the children to live with several good families. He knew that Francesca had always wanted to be a missionary, and he felt that this really was God's will for her. "Mother Cabrini," the bishop told her, "I don't know of any congregations of missionary sisters. It seems to me that you should begin one!"

Francesca didn't hesitate. "I'll look for a house immediately, Your Excellency," she happily replied.

Francesca and her companions called themselves the Missionary Sisters of the Sacred Heart of Jesus. They would go throughout the world telling everyone of Jesus' great love for humankind. Perhaps they would even go to China. Francesca's childhood dream hadn't been forgotten.

Schools, orphanages, catechism classes, and more sisters to staff them! The little community grew rapidly. Soon the sisters had several houses in Italy, including a convent and school in Rome.

One day Mother Cabrini had a visitor. It was Bishop Scalabrini, who had founded a congregation of priests to work among the Italian immigrants in America. The bishop urged Mother Cabrini to consider helping him in this missionary work. *Why America?* wondered Mother Cabrini. She still had her heart set on Asia.

"The Italian immigrants there need you," the bishop urged. "They have no one to teach catechism to the children. There is no one to take care of the sick, who are too poor to be admitted into the regular hospitals. People are taking advantage of them materially, and the immigrants are starving spiritually as well."

Mother Cabrini wasn't sure what she should do. Finally, she asked the Holy Father, Pope Leo XIII, for permission to go with her missionary sisters to China. But Pope Leo had read what Bishop Scalabrini had written about the terrible situation of the Italian immigrants in the United States. After a moment of reflection, the Pope told the little nun, "You must go not to the East but to the West!" America it would be.

After a stormy ocean voyage, Mother Cabrini and some of her sisters arrived in New York on March 31, 1889. At the sight of the Statue of Liberty, the little band forgot their weariness and their fears. But the next day, when they went to see the local archbishop, they were in for a shock. "We already have enough religious sisters working here in New York," the archbishop said. "The best thing you can do is go back to Italy!"

Mother Cabrini spoke quietly and calmly. "Thank you for your concern, Your Excellency," she responded. "But we have been sent here by the Holy Father, and only he can call us back. This is where I was sent, and this is where I will work!"

The archbishop knew he had met his match. Soon the sisters had a convent of their own. The first institution they opened was a day school. Next came an orphanage. In just four months, the sisters were caring for 400 orphans! Mother Cabrini and her sisters also visited the city prisons regularly, encouraging the prisoners and speaking to them of heaven.

Then came the wonderful offer of a beautiful piece of property on the Hudson River that could be used for another orphanage and a novitiate house. The price was low, but there was one problem: no water. Mother Cabrini smiled, and bought the property. "God will provide," she said.

And provide he did! The sisters began a novena to our Lady, and on the fifth day they marched out onto the grounds, leading workmen with hoes and shovels.

"Dig here," Mother Cabrini instructed, pointing to a certain spot.

The sisters in New York often went to visit the city prisons, encouraging the prisoners and speaking to them of heaven.

Soon the shovels were turning up rich, brown soil instead of dry sand. And then—water, clear, running water!

In the depths of her heart, Mother Cabrini thanked God. "We'll build a shrine to our Lady near the spring," she promised.

Mother Cabrini's undertakings were full of the same kind of faith that she showed when searching for the spring. She traveled constantly, from the United States to Italy to Central and South America, founding orphanages, hospitals, and schools in an amazingly short period of time and despite all kinds of obstacles. She succeeded through prayer, courage, and faith.

Her faith was great when confronted with natural dangers, too. Many times in her frequent sea journeys violent storms arose, forcing her companions to take to their berths but leaving her calm and prayerful— giving courage to everyone who saw her. When traveling from Chile to Argentina, Mother undertook a treacherous journey over the Andes Mountains on a mule. Her motto was a line from St. Paul: "I can do all things through him who strengthens me" (Phil 4:13).

Life was hard for Mother Cabrini's sisters, especially in Central America. Mother Cabrini realized this, and knew, too, that the sisters must strive to become always more fervent. Once she wrote: "Our great patron, St. Francis Xavier, said, 'He who goes holy to the missions will find many occasions to sanctify himself more, but he who goes poorly provided with holiness runs the risk of losing what he has and of falling away.' I become more convinced of this truth every day. Since experience is a great teacher, let's take advantage of the lessons it gives us and never let a day pass without examining our consciences and making serious resolutions to acquire the virtues we need."

In 1893 a revolution in Nicaragua put into power an anti-religious government that ordered Mother Cabrini's sisters to leave the country at once. Carrying a few little bundles, the sisters filed out of their convent between a double line of soldiers. The schoolchildren sobbed as they helplessly watched the sisters being sent away. From all sides, people flocked to say good-bye.

In the middle of the crowd was an anti-Catholic man named Don Jose Paos. He had come only out of curiosity. As he stood there, a young student went up to one of the sisters and asked, "How can you leave like this without even crying?"

"Why should we cry?" the sister replied. She lifted a crucifix she was carrying. "We had this with us when we came, and we have it with us now!"

Don Jose felt something stirring in the depths of his soul. He returned to his home, locked himself in his room, and refused to see anyone until the next morning. Then he went to the bishop and asked to be readmitted into the Church. Soon he was one of the most active defenders of the faith. Years later, he said, "A religion that inspires young sisters with such serenity, resignation, and peace in times of hardship and strife must be the true one."

When Pope Leo XIII celebrated his golden jubilee as a priest, Mother Cabrini paid him a visit to ask his blessing. "Let us work, let us work," the Holy Father urged her, "for after this there is a beautiful heaven." The words struck home. No matter how much she had done, there was still more to be accomplished. She must never stop, never rest, never say she had done enough.

One of the areas where knowledge of and faithfulness to religion was sadly lacking in 1902 was Denver, Colorado. Many Italian immigrants had settled there as miners and factory workers, but not enough Italian priests had followed them, and there were no Catholic schools in the area. Very few of the people went to Mass on Sundays and many children had never been baptized. Some men and women in their thirties hadn't even made their First Communion yet!

Mother Cabrini opened a school in Denver, and assigned two of her sisters to visit the homes, mines, and factories with words of gentle encouragement. Soon many families returned to Mass and the sacraments—so many that new churches were needed.

In New Orleans, many people were unkind to the sisters at first, but their opinions changed during the yellow fever epidemic of 1905. The sisters sent the orphans safely to a home outside the city and used the orphanage as a hospital for sick women and children, whom they cared for lovingly until the epidemic had passed. How grateful those people were!

Mother Cabrini died peacefully in Chicago on December 22, 1917, in one of the hospitals she had founded. It was fitting that she should die in the land to which she had come out of obedience to the Holy Father and in which she had done so much good. On July 7, 1946, Mother Frances Xavier Cabrini became the first American citizen (she had become a citizen in 1909) to be canonized a saint.

Even though young Francesca's desire to be a sister and a missionary seemed impossible, she continued to pray and to do the work she was able to do. To her great surprise, she became the foundress of a new community of missionary sisters! Even when we can't understand where our lives are going, we can trust that God knows and is with us on our way.

Bl. Miguel Augustín Pro

(1891–1927)

November 23

The well-dressed young man leaned on the railing of the *Cuba* as the ship's captain shouted, "Land ahead! Veracruz ahead!"

Within a few hours they had docked, and the passengers were herded into the customs hall. Miguel grinned and tipped his hat jauntily as he walked confidently past the armed officers. No one suspected that this "rich" young man was not what he appeared to be!

This was a good thing, because in 1926 it was against the law for Catholic priests to enter Mexico. Miguel breathed a sigh of relief and said a prayer of gratitude as his baggage came through unopened. The chalice and vestments that he had received at his recent ordination in Belgium would have cost him his life.

Still wearing his disguise, Father Miguel Pro made his way through the crowded streets. It had been twelve years since he and his fellow seminarians had been forced to flee from their homeland. But he remembered the way to the Jesuit provincial house. Arriving in time for the evening meal, he was greeted warmly by his provincial superior.

"Father Miguel, you're looking well! How did you survive such a long voyage so soon after your operation?"The young priest sat down in a chair across from his superior at the table, and the two men said their meal blessing together.

"God is good, Father. And with the Virgin Mary of Guadalupe watching over me, I had nothing to fear! Besides, since the operation in Belgium my stomach has given me no trouble at all!" Father Miguel took a bite of a freshly baked *buñuelo* roll, before asking, with a grin, "How do you like my costume?"

Father Provincial laughed. "Well, you certainly don't look like a newly ordained Jesuit priest! What guardian angel warned you to come so well disguised?"

"There were Mexican travelers visiting our house in Belgium shortly before I left. They filled us in on the thirty-three articles regarding religious practices in our new constitution. Is it true that President Calles has closed the schools?"

"Not only the schools, but the hospitals and orphanages as well. All Catholic institutions had to either close or turn themselves over to the state." Father Provincial pushed his bowl of soup to one side. "I'm especially worried about what will happen to the poor. The sisters had gradually been establishing schools in even the remotest villages. Calles says he's for the poor working people, but without education, there will be no future for our country—and the Church was the only hope of the poor for education!"

"And what about the churches?" asked Miguel. "I've heard that the president intends to close them as well."

"Yes. On July 31, the feast of our patron, St. Ignatius, the churches will be officially closed." The older man looked intently at Father Miguel. The young man's reputation for intelligence and prayer had impressed him. "Father Miguel, are you prepared to go underground? To risk your very life to bring the sacraments and the Gospel to our people?"

Miguel thought for a moment before he replied. "Yes, Father. I've offered my life to God through my vows as a religious. And through my priestly ordination, I've committed all my energy to preaching the Gospel and to celebrating the sacraments for my fellow Mexicans. I am prepared to do whatever is necessary."

"I thought you'd say that! *¡Qué bien!* Very well! Tomorrow you'll go to visit your family in Mexico City. We'll send word to you there about where we shall meet again. In the meantime, Father Miguel, don't let anyone know your true identity. The people are flocking to confession by the hundreds, trying to receive the sacraments one last time before July 31. Try to go in and out of the church at night. Your identity isn't known to the police yet; let's keep it that way."

Late that night, still dressed as a rich young man, Father Miguel set out for Mexico City. When he arrived, he exchanged his fine clothes for the dress of the poorest Mexican. His once-wealthy family was now impoverished, and Miguel didn't want to attract attention to himself while visiting them. During the day, he talked and laughed with his elderly father and teenage brothers and sisters. They had missed him while he'd been away studying for his ordination. And he missed his mother now; she had died only a few weeks before his return. At night, Father Miguel celebrated Mass and heard confessions.

As July 31 approached, the city was tense. Violence often erupted between people loyal to the Catholic Church and people who supported the government of President Calles. But most faithful Catholics chose to oppose the anti-religious government in nonviolent ways. They boycotted stores and industries known to be Calles's supporters. They refused to attend prayer services at the "national churches" established by the government. And they formed underground networks enabling priests to say Mass and celebrate the sacraments in secret.

One way Catholics kept up their courage was by distributing leaflets with parts of the Gospel, the catechism, and prayers printed in them. These leaflets were illegal. Anyone caught distributing them could be shot—with no trial.

One afternoon, a police officer spotted Father Miguel, who was disguised as a street cleaner, and picked him up for questioning. Miguel's pockets were filled with Catholic leaflets. Maintaining his disguise, he began to tell the officer stories of the crazy things he had done as a youngster. Lucky for Miguel that he was a good storyteller! As the officer was laughing uncontrollably, Father Miguel tossed the leaflets out the car window. By the time they reached the police station, the officer decided to let his delightful young prisoner go without questioning.

But Father Miguel knew it had been a close call. There were government spies everywhere. Almost all the priests in the city had either fled for their lives or had been caught and killed—often while celebrating Mass. The city officials knew there was a priest circulating in clever disguises, but so far Father Miguel had always managed to slip by the security officers posted throughout the city. In the meantime, Catholics there had never been so devoted to their prayers. Because so many of the Catholic hospitals and orphanages had been closed, the women formed groups to help care for the sick and the homeless children.

On the feast of Christ the King, 1926, the people organized a peaceful procession to the shrine of Our Lady of Guadalupe. Thousands of men, women, and children took part. Armed police were everywhere, looking for any excuse to begin shooting at the crowd of pilgrims. But there was no trouble. The people sang hymns and prayed the Rosary. Father Miguel, disguised as a worker, marched proudly with his people. *"Viva Cristo Rey!"* The familiar cry—"Long live Christ the King!"—had become the rallying motto of the persecuted Church of Mexico.

President Calles became more corrupt. Along with his supporter General Obregon, he ran the country as a military state. The people who opposed him had to

One afternoon a police officer spotted Father Miguel, who was disguised as a street cleaner, and picked him up for questioning.

think of creative ways to spread the truth to the people of Mexico. Only by doing so could they hope to band together and vote him out of office.

Most active among Calles's opponents were Humberto and Roberto Pro, Miguel's younger brothers. On December 4, 1926, they carried out a daring act. Stuffing six hundred balloons with anti-Calles leaflets, they filled the balloons with helium and released them over Mexico City. When the balloons reached a certain height, they burst. The anti-government propaganda rained down on the busy streets.

Furious, President Calles demanded that someone be arrested. Since the Pro brothers were known for their anti-Calles activities, the police went to their home first. But they found only Miguel. He was arrested and spent that night and the next day in jail. Fortunately, no one had yet discovered his identity as a priest, and he was released.

As it became clear that his attempts to crush the Catholic faith in Mexico were not meeting with success, President Calles stepped up the violent persecution. Over ten thousand soldiers were sent out to arrest and shoot anyone suspected of promoting the Catholic faith—or of opposing the government of President Calles. Hundreds of priests and religious sisters were martyred for the faith; many lay people and children were killed as well. Father Miguel Pro was placed at the top of the "most wanted" list.

One afternoon, the tension in the city reached its peak when three young men tried to throw a bomb into the car carrying President Calles and General

Obregon. The two leaders were not hurt, but their bodyguards opened fire, and two of the young men were killed. The third escaped, but was later arrested. Infuriated by this bold attack, the president ordered a sweep made of the city, and all the men ever suspected of opposing Calles were arrested, including Miguel and his two brothers. It was November 13, 1927.

For six days Miguel led his fellow prisoners in prayer and song. No longer able to hide his identity, he acted openly as a priest, hearing the confessions of prisoners and guards. At first, the prisoners hoped for release, since they had not been involved in the attack on the president and there was no evidence to convict them. But on the sixth day, Miguel announced seriously, "Today, I think, will be our last."

This stunned his fellow prisoners. Father Miguel had always encouraged them to hope for acquittal! Concerned, they gathered around him in the dirty cell.

"Don't be afraid," he told them. "We go to the Lord with clear consciences!" Then he lifted up his hand and shouted, *"Viva Cristo Rey!"* Together, the men repeated his cry, and their spirits rose. They sang and prayed until a guard's voice called out: "Miguel Pro! Come with me!"

The men were silent as Father Miguel picked up his jacket. The serious, sad eyes of the guard told him all he needed to know. After clasping his brothers' hands in a final farewell, Miguel marched down the hall in front of the guard. As he was pushed out into the bright courtyard, the priest stopped and stared. A large crowd had gathered. He recognized many important dignitaries, newspaper photographers, and even some of his faithful Catholic friends. They had all come to witness the death of a Jesuit priest who had eluded the police for over a year. His only crimes had been preaching the Gospel, forming catechists, and celebrating the sacraments in the homes of faithful Catholics.

Clutching his rosary in one hand and his crucifix in the other, Father Miguel raised his head. Begging the Virgin of Guadalupe to give him courage, he forced his trembling legs to walk toward the wall of execution. Along the way, one of the police officers fell to his knees and grabbed Miguel's legs. With tears streaming down his face, he begged, "Father, forgive me!"

"I have nothing to forgive, my friend," replied Miguel. Then he embraced the man and said, "I will pray for you all."

Father Miguel stood and faced the firing squad, stretching out his arms like Jesus on the cross. As the guns exploded, he cried out, *"Viva Cristo Rey!"*

Father Miguel had sacrificed his life out of love of God and neighbor. Intending to frighten the Catholic population into submission, President Calles ordered several of the young men who had been imprisoned with Father Miguel to be shot that day as well. Among them was twenty-three-year-old Humberto Pro, Father Miguel's brother.

But there was probably nothing that strengthened the faith of the Mexican Catholics more than the murder of their favorite priest. As news of the deaths was broadcast, hundreds of thousands of people took to the streets, shouting, *"Viva Cristo Rey!"* And, "Long live the Pope! Long live the Catholic Church!" Leading the crowds was seventy-five-year-old Señor Pro, Miguel's father. At the graves of his two sons the next day, he led the huge crowd in singing the *Te Deum*, a hymn of praise sung only on the most solemn and joyful of feast days.

Father Miguel Augustín Pro was beatified by Pope John Paul II in 1988.

The Church in Mexico still had a long struggle ahead before achieving freedom. But recognizing the holiness of their new young martyr, the people used his memory as a source of inspiration and courage. In many nations of the world today, the Church is still persecuted and people are oppressed by unjust rulers. We can pray to Blessed Miguel Augustín Pro for the grace to be proud of our Catholic faith and to use all our talents and energies to spread the Gospel of Jesus without fear.

St. Edith Stein

(1891–1942)

AUGUST 9

As the train pulled into the busy station in Breslau, Germany, Edith Stein's heart reached its breaking point. How many other summers in her fifty-one years had she arrived at this station and been greeted by loving family and friends? Now she longed for even a glimpse of the platform, but there were no windows in this train car, filled with starving, sick, and dying Jewish men, women, and children. Sister Teresa Benedicta of the Cross, as Edith was known in her community of Carmelite nuns, closed her eyes and prayed.

Unexpectedly, the door of the freight car opened. The people packed within gasped for air, groaning in pain as the bright sunlight hit their eyes. Edith clung to the doorway and leaned out, scanning the crowded platform for familiar faces, but there were none. And if anyone had recognized this brilliant philosopher, it would have been foolish indeed to speak to her. This was a freight car full of Jews, the condemned victims of Nazi Germany.

A young postal worker standing on the platform couldn't help but stare at the spectacle. He moved closer. Was that a Carmelite nun packed in with the rest of the Jews? "Hello," he called. "Where are you going? Can I get you anything?"

Edith looked intently at him, almost forgetting that not all of Germany was aware of the horrors of the concentration camps. "No, thank you," she replied. "We accept nothing. We are going to our deaths."

The stunned young man was pulled away by his friends, who were angry with him for talking to a Jew. The door of the freight car slammed shut and darkness again enveloped them. Edith hugged her sister, Rosa, as tears flowed silently down their faces. As she had done so often in the past weeks, Edith Stein renewed her offering of herself to God in atonement for the horrors of this war and for her beloved Jewish people.

Edith remembered a summer day in Breslau—the day she told her mother that she was going to join the Carmelite nuns in Cologne. That had been in 1933. Augusta Stein had been happy that Edith was home for the summer. A devout Jew, Frau Stein hadn't understood at all when Edith had been baptized a Catholic in 1922. But she'd gotten used to the idea. After the Nazis had forbidden Jews to teach in universities or hold government jobs, Augusta had been relieved when Edith had found a teaching position at a

Catholic girls' school. Her brilliant Edith, who had received a doctorate in philosophy with highest honors and had been among the first recognized female scholars of Germany, was now a Catholic. Frau Stein could accept that. But on that particular day—Edith's forty-second birthday—Frau Stein had sensed that her youngest daughter had a secret.

"So, Edith, you aren't returning to the school in Speyer. Who will teach the girls if you leave?"

"No, Mama, I'm not going back to Speyer. The school will survive without me."

"Well, why don't you stay here in Breslau with me? Surely you can find a position here?" Frau Stein bit her lip. It would be humiliating to have her daughter living openly as a Catholic in their hometown. But she would gladly endure that, just to have her Edith back home.

"Mama, you know I've already arranged to go to Cologne."

"To Cologne? Yes, I know, to the *Carmelites* in Cologne." Frau Stein let her knitting fall to her lap as she asked, her voice trembling, "And what will you be doing with the Carmelites in Cologne?"

Edith couldn't look at her mother. Turning toward the window, she said firmly, "I'm going to live with them, Mama. I'm going to be a Carmelite nun."

Fra Stein's desperate cry echoed through the house. Edith rushed to her side. As the older woman sobbed violently, Edith stooped and held her mother's head close to her heart. When at last her crying quieted, Edith led her eighty-two-year-old mother upstairs

Edith remembered a summer day in Bresla—the day she told her mother that she was going to join the Carmelite nuns in Cologne.

and helped her into bed. The next day, they embraced for the last time before Edith left for Cologne.

~~~~~~~~~~~~

The train lurched, bouncing the tired, frightened people against one another. In one corner a woman cried, and a man cursed loudly. "Edith," gasped Rosa, "I'm glad that Mama didn't live to see this evil day."

"So am I, Rosa. I'm sure that Mama is already in heaven. And I'm sure that we will see her there."

~~~~~~~~~~~~

The idea of heaven had been one of the beliefs that had led Edith to the Christian faith. As a child, she and all her brothers and sisters had said the traditional Jewish prayers with their mother. Since their father had died when Edith was only two, Frau Stein herself had taken her seven children to the synagogue every Sabbath, and she taught Edith's brothers the traditional prayers and blessings. Yet, one by one, the Stein children had abandoned their Jewish traditions. In her autobiography Edith noted that she consciously and deliberately stopped praying as a young teenager. Instead, she filled her mind and soul with the study of psychology first, then philosophy.

As one of the first women to study philosophy at a German university, Edith felt challenged to prove herself. Within a few short years, her reputation as a scholar was well established. Her teacher was the famous Edmund Husserl, whom the students called "the master."

At twenty-one, Edith had found herself surrounded by a group of peers who totally accepted her. On holidays they would take hiking trips through the German countryside. At exam time, they would encourage one another. Edith gradually became aware that her most respected friends and teachers had all struggled with their belief in God—and that most were now Christians. This puzzled Edith. For her, the answers to life's mysteries were to be found in philosophy, not religion.

In 1915, Edith's happy life as a scholar ended as World War I swept across Europe. Most of her male friends were soon in the army. Edith volunteered as a Red Cross nurse to help care for the sick and wounded. She kept in close contact with her friends, often sending them packages of food and clothing. She was saddened as many of them were killed in the fighting at the war front. It was especially sad news when one of her teachers, Adolph Reinach, was killed. Edith had become close to Adolph and his wife, Anna Reinach. She felt obliged to go and try to comfort Anna in her time of grief.

Edith had expected Anna to be devastated by the death of her husband. She was surprised to find her sad but peaceful. Anna and Adolph, she learned, had recently been baptized Christians. Now Anna was comforting Edith with her firm belief in the reality of heaven and of the resurrection of the dead. The seeds of faith were planted, and Edith began to seek the God whom she really wanted to believe in.

Edith fell asleep leaning on Rosa's shoulder and dreamed of happier days past. Just as she recalled the glorious moment when she first received the Eucharist, the train screeched to a halt. Voices screamed in the cool summer night as the doors again opened. Starved and cramped from the long ride, the women, men, and children half-fell and half-jumped to the ground.

The strongest among the hundreds of Jews in the train were herded off to one side. They would be sent to one of the work camps. The rest, they were told, would remain here at Birkenau, just outside Auschwitz. First they were all to have showers.

Edith and Rosa clung to one another. Soon the prisoners were lined up in the woods, outside the "shower houses." No one spoke, but they all knew by now that what awaited them was not a hot shower, but death by poison gas.

It was August 9, 1942. Sister Teresa Benedicta's offering of herself for her people was complete. Survivors who had been imprisoned with her remembered her serenity and calm. Overcoming her own fears, she had gathered the children around her, cleaning them and finding them food. She had prayed constantly, both with her fellow Jews and fellow Christians. She knew that the innocent Jesus on the cross was with her innocent people suffering in the concentration camps.

Edith Stein's legacy as a scholar remains in the books and essays that she wrote. Most of these were works of philosophy. She also wrote meditations and explanations of the writings of St. Thomas Aquinas and St. John of the Cross. But it is for her faithfulness to the vocation God called her to, for her tremendous love of her Jewish people, and for her example of faith at the moment of death that the Church remembers Edith Stein. She was canonized as St. Teresa Benedicta of the Cross in 1998 by Pope John Paul II.

Sometimes we may be tempted to stop praying or even to stop going to Mass. If this ever happens, we can pray to St. Edith Stein, asking her to help strengthen our faith and send us good friends who will lead us back to Jesus and help us believe in his great love for us.

St. Katharine Drexel

(1858–1955)

Drexel has been a well-known name to generations of Philadelphians. But since Katharine Drexel was proclaimed a saint, the name has spread beyond Philadelphia and throughout the world.

Katharine Drexel was born on November 26, 1858. Her sister, Elizabeth, was three years older. Their family was very wealthy because of the remarkable talents of their father, Francis Drexel. Mr. Drexel, a devout Catholic, had earned his money through hard work in the world of finance. He was well-liked and admired by his friends and associates, but his little girls loved him even more.

Elizabeth and Katharine's mother, Hannah, died when Katharine was just five weeks old. On April 10, 1860, Mr. Drexel married Emma Bouvier, the woman who would raise Katharine and Elizabeth as her own. But the sisters never lost contact with their birth mother's family. On Saturdays, the two little girls were often taken to spend the day with Hannah's parents, Mr. and Mrs. Langstroth. The Langstroths were Quakers. The Drexel girls were Catholic.

One Saturday, when they arrived, Grandma Langstroth explained that her Quaker minister would be coming for lunch. "He'll also be leading our meal prayer," she added. Elizabeth and Katharine glanced nervously at each other. Both girls were thinking the same thing: *What should we do?* When lunchtime arrived, they were ready. All through the minister's heartfelt prayer, the two little girls held their rosary beads up...just to make sure he knew they were Catholic!

On October 2, 1863, Katharine, affectionately known as "Kate," and Elizabeth received a wonderful gift—the birth of their new baby sister, Louise. From then on the three girls were always together.

Because she grew up before the time of Pope Saint Pius X, who lowered the age for children to receive the Eucharist, Kate did not make her First Communion until June 3, 1870. She was eleven years old. It was the beginning of the special relationship with Jesus in the Holy Eucharist that would mark Kate's long life.

The family custom of saying evening prayers together was a favorite part of Kate's day. So was helping her stepmother with different charitable projects. While still very young, all the Drexel children learned about the needs of others, about the poverty they had never experienced, and about their obligation to share the good things they had with others. By serving the needs of the poor who came to their home for food, clothing, and even rent money, each of the girls became convinced of the importance of helping others.

~~~~~~~~~~~~~~~~

After attending their first years of school at the Convent of the Sacred Heart, Kate and her sisters were taught at home by tutors under the direction of Mary Ann Cassidy. Miss Cassidy moved in with them and was like a member of the family. Mr. Drexel spent time with the family in the evenings and during vacations. The Drexels took two-week summer trips that brought geography and history to life. As part of their education, the girls traveled all over the United States and large areas of Europe. In the fall the family's trips continued, but for a different purpose. These trips were chances to relax and have fun together.

The Drexel family lived on Walnut Street in a very fashionable section of Philadelphia, but each summer they rented a cottage out in the country. When Kate was twelve, Mr. Drexel bought a ninety-acre farm in Torresdale, Pennsylvania. The building was remodeled into a summer home in which the family was to spend happy vacation months each year. Mr. Drexel mounted a statue of Saint Michael the Archangel over the main entrance, and the house was named Saint Michel, pronounced the French way.

During Kate's teenage years, she became very interested in her own country, and especially in its people. She had been seven years old in 1865 when the Civil War broke out. Her father had explained many things to his daughters then in a way that they could understand. "War is always a terrible thing," he had said, "but doubly so when brothers fight brothers, when Americans fight Americans." Slavery had ended after the war, but poverty and prejudice hadn't. Kate wished there were something *she* could do to help disadvantaged people.

In 1876, America's Centennial Year, Kate turned eighteen. On New Year's Eve, 1875–1876, the Drexels stood outside on the balcony of their home waving flags with the rest of their neighbors. *Time is passing,* Kate realized. *I wonder what I should do with my life.*

Since the age of fourteen, Kate had had a spiritual director named Father James O'Connor. During the summers when the family was at Saint Michel, Kate was able to visit him at his nearby parish church. During the rest of the year, Kate wrote letters, open and sincere, and the kindly priest always responded. Father O'Connor helped Kate to deepen her love for the spiritual life. She kept a diary and wrote daily about her goal to be totally centered in Jesus.

Kate finished high school on July 2, 1878. Meanwhile, Father O'Connor had been consecrated the bishop of Omaha, Nebraska. Kate continued to write to him, and he always sent her a quick reply.

As was the custom, Kate was presented to Philadelphia's high society at a special party when she reached the age of twenty. Many of the wealthy families considered this a very important event, but Kate's heart was not in expensive parties.

Not long after, Kate's stepmother became very ill. Mrs. Drexel began a struggle with cancer that was to last for three long years. Kate became her full-time nurse. She realized how heroically her stepmother was suffering. The way in which Mrs. Drexel calmly and trustingly accepted God's will deeply impressed her. It made Kate begin to think seriously about the true meaning of life and about the choices she herself still had to make. *Whatever can lead us to heaven and bring many others with us is the best choice,* Kate decided. As Mrs. Drexel lived her three-year Calvary, Kate became more and more aware of her own desire to enter the convent and become a sister.

Mrs. Drexel died peacefully on January 29, 1883. She left behind a quiet, lonely house. Because her long illness and death had been so difficult for the family, Mr. Drexel thought a change of scenery would do everyone good. He planned another trip to Europe. He, his daughters, and Johanna Ryan, who had worked for the Drexels for many years, sailed from New York in October 1883. They returned home that May. In September of 1884, the family traveled by train through the Northwest, with a detour to Yellowstone National Park. That journey covered a distance of 6,833 miles! A short time after they returned home, Mr. Drexel called his daughters together. "I've made my will," he smilingly announced. A chill swept over Kate as she listened. She couldn't bear to think about losing her father. "Each of you girls will receive a share of my estate that will ensure that you will be financially independent for life," Mr. Drexel went on. "The rest of the money will be divided between the various charitable institutions I've specified."

It was bitterly cold that February. Even the well-stoked fires blazing in the fireplaces of the family's comfortable home weren't enough to protect Mr. Drexel from catching a cold. The cold led to a lung infection called pleurisy. Mr. Drexel was placed under the doctor's care and seemed to be responding well to the medication. His three daughters took turns keeping eight-hour vigils in a small room adjoining their father's bedroom.

Kate was with him on the afternoon of Sunday, February 15. They had both been reading for several minutes when Kate felt her father looking at her. She watched as he smiled and tried to stand. But suddenly he slumped back into his chair. His glassy eyes held no expression. Kate flew down the stairs. "Elizabeth! Louise! Call the doctor!" she shouted. "I'm going for a priest!"

But by the time she returned with a priest, Mr. Drexel had already passed away. The kindly priest anointed him and prayed that he would find eternal joy and peace. Later that week, 2,000 people attended Mr. Drexel's funeral Mass.

In the days that followed, the Drexel sisters mourned their loss and consoled each other. "What would Father expect us to do now?" Kate sadly asked.

"He would want us to be happy and to move on with our lives," Elizabeth replied quietly. "He would want us to use the money he's left us to take care of those good works he mentioned in his will."

The three sisters each decided to help different groups of persons who were in need. Kate chose to use her inheritance to provide for the educational needs of Native Americans. Racial prejudice was a great problem at that time, and the Catholic Church was one of the few institutions vitally interested in helping these marginalized Americans. Kate understood that the bishops wanted priests and missionaries to build churches and staff schools for the Indians. But lack of money, and, even more seriously, lack of personnel, hampered the work. The few generous missionaries who were already working among the Native Americans appealed to Kate for financial help. She paid for chapels and schools and whatever else was needed. The missionaries then asked her to find more priests to help in the important work. Since she would be stopping in Rome during another European trip, Kate decided to ask the one person who could surely help!

The Drexel sisters had each received Pope Leo XIII's blessing at the private audience he had granted them. Now the Holy Father was smiling at Kate. In that smile she found the courage to ask him an important favor. "Your Holiness," she suddenly found herself saying, "the Native Americans are in great need of spiritual as well as material food. I beg you to send missionaries to them!" The Pope looked searchingly into the face of the earnest young woman before him. "Why not become a missionary yourself?" he asked softly. The question stunned Kate. She left the Vatican in tears and confusion.

Back home in Philadelphia Kate thought and prayed. *What does God want?* she asked herself over and over again. *What does God want?* Through the charitable work of her sister Louise, Kate became interested in helping African Americans as well as Native Americans. She kept herself very busy, but the Pope had brought up the important question of her vocation, and it wasn't going to go away. With the help of Bishop O'Connor, Kate finally reached a decision. She would become a sister. And not only that. She would begin a new congregation in the Catholic Church—one dedicated totally to Jesus in the Eucharist and to the service of Native and African Americans.

The well-established Sisters of Mercy of Pittsburgh trained Kate as a religious sister. Young women who heard of her goal came to join her at the Sisters of Mercy novitiate.

Two years passed. During that time, Kate lost her older sister, Elizabeth, who died in childbirth. This was a great suffering for Kate. Another sorrow soon followed. Bishop O'Connor, Kate's trusted spiritual father, also passed away. Good friend that he was, Bishop O'Connor had entrusted Kate's spiritual welfare to Archbishop Patrick Ryan of Philadelphia. The archbishop came to Mercy Convent in Pittsburgh to comfort Kate over the death of Bishop O'Connor. He found her badly shaken and afraid. The archbishop was kind and gentle, and genuinely interested in Kate and her new congregation. As tears stung Kate's eyes, Archbishop Ryan asked her, "If I help you, can you go on?" Kate felt a huge weight lifted from her heart. Courage seemed to flood her. "Yes," she whispered.

Kate went on to live her "yes" in all that she did. On February 12, 1891, she became the first Sister of the Blessed Sacrament, making the vows, or sacred promises to God, of poverty, chastity, and obedience. She added a fourth vow by which she pledged to be the mother and servant of Native and African Americans.

With the help of the Sisters of Mercy, Mother Katharine began to turn Saint Michel, her family's summer home, into a temporary convent for her new congregation. Ten novices and three postulants joined the little community. By the end of 1891, there were twenty-eight members. The sisters spent their days praying, attending classes, and doing laundry, cooking, and cleaning. They waited anxiously for Archbishop Ryan's permission to begin their first mission assignment.

After some delays, the Sisters of the Blessed Sacrament moved into their new, unfinished motherhouse on December 3, 1892. On the same property they built Holy Providence School, where children of poor families became boarding students. Everything was moving ahead for the young, energetic sisters who wanted to serve their Native and African American sisters and brothers.

Finally the day came that everyone had been waiting for. Archbishop Ryan gave the sisters permission to staff their first mission school! Four sisters left for St. Catherine's School in Santa Fe, New Mexico, on June 13, 1894. (This was actually a school for Pueblo Indian children that Kate had funded even before she became a sister.) There wasn't a dry eye among the sis-

ters as the train carrying the missionaries pulled slowly out of the station.

On January 9, 1895, Mother Katharine pronounced
her perpetual vows before Archbishop Ryan at the
motherhouse. She received a symbol of her pledge of
lifelong dedication. It was a silver ring, engraved on
the inside with her motto: "My beloved is mine and I
am his"—words taken from the Old Testament's Song
of Songs (see chapter 2, verse 16). Now, totally dedicated to Jesus, her beloved, Mother Katharine set her
sights on the next phase of the mission: Catholic education for African Americans.

Kate's sister, Louise, and her husband, Captain
Morrell, had purchased land in the diocese of
Richmond, Virginia, to build a school for young African
American men. Mother Katharine inquired about the
availability of land nearby for the building of a high
school for young black women. Since land was obtain-
able, she wrote to the bishop for permission to enter
and serve in his diocese. The bishop was very pleased,
and Mother Katharine bought a 600-acre plantation.
Before the construction started, she named the school
St. Francis de Sales, in memory of her father.

Classes began in October 1899. In addition, the sisters made home visits to the students' families, many
of whom were poor, some even destitute. The nuns
helped as much as possible. They offered religious
instruction to the families and also reached out to the
local prisoners. At the prison, they met a man condemned to death. He listened to the sisters and trusted them. He asked to be instructed in the Catholic

faith. The nuns taught him, answered his questions, and calmed his fears. On December 29, 1902, two days before his execution, the man was baptized.

The stories of grace continued and multiplied as Mother Katharine and her sisters established new schools and convents. They went to the Navajo nation and began work there with the help of the Cincinnati Franciscan Fathers and Brothers. Mother Katharine built St. Michael's, the first school on the Navajo reservation in Arizona. She and her sisters opened the school on October 19, 1902. Although it was the Navajo custom to educate children at home, the parents gradually responded to the sisters' efforts, and bright-eyed children slowly filled the classrooms. By the second school year, St. Michael's enrollment had doubled. Mother Katharine was overjoyed.

Meanwhile, Mother Katharine also kept in her heart the poverty of African Americans in the south. Bishops and priests continued to ask her for financial help for their badly needed charitable works. Katharine never turned down a request. She had paid half the cost of a new church for the black community of Nashville, Tennessee. A grateful Bishop Byrne came to visit her. "I have one more favor to ask, Mother," he quietly explained. "Would you open a school for black children in Nashville?" Although for practical reasons she felt she had to refuse, the word that came out of her mouth was "yes"!

On February 13, 1905, much to the distress of some of the neighbors (racial prejudice was a great problem at that time), Mother Katharine bought prop-

erty for her new school in Nashville. Immaculate
Mother Academy opened its doors on September 5,
1905. Mother Katharine faced the opposition to the
school with quiet dignity. "We have come here to stay,"
she said simply and firmly.

As the years passed, the Sisters of the Blessed
Sacrament grew steadily. On May 15, 1913, Mother
Katharine's congregation received final Vatican
approval of its rule of life. The entire community celebrated. By the time of Mother Katharine's death in
1955, there were 501 sisters, 51 convents, 49 elemen-
tary schools, 12 high schools, Xavier University in
New Orleans, 3 houses of social service, and a house
of studies in Washington, D.C.

By 1935, Mother Katharine's own health was failing. Soon to be seventy-seven, she had a heart condition that demanded a slower pace of life. There would
be no more long, rugged trips out West or down South.
But the ailing nun knew how to maintain her serenity.

It was time, she realized, for other sisters to guide
the congregation on roads the Lord had chosen for it.
She trusted God and trusted the sisters. After all, they
were the vocations the Lord had sent for this great
work. The pressures of daily life were gently lifted from
the aging foundress. The superiors informed her of
events and developments and often asked her advice.

Mother Katharine loved the little chapel next to
her bedroom and office. As the years passed, she spent
more and more hours in the presence of the Blessed
Sacrament. Once, so long ago, she had thought about
joining a cloistered order. How attractive to her was

the cloistered nuns' life of prayer and union with Jesus! But as time and events unfolded, she had resigned herself to doing for God what she believed he wanted of her. Now, as she was slipping toward eternity, the Lord gave her the close union with him that she had longed for.

Mother Katharine died peacefully on March 3, 1955, at the age of ninety-six. Since she was the last living member of the Drexel family, the remainder of the family fortune was distributed to the charitable institutions that her father had specified in his will. (Because Katharine's own Sisters of the Blessed Sacrament did not exist during Mr. Drexel's lifetime, they had not been included in his will.)

Mother Katharine Drexel was declared blessed by Pope John Paul II on November 20, 1988, and was proclaimed a saint on October 1, 2000.

Did you ever wonder what you would do if you received a fortune? Would you try to help as many people as you could? Or would you keep the money for yourself? Saint Katharine Drexel had to make a choice like this. The special virtues she teaches us are generosity and total unselfishness. She shows us how to be generous with our own life, our time, our talents, our education, and even our money. How will you imitate St. Katharine Drexel today?

Bl. James Alberione

(1884–1971)

"Michael...you must bring James...to be baptized...as soon as possible," Teresa pleaded from her bed. "We just can't let him die...without Baptism!"

"Rest now," her husband reassured, "and don't worry. I'll go and speak to Father." It was April 4, 1884, and a fifth child, tiny and frail, had just been born to Teresa and Michael Alberione, tenant farmers in the northern Italian town of San Lorenzo di Fossano.

Little James was baptized the very next day. As was the custom, after the ceremony, his mother consecrated him to the Blessed Virgin Mary.

Although James continued to be weak and sickly as he grew up, his parents never spoiled him. He was given his own small chores to do on the farm. Gradually, he grew stronger. And little by little, through the example of his mother and father, he grew in his faith and love for God and prayer.

James had a very decisive character. When he made up his mind to do something, there was no changing it! When he was six years old, his teacher asked some of her students what they wanted to be when they grew up. "What about you, James?" she prodded. "What will you become?"

"I'm going to be a priest!" the boy responded.

Some of his friends thought it was a joke. But James was serious. From then on, he did everything with this one goal in mind. His pastor even permitted James to make his First Communion when he was eight—earlier than usual for those days—because he saw that the boy was ready and very eager to receive Jesus in the Holy Eucharist.

On October 6, 1896, Signor Alberione accompanied James to the minor seminary (a special high school that prepared boys to enter the seminary) of the diocese of Turin. James liked to study, and he did well during his first years in the seminary. But trouble began when he turned sixteen. Some of his classmates, who were reading harmful books, got James to start reading them too. He began neglecting his studies and seminary life. Soon enough, the priest in charge of the seminary noticed a big change in the teenager. It was time for a serious talk.

The rector finally called him to his office. "James, it seems that you've lost the spirit and enthusiasm you once had," the priest began. "Perhaps you need more time to discover whether God is really calling you to the priesthood," he continued slowly. "For now, I'm recommending that you return home."

Home! James was shocked and confused. What was happening to him? All he had ever wanted was to become a priest...and that hadn't changed.

James spent the next six months back at the family farm. During that time he prayed and seriously thought things over. *I still feel God calling me to become a priest. I still want to be a priest,* he told himself. *I have to try again.* His pastor, Father Montersino, encouraged him.

In October of 1900, he was accepted, on a trial basis, into the seminary of the city of Alba. Because of his probationary status, James wasn't allowed to wear the black cassock that all the other seminarians wore. But it didn't matter. He was happy to be given a second chance!

The night between December 31, 1900 and January 1, 1901 would become a very important one in James Alberione's life. That night marked the passage from the nineteenth century to the twentieth. A midnight Mass was celebrated in the ancient cathedral of Alba. On that special occasion, the diocesan seminarians were allowed to remain in church after Mass and to adore the Blessed Sacrament for as long as they wished. James prayed for four hours before dawn. He reflected on the words of Pope Leo XIII: "It is necessary to unite our energies to work against those who oppose the teachings of the Church.... We must oppose evil publications with good publications."

Lord, James prayed, *I want to do something for all the people of this new century...and for the Church.* As he remained in adoration, sixteen-year-old James

felt what he described later as a "special light" coming
to him from Jesus in the sacred Host. He understood
in a clearer way Jesus' invitation, "Come to me, all of
you." James felt that Jesus was giving him a mission: to
bring the Gospel message to *as many* people as possible, as *quickly* as possible. He felt called to use the
fastest means available to make God's love known
everywhere. James also understood that others would
want to join him in this important work.

As he prayed, he realized that he could start by
printing and distributing books to teach people to
know and love Jesus and to act as Jesus would. But
how? The whole idea was still very confused in his
mind, and James felt small and helpless. Then, in his
heart, he clearly heard Jesus reminding him, "I will be
with you until the end of time!" That was enough.
James would trust God.

The next day, some of the other seminarians
noticed that James was like another person. "What's
happened to you?" one asked. "You look so different!"

"It's nothing," James answered casually. It wasn't
time yet to reveal his secret to everyone. He only told
his spiritual guide, Father Francis Chiesa, and his good
friend, Augustine Borello, what had happened. "This is
something very important, James," Father Chiesa
advised him. "Be courageous and keep praying about it."

And that's exactly what the young seminarian did.
Five years passed. On June 29, 1907, James Alberione
was ordained a priest. He was sent as assistant pastor
to a parish in the small Italian town of Narzole.
Everyone loved and respected this new priest, who

put his whole heart into everything he did. Father James was happy, too. But strangely enough, he felt restless. His thoughts kept going back to that night between the centuries when Jesus had spoken to his heart. James spent every extra minute praying, meditating, and studying. He wanted to prepare himself for whatever it was that Jesus was asking him to do.

Soon enough Father James received a letter from his bishop. In it, the bishop asked him to become a professor and spiritual director at the seminary. *There has to be some mistake,* James thought. *The bishop must not realize that I'm only twenty-four!*

James went to visit Bishop Re to clear up the matter, but what a surprise he received! "There's no mistake, Father James," the bishop assured him. "I know you're young, but I believe God is with you."

Little by little, the inspiration James had received from God became clearer. Father James realized that he was called to begin a religious congregation whose members would love and imitate Jesus as closely as possible and proclaim God's word to everyone with the quickest means available. But how would he get started? And who would join him? James waited for God to show him.

A few years later, in 1913, Bishop Re called James aside after hearing him preach a sermon on the Blessed Mother. "I have a new assignment for you," he explained. "I'd like you to take over our diocesan newspaper."

Father James was happy with this new work, but it still wasn't enough. *If only I had a print shop and helpers to join me,* he mused. *We could spend our lives spreading the message of God's love by printing good newspapers, books, and magazines! Since so many people won't come to church, we must bring God to them!*

The very next year, Father James began to see his dream come true. On August 20, 1914, he opened a small printing school in a rented room. He only had secondhand printing presses, and there were just two young students—a thirteen-year-old and a fifteen-year-old—but it was a start.

In fact, it was the beginning of a new religious congregation in the Church—the Society of St. Paul. Today the priests and brothers of the Society of St. Paul spread the Gospel in twenty-eight countries across the globe, using every means of communication: the Internet, books, magazines, videos, CDs, DVDs, radio, and TV.

Father James always insisted that he didn't choose St. Paul as the patron saint of his religious congregation. It was St. Paul himself who chose to be its "Father." Father James greatly admired St. Paul, not only because Paul imitated Jesus so closely, but also because the Apostle used every possible means to make Jesus known and loved. Father James believed that if St. Paul were living today he would go on TV and radio (and now even the Internet) to broadcast the message of Jesus. Paul would produce newspapers and write books to bring the words of the Gospel to everyone. Father James wanted all his followers to become "St. Paul living today."

As more and more boys and men joined the Society of St. Paul, Father James's plans grew even bigger. *We could spread God's word quicker if we had more people to help us,* he thought. *I believe God wants me to begin a new group of sisters to join in this mission!* And so, in June 1915, Father James started this new project with the help of a young woman named Teresa Merlo.

Another young lady and three teenage girls were the first to join Teresa. Soon the bishop of the little town of Susa, Italy, asked the group to take over his diocesan newspaper. The young women didn't know the first thing about printing. But they prayed hard as Father James advised them, and...the newspaper was a success!

When the townspeople saw how much the young women loved St. Paul, they began to call them "Daughters of St. Paul." This is how the first congregation of sisters founded by Father James got its name. (This book you're now reading, in fact, was written and published by the Daughters of St. Paul in the United States.) Father James gave Teresa Merlo a new religious name when she made her vows. From then on, Teresa was called Mother Thecla, in honor of one of St. Paul's own helpers.

Father James and his priests, brothers, and sisters continued to work hard to spread God's word everywhere. In those days TV, radio, CDs, DVDs, and the Internet hadn't yet been invented. The best way to reach large numbers of people was through books, magazines, and newspapers. And this was the method that Father James and his followers used.

One of the most important books they printed and distributed was the Bible. Father James felt that the

Bible was like "a letter that our Heavenly Father has written to us. How can it be that people don't read it?" he asked.

As time went on, not everyone was happy with the work Father James was doing—especially people who lent him money. The equipment that was needed to print and make books was very expensive. So were the buildings that Father needed to build for the members of his congregations. Father James had to continually borrow very large sums of money. But God never let him down. He was always able, even miraculously, to find a way to pay all his debts.

In 1923, just when his two religious congregations were beginning to grow, Father James came down with tuberculosis. In those days, this disease was usually fatal. In fact, the doctor told Father James that he had about a year and a half to live. After spending several weeks in rest and prayer, the priest called all his young followers together. "I have something very important to tell you," he started out. "Not too long ago, when I was praying, I saw Jesus. What he told me is also for all of you. Jesus said, 'Do not fear. I am with you. From here [Jesus was pointing to the tabernacle] I want to enlighten you. Be sorry for sin.' You must place these words near the tabernacle in each of your chapels," Father James insisted.

"Father, you're better!" one of his seminarians exclaimed in surprise. "Yes. St. Paul healed me," was all Father James would say. And he lived another fifty years!

Father James went on to do many other wonderful things for God. He wrote many books to lead people to the Lord. Besides the Society of St. Paul and the Daughters of St. Paul, he began three more congregations of sisters: the Sister Disciples of the Divine Master; the Sisters of Jesus, the Good Shepherd; and the Sisters of Mary, Queen of Apostles. He also founded a group of lay cooperators, as well as associations for married couples, single men, single women, and priests who want to grow closer to God in prayer and spread the Gospel through some form of missionary work. Today over 10,000 members worldwide belong to the Pauline Family—the religious congregations and secular institutes founded by Father James Alberione. All keep Jesus in the Holy Eucharist and the word of God as the center of their lives, in imitation of Father James. All take St. Paul as their special patron.

Father James Alberione died on November 26, 1971. Just over thirty-one years later, on April 27, 2003, Pope John Paul II beatified him (a step in the process of being declared a saint). We can be sure that from heaven Father James continues to pray for and help all who work to spread the love and message of Jesus throughout the world.

Father James had two great desires in life: to become as close as possible to Jesus himself, and to help all people everywhere come to know and love Jesus, too. We can imitate him by having a great love for Jesus in the Holy Eucharist and by reading the Gospel often, trying to live by everything it teaches us.

Bl. Teresa of Calcutta

(1910–1997)

"Betika, you're missing the beautiful mountains!" eighteen-year-old Agnes Bojaxhiu chided.

Agnes's companion obliged her by pressing her nose against the train window. "The Alps do look prettier here than they do in Albania," Betika admitted, leaning back in her seat. "We've already passed through Austria. According to the conductor, we're in Switzerland now. That means there's still France to go before we reach the English Channel."

"Then we sail to London," Agnes excitedly broke in, her brown eyes shining with joy, "and on to Ireland and Loreto Abbey!"

Agnes—Gonxha as her family called her—had been fascinated by stories of the Catholic missions all during her childhood. By the time she was twelve, she had felt God calling her to become a missionary sister. Now, in September 1928, she was on her way to

Dublin, Ireland, to enter the congregation of the Sisters of Loreto.

At the convent, Agnes studied English and was introduced to the religious life. Then, after barely two months, she and her friend Betika set out for where they really wanted to go—India! The rough ocean voyage took seven long weeks. But Agnes had never been happier. Her dream was finally coming true.

Once in India, Agnes and Betika traveled to the city of Darjeeling. At the novitiate of the Sisters of Loreto, the young women began their training as sisters. They also received new names. Agnes was now called Sister Teresa.

Sister Teresa made her temporary vows of chastity, poverty, and obedience on March 24, 1931. After that, she was sent to Calcutta. There she attended college classes. She also earned a teaching certificate while she taught at St. Mary's School. In May, 1937, Teresa made her final vows as a Sister of Loreto. Following the custom of her religious congregation, she was called "Mother" from then on.

Mother Teresa loved the children she taught. She was very happy in her life as a sister. She was also shocked by the terrible poverty that she saw all around her in Calcutta. She realized that the students she was teaching came from the more well-to-do families. There were so many others—children and adults—in greater need. Teresa began to feel that God was asking her to do something more. *But what?* she wondered. *What should I do?* The answer came in an unexpected way.

In 1946, Mother Teresa was traveling on a crowded train. She was on her way back to Darjeeling to make her yearly retreat, a special weeklong time of prayer. Suddenly, she heard God speaking within her heart: "You must leave the convent to help the poor by living among them." Teresa was amazed. She prayed about this message all during her retreat. God made it clearer and clearer to Mother Teresa that he wanted her to dedicate her life to helping the poorest of the poor.

Teresa wanted to obey God, but she also felt that God wanted her to remain a sister. This was a problem. At that time there was no religious congregation whose members actually lived with the poor. Teresa would have to begin such a congregation herself. After speaking with the Archbishop of Calcutta and receiving his advice, Mother Teresa wrote to Rome. She eventually received permission from Pope Pius XII to leave the Sisters of Loreto and found a new congregation. She admitted many years later that leaving the convent that she loved was "the most difficult thing" she had ever done.

Teresa set out alone on her new adventure. It was August 16, 1948. In place of the habit of the Sisters of Loreto, she wore sandals and a white Indian sari with blue trim. She pinned a small crucifix to her left shoulder. In Teresa's small bag was what would have equaled about $1.00 in American money in those days.

After spending almost three months in medical training in the city of Patna, Mother Teresa returned to

Calcutta. In the beginning, she stayed with the Little Sisters of the Poor at their home for the elderly. Every day Teresa would go out and visit the poor. She took care of the sick, making sure they had enough to eat. She even washed their clothing.

"Take this," a priest urged one day, pressing some money into her hand. "It's for your good work." Teresa lost no time. She used the donation to buy a two-room shack in one of the slums. That same day, she got the neighborhood children together and began teaching them outside the shack. She used the only teaching tool she had—a stick—to draw letters in the dirt.

Time passed. People began to notice the work that Teresa was doing for the poor. Donations of money, books, and desks began to arrive. Best of all, three teachers joined Mother Teresa.

Besides her teaching, Teresa kept up her visits to the sick. At that time in India, many people suffered from leprosy. When left untreated, leprosy eats away parts of the body and leaves a person deformed. Because this terrible disease was contagious, people were afraid to go near anyone who had it. In fact, the victims were often abandoned. Mother Teresa wasn't afraid. She cared for and nursed the suffering people. She saw Jesus in every person she helped.

Little by little, more young women came to join Mother Teresa. They wanted to dedicate themselves to Jesus and spend their lives serving the poorest of the poor. Teresa called her new community of sisters the Missionaries of Charity. Pope Pius XII approved the group in the fall of 1950. There were twelve members by that time. "Sisters," Mother Teresa enthusiastically told them, "our goal is to weave a chain of love around the world!" And that is just what they began to do.

The sisters led a very strict life. They tried as much as possible to live like the poor people they served. They got up very early each morning to pray and attend Mass before beginning their work. Each sister owned only two saris and a bucket with which to wash them. They had no washing machine, refrigerator, or fans. They didn't have their own bedrooms but slept in a large dormitory. Even though they were poor and worked long hours, the sisters were very happy. They did everything for the love of Jesus, and they found him in every person they served.

Like many of the cities in India, Calcutta was extremely crowded. The hospitals didn't have enough room for all the sick. Because of this, only people who had a good chance of getting well were admitted. Those who were in more serious condition were often left to die right on the streets.

This greatly disturbed Mother Teresa. She made up her mind to do something about it. "Please give me a building that my sisters and I can use as a hospital for the dying," she pleaded with the city officials. She finally received what she was asking for. The building she was given was actually part of the property of a Hindu temple. Mother Teresa named her new hospital *Nirmal Hriday*—Place of the Pure Heart—in honor of the Immaculate Heart of Mary. From that time on, Mother, her sisters, their helpers, and even the police would carry the dying to this hospital. There every person was cared for with love and respect until he or she went home to God.

Another great problem worried Mother Teresa. Many people in Calcutta at that time were abandoning their children. Some of these unwanted babies suffered from mental or physical handicaps. Mother and her sisters began homes for children. Besides taking care of the children who had no place to live, the Missionaries of Charity welcomed unwed mothers who were expecting babies. From their homes for children they also distributed food to the poor.

"All human life is precious and valuable," Mother Teresa loved to repeat. "God loves every person and is close to each person." Mother always defended and tried to help the weakest members of society. She stood up for the rights of unborn babies and never tired of explaining that abortion is a terrible evil that we must all work to overcome.

Mother Teresa had a special love for people with leprosy, who were true outcasts in Indian society. As soon as she had enough sisters to help her, she expanded her work among the millions of people who suffered from this disease. Again she went to the government officials to ask for help. With the donations that she and her sisters were able to collect, and with thirty-four acres of land that the officials gave her, Mother Teresa began *Shanti Nager*—City of Peace. In this "city," persons suffering from leprosy could live and receive the medical treatment they needed. Here they were also taught skills that would help them earn a living when they were well enough to reenter society.

As more and more young women came to join the Missionaries of Charity, Mother Teresa expanded her work for the poor throughout the world. From Tanzania to London, from Yemen to the Bronx, her sisters in their white saris can be seen on the streets of the world's most destitute neighborhoods doing whatever they can to relieve the people's sufferings.

Mother Teresa's heart embraced the whole world. Because the needs were so great, she also founded a congregation of brothers and priests to serve the poorest of the poor. They are known as the Missionaries of Charity Brothers.

How did this tiny Albanian woman (she was barely five feet tall) find the strength to do all that she did for the Church and the world? Mother's secrets were her prayer and her strong love for Jesus. She did everything for Jesus and had great faith in his presence in the Holy Eucharist. Mother Teresa encouraged all her sisters to have this strong faith too.

In the rule that she gave her sisters to live by, Mother Teresa established the practice of making a daily Hour of Adoration before Jesus in the Blessed Sacrament. She realized that her sisters could never sacrifice themselves so totally for others without the help and grace of God. In every chapel of the Missionaries of Charity throughout the world, there is a crucifix. Beside the crucifix are the words Jesus spoke when he was dying on the cross for us: "I thirst." Mother Teresa once explained why these words were so important to her and her sisters. "Jesus is thirsting for our love," she said, "and this is the thirst of everyone, poor or rich alike. We all thirst for the love of others." The mission of Mother Teresa and her sisters was simply to put love into action.

During her lifetime, Mother Teresa received many awards for her work among the poorest of the poor. The most famous of these was the Nobel Peace Prize, which she was given in 1979. Mother traveled by plane to Oslo, Norway, to accept the award. A crowd of very important people from all over the world was there to hear her acceptance speech. Mother spoke for an hour—without notes—about the world's need for peace and love. "There is so much suffering," she said, "so much hate, so much misery. To remedy this we must start in our homes with prayers and sacrifices. Love is born in homes." Mother Teresa asked that the banquet that was traditionally part of the award celebration not be held. Instead, she used the money that would have been spent on the banquet to feed 2,000 poor people on Christmas Day!

For many years, Mother Teresa led her sisters to places where other people were afraid to go. She brought them to leprosy colonies, to AIDS hospitals, and to the slums of the world. When natural disasters such as earthquakes, floods, or famine struck a country, Mother Teresa's Missionaries of Charity were often among the first to respond with help.

Mother Teresa and her sisters also rushed to bring relief to people in nations torn by civil war. In 1982, at the peak of fighting in Beirut, Lebanon, Mother Teresa learned that thirty-seven mentally ill children were trapped in a building without food or water. Mother volunteered to go and rescue them—and she did! When she and her sisters drove up in a Red Cross van, the shooting suddenly stopped. Mother Teresa was able to bring all the children to safety.

Worn out by a life of selfless service to others, Mother Teresa went home to God on September 5, 1997. She was eighty-seven years old. A plain stone marks her grave at the motherhouse of the Missionaries of Charity in Calcutta. On it are carved the words, "Love one another as I have loved you." Today more than 4,000 Missionaries of Charity sisters, 400 priests and brothers, and at least 100,000 co-workers carry on throughout the world the many works of love that Mother Teresa started.

Instead of waiting the usual five years after death before beginning the process to officially name Mother Teresa a saint, Pope John Paul II began it just two years after Mother's death. On October 19, 2003, he declared her "Blessed," one step away from being named a saint.

Blessed Teresa teaches us what it means to "put love into action." She shows us how even the smallest acts of love and kindness can make a real difference in the world. She shows us how to see Jesus in every person we meet.

Index

Although we can pray to any saint to intercede for any need or intention, some saints have become especially popular for particular needs. The following is an alphabetical listing of the saints in this book, their feast dates, what they are the patrons of, and special needs we may call upon them for.

Pauline BOOKS & MEDIA

The Daughters of St. Paul operate book and media centers at the following addresses. Visit, call or write the one nearest you today, or find us on the World Wide Web, www.pauline.org

CALIFORNIA

3908 Sepulveda Blvd, Culver City, CA 90230 — 310-397-8676
2460 Broadway Street, Redwood City, CA 94063 — 650-369-4230
5945 Balboa Avenue, San Diego, CA 92111 — 858-565-9181

FLORIDA

145 S.W. 107th Avenue, Miami, FL 33174 — 305-559-6715

HAWAII

1143 Bishop Street, Honolulu, HI 96813 — 808-521-2731
Neighbor Islands call: — 866-521-2731

ILLINOIS

172 North Michigan Avenue, Chicago, IL 60601 — 312-346-4228

LOUISIANA

4403 Veterans Memorial Blvd, Metairie, LA 70006 — 504-887-7631

MASSACHUSETTS

885 Providence Hwy, Dedham, MA 02026 — 781-326-5385

MISSOURI

9804 Watson Road, St. Louis, MO 63126 — 314-965-3512

NEW JERSEY

561 U.S. Route 1, Wick Plaza, Edison, NJ 08817 — 732-572-1200

NEW YORK

150 East 52nd Street, New York, NY 10022 — 212-754-1110

PENNSYLVANIA

9171-A Roosevelt Blvd, Philadelphia, PA 19114 — 215-676-9494

SOUTH CAROLINA

243 King Street, Charleston, SC 29401 — 843-577-0175

TEXAS

114 Main Plaza, San Antonio, TX 78205 — 210-224-8101

VIRGINIA

1025 King Street, Alexandria, VA 22314 — 703-549-3806

CANADA

3022 Dufferin Street, Toronto, ON M6B 3T5 — 416-781-9131

¡También somos su fuente para libros, videos y música en español!